America Noir

America Noir

Underground Writers and Filmmakers of the Postwar Era

David Cochran

SMITHSONIAN INSTITUTION PRESS
Washington and London

Copy editor: Tom Ireland
Production editor: Ruth Spiegel
Designer: Janice Wheeler

Portions of this work have appeared in different form in *Midwest Quarterly*, *Clues*, and *North Dakota Quarterly* and are reprinted with permission.

Library of Congress Cataloging-in-Publication Data
Cochran, David, 1961–
    America noir: Underground writers and filmmakers of the postwar era / David Cochran.
    p. cm.
    Includes bibliographical references (p.   ).
    ISBN 1-56098-813-4 (alk. paper)
    1. American fiction—20th century—History and criticism.   2. Popular literature—United States—History and criticism.   3. Literature and society—United States—History—20th century.   4. Detective and mystery stories, American—History and criticism.   5. Motion pictures—United States—History and criticism.   6. Fantasy fiction, American—History and criticism.   7. Film noir—United States—History and criticism.   I. Title.
PS374.P63 C63   1999
813'.5409 21—dc21   99-044320

British Library Cataloguing-in-Publication Data available

Manufactured in the United States of America
06   05   04   03   01   00   5   4   3   2   1

∞ The paper used in this publication meets the minimum requirements of the American National Standard for Infomation Sciences—Permanence of Paper for Printed Library Materials ANSI Z39.48-1984.

For Angie

The real friend . . . is,
as it were, another self.
      Cicero

Contents

Acknowledgments

This work has been a very long time in the making, and I have piled up many debts in the process. My family has proven endlessly supportive of my studies and writing. The constant encouragement of my mother and late father, Bette Cochran Reeves and Don Cochran, sustained me. My stepfather, Earl Reeves, has alternately supported and challenged my conclusions with his vast knowledge of Cold War–era political culture, while my children, Jessica, Ian, and Rachel, have been my personal cheering section and were always willing to play hooky or watch *The Twilight Zone* with me.

Mark Hirsch, my editor at Smithsonian Press, supported the project from the beginning, while Kate Gibbs, Tom Ireland, and Ruth Spiegel guided it through the final stages of preparation. I greatly appreciate the expert assistance they have provided. Greg Reeves, Theresa DeFoe, Darren Hackler, and my brother and sister-in-law, Steve and Patty Cochran, helped find many of the sources I needed. I couldn't have finished without their kindness.

Numerous friends and colleagues read all or parts of the work in manuscript form, and their expert criticism helped focus my argument and clarify my writing. Thanks to Robert M. Collins, Jonathan Sperber, Tom Quirk, James Gilbert, Eli Zaretsky, Robbie Lieberman, David Roediger, Erik Schmeller, Bev Whalen-

Schmeller, and Jonathan Wiesen. Steve Watts, especially, deserves thanks for his constant encouragement, discerning eye, and insights into the intricacies of the relationship between high and popular culture. He believed in the work even when I didn't. I am, of course, responsible for any errors of fact or interpretation.

My greatest intellectual debt grows out of an extended conversation that has gone on for several years, over endless cups of coffee and pitchers of beer, with Rick Cotner, Jeff Daniel, and Jim Struttmann. In the process, each read parts of the manuscript in various forms, but more fundamentally, the entire project would not have been possible without my being able to think aloud and test my conclusions on this brilliant and opinionated bunch.

Angie Calcaterra, my gentlest critic and best friend, always believed in the project and knew instinctively when to push me to work on it and when to take me away from it. The book would not have been possible without her loving support.

Preface

Mapping the Underground Culture

Nevertheless it is clear that such persons as the writer of these notes not only may, but positively must, exist in our society, when we consider the circumstances in the midst of which our society is born. I have tried to expose to the view of the public more distinctly than is commonly done, one of the characters of the recent past.—Dostoevsky, *Notes from the Underground*

Writing in 1957, the maverick film critic Manny Farber decried the self-conscious artiness of mainstream American cinema and the critical disdain for what he labeled "underground films"—well-directed, action-oriented, tough-guy movies. "[These films'] dismissal has been caused by the construction of solid confidence built by daily and weekly reviewers. Operating with this wall, the critic can pick and discard without the slightest worry of looking silly. His choice of best salami is a picture backed by studio build-up, agreement amongst his colleagues, a layout in *Life* mag . . . and a list of ingredients that anyone's unsophisticated aunt in Oakland can spot as comprising a distinguished film. This prize picture . . . has every reason to be successful. It has been made for that purpose."[1] Beneath the critical and popular success of such formalized, big-budget productions, Farber identified a group of directors whose hard-boiled thrillers offered a darker picture of postwar American life. "At heart," he observed, "the best action films are slicing journeys into the lower depths of American life: dregs, outcasts, lonely hard wanderers caught in a buzzsaw of niggardly, intricate devious movement."[2] Such directors as Howard Hawks, Raoul Walsh, Anthony Mann, and Robert Aldrich had discovered "private runways to the truth while more famous directors" took a "slow, embalming surface route."[3]

Farber heard a variety of voices in American culture, but he also saw a tendency for mainstream cultural arbiters to ignore or actively drive out more critical views. The postwar era witnessed an explosion of new forms of mass media—in paperback and comic-book publishing, filmmaking (for example, with the popularity of drive-in theaters), and television—which precipitated a cultural crisis. For a wide range of prominent intellectuals of many political stripes, the growth of these mass-cultural forms posed a serious threat to the republic by debasing traditional high culture, depersonalizing the author, dehumanizing the audience, appealing to the lowest common denominator, and offering new opportunities for the growth of mass totalitarian movements. Thus, especially among left intellectuals, an all-out war was declared in defense of traditional high-cultural values and against the incursions of mass culture.

In the view of these elite critics, the formulaic quality and profit orientation of mass culture precluded the possibility that a cultural product could express the author's individual personality. Dwight Macdonald, for instance, in contrasting the detective stories of Edgar Allan Poe with those of Erle Stanley Gardner, commented that, even though both wrote for money, Poe's stories reflect his "neurotic anxieties," whereas it was "simply impossible to imagine Mr. Gardner afflicted with anything as individual as a neurosis."[4] But not all mass culture was of one type. The criteria for success (or at least continuous employment) in most mass-cultural genres were actually minimal: the work needed to be produced quickly and cheaply and return a profit. Otherwise the author was largely free to express whatever point of view he or she wished. Various genres reflected a wide diversity of visions. Crime novels, for instance, ran the gamut from the sterile legal whodunits of Gardner to the right-wing sadism of Mickey Spillane to the vaguely Marxist critique of American culture in the Travis McGee stories of John D. MacDonald. Science fiction literature featured the protofascist conservatism of Robert Heinlein, the technocratic liberalism of Isaac Asimov, and the psychedelic leftism of Philip Dick. Much popular culture was, as Macdonald complained, homogenized to the point that it was devoid of personality. But if one could not imagine Gardner as a neurotic, there was little trouble imagining Jim Thompson, Charles Willeford, David Goodis, or Philip Dick as such.

Within the various genres of mass culture, then, there were a variety of competing voices. As Farber indicated, some of them were far darker and more critical than the period's dominant cultural tendencies. In the view of elite critics, popular culture aimed to simply divert audiences, to allow them briefly to forget the tedium of their everyday lives. Thus, it could not raise troubling questions about the nature of existing political, economic, social, or cultural institutions. But such a view represented a vast oversimplification of the nature and content of popular culture in the Cold War period. For within the burgeoning mass culture there developed a broad-based critique of American Cold War society—a vision that, ironically, in many ways mirrored the elite criticism of American culture. Borrowing Farber's phrase, I call this dissident cultural tradition the "underground culture."[5]

Among the artists who worked within a variety of popular-cultural forms and genres in the underground culture were *roman noir* authors Jim Thompson, Charles Willeford, Chester Himes, and Patricia Highsmith; science fiction and fantasy writers Ray Bradbury and Charles Beaumont; B-film directors Samuel Fuller and Roger Corman; Richard Condon, author of several popular bestsellers; and television screenwriter and producer Rod Serling.[6] Each of these ten representative figures, laboring within genres dismissed as hopelessly corrupted mass-cultural forms by elite critics, managed to produce art that went to the heart of the cultural contradictions of Cold War society, that thrived on chaos, ambiguity, irony, and juxtaposition—characteristics notably absent from the period's dominant middlebrow culture. The advantage of focusing on individual artists is captured by Lionel Trilling, who wrote, "A culture is not a flow, nor even a confluence; the form of its existence is struggle, or at least debate—it is nothing if not a dialectic. And in any culture there are likely to be certain artists who contain a large part of the dialectic within themselves, their meaning and power lying in their contradictions; they contain within themselves, it may be said, the very essence of the culture, and the sign of this is that they do not submit to serve the ends of any one ideological group or tendency."[7] In the same way, these figures worked dialectically—as both creations and creators of the broader social arena—to influence the cultural debate of the Cold War period. In their work they uncovered the paradoxes and challenged the official pieties of the dominant postwar culture. In their contradictions they contained multitudes.

Introduction: Within the Shell of the Old

The Creation of the Cold War Consensus and the Emergence of the Underground Culture

Throughout 1952, *Partisan Review* sponsored a symposium, "Our Country and Our Culture," featuring a veritable Who's Who of left-liberal intellectuals reflecting on the nature of postwar American culture and their role in it. The discussion was based on two premises: that intellectuals and artists no longer felt alienated from the dominant culture, as they traditionally had; and that the greatest threat to America lay in the emergence of "mass culture." "The problem as we see it is this," the editors wrote. "Mass culture not only weakens the position of the artist and the intellectual profoundly by separating him from his natural audience, but it also removes the mass of people from the kind of art which might express their human and aesthetic needs. Its tendency is to exclude everything which does not conform to popular norms; it creates and satisfies artificial appetites in the entire populace; it has grown into a major industry which converts culture into a commodity."[1]

Perhaps the most interesting aspect of the symposium was that, except for Norman Mailer, no one disagreed with the first premise. In other words, by 1952 there existed a common assumption on the part of the nation's leading intellectuals of a broad political and cultural consensus. Furthermore, it was generally agreed, this consensus was based on the political realities of the Cold War. "The task of the intellectual," Sidney Hook stated in his contribution, "is still to lead an intellectual life, to criticize what needs to be criticized in America, without forgetting for a moment the total threat which Communism poses to the life of the free mind."[2] A few writers, like C. Wright Mills and Irving Howe, viewed the consensus with varying degrees of distaste, but most, like Hook, saw it as the fundamental basis on which all serious and honest criticism of American culture must rest.

The specter of mass culture, though, haunted Cold War intellectuals. For those with some residual unease regarding their integration into the dominant political and economic paradigm, a critical stance vis-à-vis mass culture allowed them to continue thinking of themselves as opponents of the major cultural tendencies. Many viewed the creation of an undifferentiated mass audience as a new opportunity for demagogic leaders to manipulate the populace, a process they saw at work in the popularity of Joseph McCarthy. Finally, they feared that the spread of mass culture would destroy the aesthetic standards that had marked traditional high culture. Throughout the *Partisan Review* symposium— and more broadly, throughout the cultural discourse of Cold War intellectuals in the two decades after World War II—ran a fear of popular culture and a debate over how best to deal with the problems it posed.

The debate over mass culture and the emergence of the underground culture cannot be understood apart from the broader history of the Cold War years. By reconstructing the political and cultural milieu of the postwar era, we can trace the process by which political dissent was defeated or integrated into the dominant consensus and the way in which the war on mass culture became a central aspect of the Cold War for intellectuals. In turn, such developments gave rise to an underground culture that flourished in several forms.

Forging the Consensus

In the immediate aftermath of the war, a wide range of options, both political and cultural, lay open before Americans. In terms of foreign policy, a variety of proposals were made on how to deal with the Soviets and the reconstruction of Europe, from the continuation of wartime cooperation, proposed by such people as former vice president Henry Wallace and Senator Claude Pepper, to the neoisolationism of Senator Robert Taft.[3] In domestic politics, the war's aftermath was marked by an unprecedented wave of wildcat strikes and labor militancy.[4] In other words, such political actions as conducting the Cold War or passing the Taft-Hartley Bill were neither preordained nor carried out in a fit of absent-mindedness, but they resulted from struggles in which the dominant political and economic classes sought to assert their control and narrow the range of options available.

Culturally, as well, Americans faced a bewildering array of alternatives. As William Graebner has argued, the uninterrupted series of crises that had befallen Americans—the Depression, World War II, the Cold War—left an underlying sense of doubt pervading American thought. Out of this anxiety emerged, according to Graebner, "a culture of profound contingency, in which everything, one's employment, one's values, one's very life, seemed dependent on the vagaries of chance."[5] In this world of contingency, the social order barely contained a fundamental moral chaos. The perfect cultural expression of this vision, as Graebner has noted, was film noir, a cinematic genre popular from the mid-forties to the early fifties, focusing on tales of crime, greed, and jealousy, populated by antiheroes and femmes fatales. In films noirs, people meet the most merciless fate for the most mundane reasons. In Rudolph Maté's *D.O.A.* (1950), for example, a tax consultant is administered a slow-acting poison by an unknown assailant and has only a short time to solve his own murder. In the end, he discovers he has been killed for the seemingly innocuous act of notarizing a bill of sale. As the protagonist of Edgar Ulmer's brilliant, low-budget *Detour* (1945) concludes, "That's life. Whichever way you turn, fate sticks out a foot to trip you."

From the end of the war through the mid-fifties, these alternative political and cultural visions were gradually isolated or co-opted. At its most obvious and heavy-handed, this process took such forms as the investigation by the House Committee on UnAmerican Activities (HUAC) into communist subversion in the film industry; President Truman's order for security checks on federal employees; the Taft-Hartley Bill's requirement that labor leaders sign loyalty oaths; and McCarthy's Senate investigations of the State Department, media, and military.

This culture of countersubversion and investigation did not just work to ferret out communists, but often also to squelch any perceived criticism of capitalism. Appearing as an expert witness before HUAC's hearings on Hollywood, for instance, Ayn Rand not only criticized wartime films for depicting smiling Russians, but also attacked *The Best Years of Our Lives* (1946) as anticapitalist for portraying a banker refusing a loan to a wounded veteran. According to her pamphlet *Screen Guide for Americans* (1950), distributed by the Motion Picture Alliance, Rand preached, "Don't give your character—as a sign of villainy, as a damning characteristic—a desire to make money. . . . It is the moral duty of every decent man in the motion picture industry to throw into the ash can, where it belongs, every story that smears industrialists."[6]

Less obviously, but equally important on a cultural level, film noir, the chief artistic expression of the culture of contingency that had marked the immediate postwar years, gradually gave way to more standard police and spy thrillers. In the culture of the Cold War, the chaos and ambiguity of noir undermined the moral absolutes of the struggle with the Soviets and thus were not appropriate.[7] But as Americans suppressed critical views of capitalism and repressed the underlying doubts of the postwar years, both attitudes resurfaced in the emerging underground culture.

For the most part, liberal intellectuals disdained such naked attacks on radicalism as those carried out by McCarthy or HUAC, while simultaneously waging their own, more subtle war against political unorthodoxy. Fundamental challenges to the Cold War, they agreed, needed to be discredited. Right-wing isolationism was described as an abdication of America's postwar responsibility and certain to result in Soviet gains. On the other hand, the progressivism of Henry Wallace and his followers was labeled dangerously naive because it was based on a faulty understanding of human nature. "Why was progressivism not prepared for Hitler?" Arthur Schlesinger Jr. asked, in explaining why it was equally unprepared to deal with Stalin. "The eighteenth century had exaggerated man's capacity to live by logic alone; the nineteenth century sanctified what remained of his nonlogical impulses; and the result was the pervading belief in human perfectibility which has disarmed progressivism in too many of its encounters with actuality. As the child of eighteenth-century rationalism and nineteenth-century romanticism, progressivism was committed to an unwarranted optimism about man."[8]

Though they held their noses at some of the unsavory antics of HUAC and the McCarthy investigative committees, liberal artists and intellectuals were also committed to identifying and denouncing communism. Elia Kazan, the brilliant film and stage director, an ex-communist turned liberal whose work consistently expressed his political commitments, drew plaudits from many liberals for his willingness to cooperate with HUAC. In an advertisement published in the *New York Times* on April 12, 1952, Kazan justified his decision: "The employment of a lot of good liberals is threatened because they have allowed themselves to become associated with or silenced by Communists. Liberals must speak out. . . . Firsthand experience of dictatorship and thought control left me with an abiding hatred of these. It left me with an abiding hatred of Communist philosophy and methods and the conviction that these must be resisted always."[9]

For Cold War liberals, consensus-building was based not solely on isolating subversive political tendencies, but also on domesticating and integrating formerly critical cultural and political forms. With few exceptions, leftist intellectuals became reconciled with the dominant status quo. Dwight Macdonald, for instance, who entered World War II a Trotskyist and came out a revolutionary pacifist, proclaimed in 1952, "I choose the West because I see the present conflict not as another struggle between basically similar imperialisms as was World War I but as a fight to the death between radically different cultures."[10] Similarly, art critic Harold Rosenberg, a former Trotskyist and leading champion of modern art—who remained a Marxist throughout the Cold War period, associating with the anti-Soviet socialists around the journal *Dissent*—worked for twenty years after the war as program consultant for the Advertising Council of America, where he was perhaps most famous for creating Smokey Bear.[11] And, by the early fifties, John Steinbeck had foregone the class-consciousness of his Depression-era novels *In Dubious Battle* and *The Grapes of Wrath* for such ringing proclamations of the liberal values of freedom and individualism as these words of the narrator of *East of Eden* (1952): "This I believe: that the free, exploring mind of the individual human is the most valuable thing in the world. And this I would fight for: the freedom of the mind to take any direction it wishes, undirected. And this I must fight against: any idea, religion, or government which limits or destroys the individual."[12]

Critical artists were also integrated into the liberal consensus. As Serge Guilbaut has shown in his discussion of the relationship between abstract expressionism and Cold War politics, the search for a new artistic language paralleled liberal attempts to establish a new political discourse in the postwar period. Beginning in the late thirties, artists impatient with the strictures—both political and artistic—of socialist realism had cast about for a new theory of art. Influenced by art critics like Clement Greenberg, an increasing number of artists rejected socialist realism for a more idealized vision of artistic expressionism, in which recognizable subjects were done away with altogether and the artist himself became the subject. Such avant-garde artists as Jackson Pollack, Robert Motherwell, and Willem de Kooning created a new style celebrating individualism and freedom, principles that dovetailed nicely with the new liberal vision. Abstract expressionism became the visual manifestation of Cold War liberalism, and it was exhibited under semiofficial auspices throughout Europe as evidence of American culture's freedom and vitality.[13] In a similar way, even an artist like Ben Shahn, who maintained his leftist politics and recognizable subject matter, could be exhibited in Europe with government sanction as an example of American political and cultural freedom.[14]

The end result of this carrot-and-stick policy of integration and isolation was the creation of a broad cultural consensus with a right and left wing. Within this consensus there still existed acrimonious debates on a variety of issues. Conservatives, for instance, did not always share the liberals' appreciation for modern art, believing that its attack on traditional values and moral absolutes served to undermine American society.[15] Liberals, in turn, often believed that conservative anticommunists like McCarthy and Nixon, by ignoring civil liberties in their zeal to unmask traitors, did more to hurt the anticommunist cause than help it. But despite such differences, liberals and conservatives were united on two basic beliefs: American capitalism fundamentally worked and would continue to do so without any major redistribution of power or wealth through the engine of economic growth; and the major threat to this system came from without, in the form of the international communist threat.[16]

Liberals within the consensus viewed themselves as, in Schlesinger's words, a "vital center" between the extremes of left and right. Priding themselves on their political realism, liberals argued that American society must be willing to reform itself to preclude the desire for more radical social changes. They recognized society and humanity in all their complexity and rejected the more simpleminded political theories and cultural forms, which denied this subtlety, nuance, and paradox.[17] For Cold War liberals, Freud and Tocqueville replaced Marx, Henry James replaced Theodore Dreiser, and *1984* replaced *Looking Backward.*

The natural social order, according to liberal theory, was one of struggle between competing interest groups. In Max Lerner's phrase, this was a "democratic class struggle . . . in which the working class and its allies use every economic and political means to better their own position and the nation's welfare."[18] For Schlesinger, it was a concept of pluralism, in which conflicts between different classes were mediated by the state, a process that ensured a gradual democratization of political power and cultural resources.[19] In this pluralistic struggle, groups acted out of motives of self-interest rather than ideology. It was this failure of grand ideologies to inspire Americans that signaled what Daniel Boorstin called "the genius of American politics" and had kept Americans free of totalitarianism.[20] For this reason, there was a fundamental distrust of ideologues and "true believers."[21] Such people could not accept the uncertainties and anxieties of living in a free society and were attracted to the rigidly structured unfreedom and sense of purpose offered by totalitarianism, whether of the left or right. "The final triumph of totalitarianism," according to Schlesinger, "has been the creation of man without anxiety—of 'totalitarian man.'"[22]

Paradoxically, though accepting this concept of pluralism, liberal intellectuals also argued that Americans were fundamentally unified. William Graebner has said that in the postwar period "Americans were virtually obsessed with creating, or affirming the existence of a 'culture of the whole.' . . . They labored to construct or imagine intellectual, technological, political and social systems that would encompass and enfold culture on a nationwide and even worldwide basis."[23] Thus the historian Henry Steele Commager set out to trace, in the title of his classic 1950 study, *the* American mind on the supposition that all Americans were fundamentally of one mind.[24] Other historians founded what came to be called the "consensus school," based on the belief that American history has been marked by a generally shared set of common beliefs, though they disagreed on the beneficence of this consensus.[25] And the new discipline of American Studies set out to trace the "myths and symbols" that had provided unifying themes for Americans.[26]

The bedrock principle of American society, according to Cold War intellectuals, was freedom. But influenced by the writings of Erich Fromm, they did not view this freedom as unambiguously liberating. For many it was terrifying. As Schlesinger wrote, "This freedom has brought with it frustration rather than fulfillment, isolation rather than integration. 'Anxiety,' writes Kierkegaard, 'is the dizziness of freedom'; and anxiety is the official emotion of our time. . . . Against totalitarian certitude, free society can only offer modern man devoured by alienation and fallibility."[27]

The liberal consensus, then, was actually built on a series of fundamental paradoxes. The belief in consensus and unity was undermined by a concept of cultural pluralism that viewed society as being in a constant state of struggle. The emphasis on freedom of thought and inquiry was premised on an uncompromising anticommunism. But the most basic contradiction of Cold War liberalism, as Irving Howe pointed out in his contribution to *Partisan Review*'s "Our Country and Our Culture," lay in the disparity between the situation it described and the solutions it proposed. As Howe wrote, "The intellectuals of liberalism must face this problem: how can they believe the ADA program offers a proper amelioration for our social problems while they find in Kafka the image of the quality of our life?"[28] (ADA, Americans for Democratic Action, was a liberal anticommunist organization founded in 1947.) In other words, within the dominant Cold War consensus, or at least the liberal half of it, a modest political program masked an underlying (though rarely consciously admitted) vision marked by chaos, anxiety, and alienation. The emergent underground culture would build on this tension, stressing the Kafkaesque nature of the situation and deconstructing the reformist proposals of consensus liberalism.

The Problem of Mass Culture

For liberal intellectuals, mass culture represented another paradox: their professed belief in democracy was belied by their fear of cultural leveling. The concern over popular culture was not universal among liberal intellectuals, but even those who supported mass-mediated culture tended to view the process as a means for bringing high culture to the masses. Nearly all opposed the quality of what they deemed the lower forms of popular culture. Daniel Bell, for instance, in attacking the very notion of "mass culture," stressed that he was speaking only in an anthropological sense—"as a change from parochial to more universal cultural forms"—and was not challenging the widely perceived decline of "the humanist quality of culture."[29] In his introduction to an influential collection of essays on the topic, David Manning White defended mass culture on the basis that it was being used to disseminate serious culture—such as ballets, Shakespeare, classical music, and quality paperbacks—while going to pains to say he was not defending the quality of such lower cultural forms as comic books.[30]

The left-liberal critique of mass culture dated back to the split between Stalinists and Trotskyists in the late thirties. In his classic essay, "Avant-Garde and Kitsch" (1939), Clement Greenberg staked out the American Trotskyist position on mass culture, which he labeled "kitsch." This kitsch was the product of modern, urban, industrial society: "To fill the demand of the new market a new commodity was devised: ersatz culture, kitsch, destined for those who, insensible to the values of genuine culture, are hungry nevertheless for the diversion that only culture of some sort can provide. Kitsch is mechanical and operates by formulas. Kitsch is vicarious experience and faked sensations. Kitsch changes according to style but remains always the same."[31] According to Greenberg, kitsch is universally popular because it demands no effort on the part of the viewer and poses no threat to his fundamental beliefs. In it, the viewer "recognizes and sees things in the way in which he recognizes and sees things outside pictures—there is no discontinuity between art and life."[32]

In the postwar period this view was expanded and gained wider currency among intellectuals increasingly distrustful of mass movements. Ex-leftists, simultaneously seeking to atone for their former faith in the masses while not altogether comfortable with their integration into the dominant cultural consensus, seized upon mass culture as a means of maintaining a critical stance toward American society, seeing it as the major domestic threat to Americans' freedom. "At its worst," Bernard Rosenberg wrote, "mass culture threatens not merely to cretinize our taste, but to brutalize our senses while paving the way to totalitarianism."[33]

Mass culture, in the view of its critics, grew out of the increasing regimentation and routinization of work in modern capitalist society. A major source of its development, in the words of Jacques Barzun, "is fatigue, the special sort of industrial and democratic fatigue, which is not being tired but drained and mindless, and yet jerky and demanding as well. All forms of soothing syrup masquerading as art have been designed, for the most part unconsciously, to allay this fatigue, to occupy without really using the attention. This, and not religion, is the opiate of the people."[34] As Howe argued, popular culture needed to be entertaining enough to take a person's mind off the boredom of his job without being so fascinating as to highlight the emptiness of his everyday life. "Leisure time must be so organized as to bear a factitious relationship to working time: apparently different, actually the same. It must provide relief from work monotony without making the return to work too unbearable: it must provide amusement without insight and pleasure without disturbance—as distinct from art which gives pleasure through disturbance."[35]

"A product of popular culture," according to Leo Lowenthal, "has none of the features of genuine art, but in all its media popular culture proves to have its own genuine characteristics: standardization, stereotypy, conservatism, mendacity, manipulated consumer goods."[36] As Dwight Macdonald argued, while bad art has been with us always, mass culture (or as Macdonald dubbed it, "masscult"—that is, not even a true culture) was qualitatively different. In preindustrial times, bad art had been of the same fundamental type as good art, just not as skillfully executed. Masscult, on the other hand, was "bad in a new way: it doesn't even have the theoretical possibility of being good. . . . It is not just unsuccessful art. It is non-art. It is even anti-art."[37] It worked at the lowest common denominator of popular taste. And, by the means of its production, it necessarily debased higher culture forms. Macdonald described an issue of *Life* magazine that followed a nine-page color article on Renoir with a photo of a horse on roller skates. "Defenders of our Masscult society . . . see phenomena like *Life* as inspiriting attempts at popular education—just think, nine pages of Renoirs! But that roller-skating horse comes along, and the final impression is that both Renoir and the horse were talented."[38]

As Andrew Ross has pointed out, the intellectuals' proposed policy toward mass culture paralleled the Cold War strategy toward the Soviet Union—containment.[39] From Hollywood in the West to the Museum of Modern Art in the East, an intellectual iron curtain of disdain descended to protect the sanctity of high culture from the degrading influence of mass culture. "There is only one way to quarantine kitsch," Harold Rosenberg commented. "By being too busy with art."[40]

The problem of containment, however, was complicated. As both Macdonald and Greenberg pointed out, the space between high culture and masscult was not empty, but occupied by a broad, amorphous middlebrow culture (or "midcult," as Macdonald labeled it) that had, in terms of social power, become the dominant culture. This middlebrow culture, as Greenberg said, "is defined roughly by the fact that, though its audience shrinks from the trials of high-brow culture, it nonetheless refuses to let its culture be simply a matter of entertainment and diversion on the lowbrow order. Middlebrow culture has to do in one way or another with self-improvement, and is born almost always out of the desire and effort of newly ascended social classes to rise culturally as well."[41]

Midcult, as Macdonald defined it, is ersatz culture posing as the genuine article. It freely mixes high and mass culture; the result, however, is not the elevation of popular culture but the denaturing of true culture. Like masscult, it is formulaic, featuring the "built-in reaction." "It is impossible not to identify the emotion [it] wants to arouse. . . . One is never puzzled by the unexpected"— and its sole standard of success is popularity.[42] Greenberg wrote of the consumer of midcult: "In his reading, no matter how much he wants to edify himself, he will balk at anything that sends him to the dictionary or a reference book more than once. . . . Towards his entertainment, no matter how much he wants it to be 'significant' and 'worthwhile,' he will become recalcitrant if the 'significance' is not labeled immediately and obviously, and if too many conditioned reflexes are left without appropriate stimuli. What the middlebrow, even more conspicuously than the lowbrow, wants most is to have his expectations filled exactly as he expects to have them filled."[43]

Macdonald warned that the relationship between high culture and midcult is also complicated. Canonized high-culture texts are welcomed into the world of midcult if they have been clearly designated masterpieces by properly accepted cultural authorities. In most cases, anything potentially subversive in the art has been eliminated before it is deemed appropriate. As Howe commented, "In the recent effort of academic critics to house-break our great writers, Hawthorne [has been] transformed into a nimble rotarian and Melville into a good burgher suffering not from spiritual agonies but from an inability to meet his bills."[44] Furthermore, as Macdonald complained, midcult audiences had lost the ability to identify and appreciate new artistic forms on their own. Thus local symphonies played Mozart or (perhaps) Stravinsky, but not contemporary modernist composers like Elliott Carter.[45] Finally, "midcult exploits the discoveries of the avant-garde."[46] In its quest for the new and vital, midcult incorporates the most recent trends in the arts, but in the process of integrating them, cuts off any critical element they might have had. Writing in the late fifties, Macdonald remarked that both abstract expressionists and beatniks had succumbed to this process. "The more they try to shock the Midcult's audience, the more they are written up in the Lucepapers; they are 'different,' that potent advertising word whose charm reveals how monotonous the landscape of Midcult has become."[47] In short, Greenberg argued, "It would seem . . . that it is middlebrow, not lowbrow, culture that does most nowadays to cut the social ground from under high culture."[48]

Culture Wars

What is to be done? The question plagued left-liberal intellectuals facing the problem of mass culture. A (very) few mavericks like Norman Mailer admonished artists and intellectuals to maintain a critical, outsider stance toward the dominant culture by aligning themselves with such marginal subcultures as black jazz musicians.[49] Others, like Greenberg and Macdonald, declared intellectual war on masscult and midcult in defense of traditional cultural standards. Still others, most of whom did not have the same disparaging attitude toward middlebrow culture as did Macdonald and Greenberg, sought to marshal the power of the state to eliminate some of the most disturbing forms of popular culture.

Frederick Wertham serves as an example of this latter tendency. A noted psychiatrist and neurologist with a long commitment to civil rights and other reform causes, Wertham had opened a free psychiatric clinic in Harlem during the forties because of his concern that the poor were being deprived of health care.[50] In his work with juvenile delinquents, Wertham noted the strong influence of comic books on children's psycho-social development and behavior, leading him into a closer examination of the comics' content. He was appalled to discover the dominant themes of the comic books included "violence; sadism and cruelty; the superman philosophy, an offshoot of Nietszche's superman who said, 'When you go to women, don't forget the whip.'"[51] Wertham made a direct connection between the spread of comic books and the rise of juvenile delinquency in the postwar period.

In a series of articles for the popular press and his influential book *Seduction of the Innocent* (1954), Wertham sought to publicize his conclusions and effect some remedial program. Enlisting in the crusade was a wide range of left-liberal intellectuals and conservative pressure groups. C. Wright Mills wrote a glowing review of Wertham's book for the *New York Times Book Review,* saying, "Dr. Wertham's cases, his careful observations and his sober reflections about the American child in a world of comic violence and unfunny filth testify to a most commendable use of the professional mind in the service of the public."[52] In 1955, Senator Estes Kefauver convened a Senate subcommittee to investigate the social effects of comic books in hearings that gained widespread publicity. By that same year, thirteen states had passed some form of legislation regulating the publication, distribution, and sale of comic books.[53] Even more chilling, the comic industry itself established the Comics Code Authority, a self-regulating agency by which the industry established guidelines specifying acceptable standards for the content of comics. The result was that most of the darker, more topical, and potentially more critical comics were driven off the market.[54]

Running throughout the anti–comic-book campaign was the glaring absence of an ability to perceive irony on the part of the censors. In *Seduction of the Innocent,* Wertham quoted several lines from comics that were obviously intended as satire, but the humor was completely lost on him. For instance, in one example, a Ma Barker–type character says to her sons, "I brought you kids up right—rub out those coppers like I taught you!"[55] Similarly, William Gaines, publisher of Entertaining Comics, responded to the growing efforts at regulation by running an editorial in his comics claiming that those advocating censorship were obviously "red dupes," noting that the *Daily Worker* also endorsed censorship. The piece was a parody of both anti-red and anti–mass-culture hysteria, but the early fifties were not marked by a strong sense of satire, and Gaines found himself called before the Kefauver committee.[56]

The crusade against comic books shows the way elite cultural criticism of mass culture filtered into the larger social arena. Wertham was motivated by many of the concerns underlying those of left-liberal intellectuals: that mass culture inured people to the dehumanizing aspects of modern society, that it taught violence, and that it paved the way for the acceptance of totalitarianism. As James Gilbert has pointed out, implicit in Wertham's writings was an indictment of capitalist culture for "substituting market relations for moral relations."[57] According to Gilbert, throughout the left critique of mass culture, from highbrows like Macdonald and Greenberg to popularizers like Wertham, ran a common theme of disillusionment with former idealism. "The mass society, so fervently promoted by many intellectuals in the 1930s, had arrived. But it was not liberating. The common man had shed his heroism, and conservatism made the taste of the proletariat insipid. The radical dreamers of the 1930s awakened to the dystopia of suburbia."[58]

Going Underground

The numerous paths—political and cultural—that had lain before Americans in the immediate postwar period had been largely closed off by the early fifties, leaving the Cold War consensus dominant. Artists had learned their best strategy was to avoid anything that smacked of political controversy or presented too dark and unflattering a vision of American society. As actress Judy Holliday commented after testifying before HUAC for having campaigned for Henry Wallace in 1948, "I don't say 'yes' to anything now except cancer and cerebral palsy."[59] This culture of suppression worked at a wide variety of levels, from official government committees to vigilante groups, employers, and local police departments. It spanned a broad range of issues, political and cultural. And it continued, at least at some levels, throughout the two decades after World War II—Lenny Bruce, for instance, was still being hounded by police departments in San Francisco and New York until his death in 1965.[60]

Culturally, the purpose of this policy of censorship was to repress the darker aspects of American social thought—the strong sense of doubt and contingency, the fears born of World War II, the atomic bomb, the Cold War—and replace them with a much more affirmative vision. But the violence, chaos, moral ambiguity, and alienation that marked such disparate popular-cultural forms as film noir and comic books did not disappear. Rather they were driven underground, resurfacing in other popular-cultural venues.

This return of the repressed encompassed a wide-ranging cultural critique of American society of the most fundamental type. It took the very basis of the Cold War consensus—that American society fundamentally worked—and challenged it at every level in terms of economics, technology, foreign policy, quality of life, modal personality, and race relations. What Geoffrey O'Brien has written of the hard-boiled paperbacks of the postwar period is more generally true of the underground culture: "The paperbacks . . . tell of a dark world below the placid surface, a world whose inhabitants tend to be grasping, dissatisfied, emotionally twisted creatures. Here, all is not well; from the looks of it, all could not be much worse. . . . Worse yet, at the heart of it all, there is an implied lack of meaning. Unlike the settling of the West or the Second World War, the events transcribed by hardboiled fiction serve no particular purpose; they just happen. A nation gets the epic it deserves, and not necessarily the one it wants."[61]

At a time when modernist art had been largely canonized and integrated into the dominant consensus, the underground culture kept alive the critical impetus of modernism. The concept of the grotesque, for instance, so central to such classic modernist texts as *Winesburg, Ohio* and *The Sound and the Fury,* had largely disappeared from postwar modernism; as Macdonald described it, the quiet desperation of Winesburg had been supplanted by the smarmy unctuousness of *Our Town.*[62] But the worlds of Jim Thompson, Charles Willeford, Chester Himes, Patricia Highsmith, Samuel Fuller, and Richard Condon were filled with grotesque characters, products of a social order that twisted and perverted people physically and psychologically. And at a time when the overblown midcult bestsellers of authors like Herman Wouk, James Michener, and James Gould Cozzens appealed, in Paul Fussell's words, to an audience "untrained in irony,"[63] the underground culture thrived on irony, ambivalence, paradox, and complexity. Artists working in the underground culture accepted the vision proposed by liberal intellectuals like Arthur Schlesinger Jr. that freedom was premised on anxiety and alienation. They rejected, however, the liberals' reform program as woefully inadequate.

Fascinatingly, in many ways the emergent underground culture actually mirrored the elite critique of middlebrow and mass culture. Authors like Condon, Charles Beaumont, and Ray Bradbury attacked the dehumanizing and totalitarian aspects of mass culture. Others, like Willeford, Highsmith, and Fuller, made frequent reference to traditional high-cultural texts but not, in midcult fashion, to give their works a patina of respectability while cutting away any critical aspects of high culture. Rather they used high culture in various ways as a means of criticizing the dominant cultural sensibilities. Finally, artists in the underground culture largely avoided the midcult sins of the built-in reaction and incessant editorializing. A tone of moral neutrality, for instance, pervaded the work of Thompson, Willeford, and Highsmith as they described their characters' murderous activities.

Over the course of the two decades after World War II, an alternative paradigm fitfully took shape within the popular-cultural forms most despised by both elite and middlebrow cultural critics. At least until the early sixties, this underground culture remained fairly inchoate. There were few direct links between the works of the ten representative artists, and certainly they would not have seen themselves as part of a common cultural avant-garde. Rather their art should be seen in terms of what Raymond Williams has called "structures of feeling," the gap between the abstract, fixed social forms that are used to understand society and the actual lived experience of individuals. While necessary for understanding social relations, such abstractions still allow much of human experience to slip through the explanatory cracks. As Williams explained: "Practical consciousness is always more than a handling of fixed forms and units. There is frequent tension between the received interpretation and practical experience. Where this tension can be made direct and explicit, or where some alternative interpretation is available, we are still within a dimension of relatively fixed forms. But the tension is as often an unease, a stress, a displacement, a latency: the moment of conscious comparison not yet come, often not even coming." Art and literature, according to Williams, with their emphasis on multiple voices, irony, and juxtaposition, often provide the first indication of the formation of new structures of feeling.[64] In the work of the artists in the underground culture, the tensions within the dominant cultural consensus were exposed dramatically. And, though politically it failed to offer an alternative vision, the underground culture would play a crucial role in the development of a counter-hegemonic culture in the sixties and, in the longer run, the growth of postmodernism.

Part One

The Killer inside Me

Roman Noir
Authors

Slipping Deeper into Hell

Jim Thompson's Theology of Absurdity

In Jim Thompson's 1965 novel *Texas by the Tail,* a minor character relates the story of how the oil boom hit Big Spring, Texas. A middle-aged man and his nineteen-year-old son invest their money in a portable oil rig. In drilling their well, they encounter a variety of mishaps: "The boiler blew up. The rig caught on fire. The mast snapped. The tools were lost in the hole a dozen times. The drill cable bucked and whipped, cleanly slicing off a tool-dresser's head." But eventually the well is drilled and begins producing a respectable quantity of oil. The father then asks what the son plans to do. The son replies that, of the millions the well is now worth, he will settle for $182,000. When the father asks why that particular amount, the son responds:

> "I've been keeping a little black book since I was seven years old. There are one hundred and eighty-two names in it, one for every rotten bastard who's given me a hard time. I've shopped around, and I can get them bumped off for an average price of one thousand dollars."
>
> "Son—" the father shook his head, aghast. "What happened to you? How can you even think of such things?"
>
> "Thinking about it is all that's kept me alive," the kid said. "I can die happy knowing I'm taking all those bastards to hell with me."

At this point, the father explains that in drilling the well the two had mortgaged everything and so were broke. "'Goddam,' the kid said. 'Those one hundred and eighty-two bastards could be dead right now for what this well cost!'" The boy feels he should be angry, but "somehow, he wanted to howl with laughter, because when you thought about it, you know, it was really funny as hell." As father and son leave town on foot, they look back at Big Spring, already developing into a vibrant oil town.

> "We did that son," [the father says]. "You and I. We caused a city to bloom in the wilderness. We've made history."
> "We should have stood in bed," the kid said. But then he laughed and gave the old man an affectionate slap on the back.[1]

In significant ways, this story serves as a parable for Thompson's worldview. Set in the context of a robust frontier capitalism that is utterly merciless toward its victims, Thompson depicted a universe marked by a strong sense of irony. His characters keep hidden their psychopathic natures, nursing private grudges that threaten to burst forth in a frenzy of homicidal rage. And yet this universe is also marked by a mordant humor, and the one potential saving grace is the recognition of that humor. Repeatedly in Thompson's fiction, characters face the grim and brutal reality of life's absurdity, which they find so terrible that the only possible response is hysterical laughter. And while this laughter is occasionally cathartic, as in the Big Spring story, at other times it signals either resignation in the face of the tragic fate that befalls most Thompson characters, or else a further descent into madness.

Thompson's dark vision undermined the dominant postwar culture at a variety of levels. In face of the faith in official institutions and the logic of official patterns of thought, Thompson created an absurd universe based on a fundamental core of insanity. His portraits of the marginal, alienated, and sociopathic inhabitants of America's barren wastelands refuted the contemporary optimism of the "affluent society." In contrast to the official economic culture, he argued that capitalism deformed both the environment and human nature, and he specialized in showing the psychic ravages inflicted on the victims of the American economic and political system. Occasionally, he placed his stories in the context of American Cold War policies, both foreign and domestic. At a time when the dominant culture viewed the family as a potential haven for domestic peace in its suburban enclave and a bulwark against communism, he showed the family as the center of the violence and chaos characterizing his view of American society. His savage parodies of the ethic of "personality" subverted what had become the dominant social character type. Finally, Thompson's works were marked by a twisted theology emphasizing innate sinfulness, an inscrutable and wrathful God, and the ubiquity of hell, which stood in sharp distinction to the increasingly vapid religion of the dominant culture.

Bad Boy

Thompson's literary journeys among the socially dispossessed grew out of his life experiences. Born in 1906 in Anadarko, Oklahoma Territory, Thompson was the son of a local politician, lawyer, and oil man who gained and lost several fortunes. Thus Thompson learned early on about the fundamental insecurity of American capitalism. Growing up in Oklahoma, Texas, and Nebraska, he worked a variety of jobs that provided much of the raw material for his novels later. For example, working as a bellboy at the height of prohibition involved him in various illegal activities with potentially serious consequences. As Thompson would say: "To survive in that world [a boy] had to be very, very lucky and have a fair degree of intelligence. But more than anything else, he had to be able to 'take it,' to absorb the not-to-be-avoided abnormal without being absorbed by it. Or, to state the matter simply, he needed a strong sense of humor. If he had that, he was usually all right. Far from harming him, the hotel life would do him a lot of good."[2] It is doubtful how much good the hotel life did for Thompson, because during his career as a bellboy he developed a serious drinking problem that plagued him for the rest of his life. But he viewed his experiences in the hotel as a microcosm of his vision of the universe. In an apocryphal story that concludes the first volume of his fictionalized autobiography, *Bad Boy* (1953), Thompson claimed that while working in a Fort Worth hotel, a bootlegging scheme in which he was involved went awry, and he had to flee town with his mother and sister, just ahead of federal agents and gangsters. In typical fashion, while they were running for their lives in a car that kept breaking down, Thompson burst into laughter. When his mother asked why, he responded, in the book's final line, "I don't know. I guess I just don't know of anything else to do."[3]

Thompson enrolled at the University of Nebraska in 1929, where he gained valuable experience writing for the school's literary magazine. Forced to drop out of college during the Depression, he worked for several years as a manual laborer on the oil pipelines in west Texas while occasionally writing for true detective magazines before landing a job on the Oklahoma Writers Project in 1936 for the Works Progress Administration. Thompson quickly was appointed the project's guide book editor and in 1938 was named director of the entire Oklahoma Writers Project. While working for the WPA, he carved out a reputation as a radical. In November 1936, for example, he wrote a strong protest to the national director of the WPA against the firing of five members of the St. Louis project for organizing a union. "I wish to protest," the letter began, "against the recent outrage in St. Louis which for sheer tyranny and the usurpation of human rights has not been equaled since the Homestead strike."[4] As state director, Thompson oversaw the writing of the decidedly pro-union *Labor History of Oklahoma.* During this period, he was also an active member of the Communist party.[5]

Thompson departed the WPA in 1940 and moved to San Diego, where he eventually found employment in a wartime aircraft factory. Working as a timekeeper at night, he wrote during the day, completing his first published novel, *Now and on Earth* (1942). Largely autobiographical, the story concerns Jim Dillon, a worker in an aircraft factory struggling to support his extended family and write a novel. In many ways, *Now and on Earth* is a proletarian novel, focusing on the oppressive nature of capitalism and how poverty breeds dysfunctional families.[6] But Thompson deviated from the standard proletarian novel format in that Dillon does not respond to this oppression by developing a class consciousness or any other type of positive action. Instead, the novel ends with Dillon fully recognizing the deforming nature of capitalism. At one point he wonders about the effects of raising children in such an environment, of "growing up amidst this turmoil, these hatreds, this—well, why quibble—insanity?" Then he asks himself, "Were you ever happy? Did you ever have any peace? And I had to answer, Why no, for Christ's sake; you've always been in hell. You've just slipped deeper."[7]

A modest critical success, *Now and on Earth* did not earn Thompson enough money to allow him to quit his job at the factory. For the rest of the forties, he worked a variety of jobs while writing two novels, *Heed the Thunder* (1946) and *Nothing More Than Murder* (1948), his last two books to be published in hardcover editions. The former is a study of the dark underside of life in a small Nebraska town in the early twentieth century. The latter was Thompson's first foray into the crime novel genre. Neither was an overwhelming success financially or critically, and in his disappointment Thompson sank deeper into alcoholism. Then, in 1952, he discovered his métier when the paperback publisher Lion Books paid him $2,000 for his noir thriller *The Killer inside Me.* Between

1952 and 1955, he published thirteen paperbacks, eleven for Lion. After this spurt, he continued writing paperbacks but also sought to break into Hollywood as a screenwriter. He coauthored the screenplays to two Stanley Kubrick films, *The Killing* (1956) and *Paths of Glory* (1957), as well as writing scripts for such television series as *MacKenzie's Raiders* and *Dr. Kildare*.[8] But his experiences in Hollywood were disappointing, and his fiction never escaped the paperback market. By the late sixties he was reduced to writing novelizations for television (*Ironside,* 1967) and movies (*The Undefeated,* 1969, and *Nothing but a Man,* 1970). Occasionally he seemed on the verge of being rescued from oblivion, as when Sam Peckinpah made a 1972 movie based on Thompson's 1958 novel *The Getaway.* But at the time of his death in 1977, none of Thompson's twenty-nine novels remained in print.[9]

Thompson's critical reputation began to improve shortly after his death. The French appreciated his genius long before American audiences. Alan Corneau's 1979 film *Serie noire* was based on Thompson's novel *A Hell of a Woman* (1954), and Bertrand Tavernier directed *Coup de torchon* (1982), adapted from *Pop. 1280* (1964). Following the French lead, Americans soon rediscovered Thompson, making up in enthusiasm for what they lacked in timeliness. Geoffrey O'Brien commented in 1985, "Thompson might be, then, a low-budget Dostoevsky in a distinctly American mode, our very own underground man, choking on industrial fumes, blinded by neon bar signs, eking out a living as a door-to-door salesman or a third-rate con man."[10] Nearly all of Thompson's books were reprinted in the late eighties and early nineties as part of Vintage's Crime/Black Lizard series, and appreciations appeared in the *New York Times Book Review,* the *Voice Literary Supplement, Film Comment,* the *New Republic, Time,* and *Newsweek.*[11] In the early nineties, Hollywood produced major film versions of Thompson's *The Grifters, After Dark, My Sweet,* and *The Getaway.* The Thompson renaissance, in fact, was carried to such extremes that mystery novelist and critic Lawrence Block felt compelled to caution, "Just keep in mind that it ain't Shakespeare."[12] As crime novelist Donald Westlake commented, this renewed interest "fits Jim's view of life. He gets his fifteen minutes of fame thirteen years after his death."[13]

That Delicate Gear between Comedy and Tragedy

Thompson often set his stories in the context of Cold War politics. In *The Criminal,* a reporter interviews a teenage boy accused of rape and murder. At a time when juvenile delinquency was a major concern, Thompson related the transformation of the teen zeitgeist to the realities of living in the postwar, atomic age. As the reporter comments: "The kid was about on a par with a good many teenagers I've seen. They aren't watchful exactly. There is rather a look of resigned hopelessness about them: they look as though no good can possibly come to them, albeit they would certainly welcome a little and are rightly entitled to it. I do not recall that kids looked that way in my day. I think it must be the times, this age we live in, when the reasons for existence are lost in the struggle to exist."[14] In his novella, "This World, Then the Fireworks," a psychopathic protagonist commits a murder that is designed to look like an accident. But he is dissatisfied with the neatness of the killing. "It was too simple," he thinks, " . . . and there is already far too much of such studied and stupid simplicity in life. Drop-a-bomb-on-Moscow, the poor-are-terribly-happy thinking. Men are forced to live with this nonsense, this simplicity, and they should have something better in death."[15]

Growing out of the context of the Cold War, the dominant reality of Thompson's universe is complete absurdity. One looks in vain for logic or meaning. In the dying words of a character in his screenplay for Kubrick's *The Killing,* life is "just a bad joke without a punch line." In *The Alcoholics* (1953), Dr. Peter Murphy, head of El Healtho Sanitarium, marvels at how alcoholics defy all the laws of medical science. By all rights, the amount of alcohol they continually consume should be many times more than enough to stop their hearts and render their brains nonfunctional. "Everyone knew these things. Everyone but the alcoholics. . . . Everything happened to them except the one thing which a logical science declared should happen."[16] Thompson's universe as a whole fits his description of the prison in *Recoil* (1953): "It was a madhouse in which the keeper, and not the inmates, was mad."[17]

This absurdity manifests itself in both the storylines and the characters' behavior. Labyrinthine criminal plots are often carried out only, in the end, to serve absolutely no purpose. In *Nothing More Than Murder,* the narrator discovers that his plot to fake the murder of his wife by killing another woman, so that he can take over sole possession of the theater he and his wife run, will accomplish nothing because a large theater chain is intent on running him out of business. "What got me, what made me feel like I was going crazy," he thinks, "was the realization that the woman was going to die for nothing. Her death wasn't going to mean a thing. It was just murder, nothing more than murder, with none of us better off than if she had lived."[18]

Thompson also frequently pointed up the absurdity of his worldview through the ironically self-referential technique of writing himself into his stories. Invariably, when appearing in his own novels, he described himself as an alcoholic whose drunken ravings penetrate to the absurd core of life. He makes his first appearance in *Nothing More Than Murder,* where the narrator comments: "The Literary Club brought an author here once. . . . He was a big gawky guy named Thomas or Thompson or something like that, and I guess he'd put a few under his belt because he sure pulled out all the stops. He spent most of his time talking about people who asked him for free books and seemed to think he ought to be tickled to death to give 'em away. He said that sarcasm was wasted on such people and that the homicide laws ought to be amended to take care of them."[19] On the last page of *The Alcoholics,* Thompson appears at the sanitarium suffering delirium tremens, having been beaten and rolled, babbling incoherently about being a writer. "Doctor Murphy regarded him fondly. 'A grade-A nut,' he said. 'A double-distilled screwball. Just the man to write a book about this place.'"[20] With his appearance in *Savage Night* (1953), Thompson, as author and character, reached new heights (or sank to new lows) in the grotesque nature of his metaphors. The narrator, hit man Carl Bigelow, remembers the time he was hitchhiking when a drunk Thompson picked him up. "He was a writer, only he didn't call himself that. He called himself a hockey peddler. . . . He went on talking, not at all grammatical like you might expect a writer to, and he was funny as hell." Thompson tells Bigelow he has a farm in Vermont where he grows "the more interesting portions of the female anatomy." He also keeps goats on the farm and uses their manure to fertilize the crops, feeding the goats pure grain alcohol. But the stench drives the goats insane, and at night they howl. When Bigelow asks why he does not harvest other anatomical parts, Thompson replies, "Oh, I used to grow other things. . . . Bodies. Faces. Eyes. Expressions. Brains. I grew them in a three-dollar-a-week room down on Fourteenth Street and I ate aspirin when I couldn't raise the dough for a hamburger. And every now and then some lordly book publisher would come down and reap my crop and package it at two-fifty a copy."[21] As this quote indicates, Thompson never adjusted psychologically to writing pulp fiction. He compares his earlier, serious novels to entire persons, but his crime novels are equated only with sexual organs. In a line repeated in several Thompson novels, he tells Bigelow, *"Yes, there is a hell, my boy, and you do not have to dig for it."*[22] At the novel's end, Bigelow escapes to Thompson's farm, where he suffers a rapid descent into insanity and his own personal hell, listening to the goats howl.

Like other black humorists such as Joseph Heller and Kurt Vonnegut,

Thompson underlaid this absurdist worldview with one bedrock reality—death. His books are immersed in death, not only in the large number and often graphic description of murders in his stories, but also in the general view of humans under a sentence of death. In *Ironside,* he wrote, "Add three billion to the planet's mass, and subtract kindness and caring, and you were left not with an unkindly, uncaring three billion, but death."[23] The narrators or main characters of Thompson's stories are often already dead. Occasionally this death is literal. In *After Dark, My Sweet* (1955), for instance, the narrator is killed in the final scene. Since the story has been told in past tense, it becomes apparent that the entire novel has been told from beyond the grave.[24] At other times this death is figurative. In the final line of *Nothing More Than Murder,* the main character, having been caught in his murder scheme and facing a death sentence, thinks, *"They can't hang me. I'm already dead. I've been dead a long, long time."*[25] At the end of *The Killer inside Me,* the psychopathic narrator, Lou Ford, awaiting his inevitable arrest and probable death, thinks, "How can you hurt someone that's already dead."[26]

Faced with the absolute meaninglessness of life, Thompson's characters repeatedly burst into hysterical laughter, often seen as the only alternative to being consumed by the tragedy of the situation. In *Texas by the Tail,* Mitch Corley discovers that his wife Teddy has been working nights as a prostitute: "His emotions locked on the delicate gear between comedy and tragedy, the hideous and hilarious. Then there was a kind of inward back-thrust, the 'kick' of a mechanism that had built up more compression than it was meant to handle. And he began to laugh. He laughed as though his life depended upon laughing well, as, in a sense, it did. He was still laughing, laughing and weeping, when Teddy got up and slugged him with the pisspot."[27] Corley's laughter is liberating because it allows him to leave Teddy and begin a new life. But other characters laugh in resigned acceptance of the inexorable momentum toward death that marks most of Thompson's stories. When Carl Bigelow finds himself locked in a freezer in *Savage Night,* he begins laughing because, as he says, "it was the damndest funniest thing in the world and it was a relief to get it all over."[28] As Nick Corey, the murderous sheriff in *Pop. 1280,* observes, "What else is there to do but laugh an' joke . . . how else can you bear up under the unbearable? It was a cinch that cryin' didn't do no good."[29] Such a view reflects Morris Dickstein's description of literary black humor, which "is pitched at the breaking point where moral anguish explodes into a mixture of comedy and terror, where things are so bad you might as well laugh."[30] Black humor is usually discussed in terms of the high-culture texts of such authors as Nabokov, Pynchon, Barth, Heller, and Vonnegut, but Thompson's indicates that this worldview existed at a variety of levels in postwar American culture. Thompson offered a grassroots, pulp version of black humor, much less concerned with literary gamesmanship and erudition than the elite version and more with the effects of routinized horror and irrationality on society's victims.

Extracting Payment for the Hell I Dwelt In

In the postwar period, modernist authors had largely evolved, in Richard Pells's words, into "well-adjusted servants of the modern state."[31] Hemingway devoted his energies to portraits of heroic elderly fisherman as symbols of humanity writ large, while Dos Passos had become an apologist for American Cold War policies. Modernist texts were being canonized, and modernism itself was losing most of its critical impetus. Thus the dilemma for modernism, according to Irving Howe, became how to find a critical position from which to comment meaningfully on mass society, which was, by definition, overwhelmingly and amorphously banal. "How can one represent malaise," Howe wondered, "which by its nature is vague and without shape?"[32] In this context, modernism's oppositional impulse was inherited by pulp writers like Thompson, Charles Willeford, and Chester Himes.

Several of Thompson's stories are rewritings of modernist classics. His portrait of the grotesqueries of small-town life, *Heed the Thunder,* updates *Winesburg, Ohio.* In both *The Criminal* (1953) and *The Kill-Off* (1957), Thompson used multiple narrators, a technique for which he owed a debt to Faulkner.[33]

With *The Nothing Man* (1953), Thompson revised and updated Hemingway's *The Sun Also Rises.* Like Hemingway's Jake Barnes, Clinton Brown has been emasculated during the war. Unlike Barnes, though, Brown does not seek solace by retreating to Europe or going fishing. In fact, Brown does not want any kind of solace. He follows his former commanding officer, Dave Randall, around, tormenting him, never allowing Randall to forget that he ordered Brown into the minefield where he sustained his injury. Both now work for a small-time California newspaper, Randall as editor, Brown as columnist. In between writing his weekly column and pursuing his deliberate, sardonic sycophancy of the paper's publisher, Brown drinks heavily and unleashes his biting sarcasm on Randall. At one point he asks Randall if he can head his column with the phrase,

"I regret that I had only his penis to give to my country," written in Latin.[34] Another time Brown wonders, "Was every move I made . . . designed to extract payment from the world for the hell I dwelt in?"[35]

Brown is only one of the many grotesque characters inhabiting Thompson's universe. The concept of the grotesque had always played a crucial role in modernism. In the works of such authors as Faulkner, Sherwood Anderson, and Nathanael West, psychologically twisted and emotionally ravaged characters subvert the official optimism of twentieth-century American culture. In the postwar period, modernist authors largely lost their interest in the grotesque (except for a maverick few, like Nelson Algren), preferring to focus instead on the private angst of the middle class. But Thompson insisted on seeing the grotesque as central to postwar culture. In contrast to the dominant image of the affluent middle class, his characters stand as the poor relations and crazy aunts locked in the attic. Like Chester Himes, Thompson often gave characters physical deformities as outward evidence of twisted psyches. In *Savage Night,* Carl Bigelow is a toothless, nearly blind, five-foot-tall hit man, and his lover, Ruthie, has a withered leg with a tiny baby's foot where the knee should be.[36]

But Thompson's most terrifying grotesques are those whose outward appearance completely belies their twisted nature. The most brilliantly conceived of these characters is Lou Ford in *The Killer inside Me.* A deputy in a small Texas town, Ford comes across to other townspeople as a boring simpleton prone to talking in the most banal clichés. In fact, he can read several languages and works advanced calculus problems as a hobby. He adopts his outward persona only as a way of needling people, deliberately seeking to drive them crazy as a means of staving off what he terms "the Sickness." This mental illness began at the age of fourteen, when Ford was seduced by the housekeeper, and his father had never forgiven him. Ford started striking out at all women and, at fifteen, was caught molesting a three-year-old girl. His foster brother was accused and convicted of the crime, but to Ford, all women bear the guilt of that first woman, and all have to pay for her sin.[37] Throughout his adult life, he fought successfully to repress the Sickness until he met Joyce, a prostitute, at which point the Sickness returns, and he has to kill not only Joyce, but also his "respectable" lover, schoolteacher Amy Stanton. As Ford explains to one character just before killing him, the main problem with the world is that people do not recognize the absurdity. "We're living in a funny world, kid, a peculiar civilization. The police are playing crooks in it, and the crooks are doing police duty. . . . Yeah . . . , it's a screwed up, bitched up world, and I'm afraid it's going to stay that way. And I'll tell you why. Because no one, almost no one sees anything wrong with it. They can't see that things are screwed up, so they're not worried about it.'"[38]

Similarly, in *Pop. 1280,* Nick Corey, the sheriff of a small southern town, masks an inner genius beneath a dullard's exterior. Realizing the sheriff's office is a sinecure in which people do not expect him to do anything, Corey enforces the law only against the poor and minorities, groups with no social power.[39] Under this guise he carries out a series of cold-blooded murders for which he frames various others.

Thompson further highlighted the importance of the grotesque in his worldview through the marginality of his characters and settings. Many of his stories are set in barren west Texas or Oklahoma. *The Kill-Off* takes place in a small, declining vacation spot, and *The Grifters* is set in a spiritually barren southern California. These marginal lands, far from suburbia, are populated with grifters, prostitutes, and cold-blooded killers, losers even at crime. In such settings Thompson refuted the optimism of the dominant cultural view of Americans as a "people of plenty," both materially and spiritually.

Creating a Career out of Selling Himself

Just as Thompson often specifically placed his stories in context of postwar international politics, at other times he used domestic Cold War issues to establish his mise-en-scène. In *A Swell-Looking Babe* (1954), the father of the protagonist, Dusty Rhodes, is a victim of anti-red blacklisting, having lost his job as a school principal for signing a petition to allow the communist-front Free Speech Committee to hold a meeting in the school auditorium.[40] In *Recoil,* a right-wing organization, the National Phalanx, and its demagogic leader have created a major national issue by attacking school textbooks for their subversive tendencies. Meanwhile, the political machine that controls the state government is using the National Phalanx and the textbook issue to divert attention from its corrupt relationship with the oil industry.[41]

Thus, in many ways, Thompson always maintained the leftist sympathies he had shown in the thirties. His works resemble Depression-era proletarian literature in their determinism and in their portrait of the squalor created by capitalism. But Thompson avoided any redemptive acts on the part of his working-class subjects. In fact, he laid bare one of the major paradoxes of Marxist thought. As Dwight Macdonald once argued, there exists a fundamental contradiction in socialism. If capitalism is as brutal and dehumanizing as its critics maintain, then it must have done irreparable damage to its victims. But if the history of the workers under capitalism is one of heroic resistance, can the system really be so oppressive?[42] Thompson focused on the first part of the question and argued that the system had irreparably degraded its victims, and his work depicted the psychic ravages of capitalism on society's marginal people. Political action on the part of these victims was problematic because they had been degraded and deformed by social forces more than any other group.

This metapolitical vision was firmly based on Thompson's understanding of the American economic system, with its emphasis on short-term profit with no consideration for long-term consequences. In *Heed the Thunder,* one character thinks back over how, through greed, the beautiful land the white people had discovered had been deforested, the soil exhausted, the creeks dammed, and the people starved. "I remember when the hay-flats—what we call the sand-hills now—was fair land. It wasn't as deep as the valley and more loamy, but it was fair land." The soil was perfect for hay, but people believed they would earn more money by growing grain. So they had, and, in the process, they destroyed the land until it was marked by "sand and cactus an' buzzards and rattlesnakes an' months on end of drought, an' half-starved rickety kids that's going to grow up to do with what's been given to them. . . . And now we ship in most of our hay. Prob'ly from fellows who ought to be growin' wheat."[43] For Thompson, then, the warped and sociopathic culture of postwar America was a direct outgrowth of the system of economic relations. In *South of Heaven* (1967), the narrator hides out by the Pecos River in west Texas. In the cool of the evening he notices a wide variety of animals coming to a pool in the river to get water and marvels at the harmony of birds, rabbits, wolves, and coyotes peacefully coexisting. "This was the end of the day, and everyone had fought and fed enough, and now was the time of truce. . . . I watched and kind of wondered if there were any natural enemies, or whether there was even any enemy anywhere but hunger."[44]

In several stories, Thompson extended his critique with savage parodies of what had become the dominant character type under twentieth-century consumer capitalism. As Warren Susman has argued, in the nineteenth-century, producer-capitalist economy, most cultural sources had stressed the necessity of developing a good character, with emphasis on the internal cultivation of a strong sense of morality. But in the twentieth century, this ethic was gradually supplanted by an emphasis on personality, which was other-directed, stressing the need to fit in and get along. According to Susman, "The social role demanded of all in the new culture of personality was that of a performer. Every American was to become a performing self."[45] But the underside of the cult of personality was manipulation. One worked to please others to get them to do one's bidding. This theme—the fear of the "confidence man"—had been common in American culture at least since the mid-nineteenth century, but it reached its psychopathic apogee in Thompson's fiction.

In Thompson's universe, most characters are performers, wearing masks that allow them to fit in, while covering their darker, manipulative sides. For Lou Ford in *The Killer inside Me* and Nick Corey in *Pop. 1280,* the outward image of boring good old boy covers their inner, homicidal, Machiavellian genius. In *The Nothing Man,* Clinton Brown solidifies his position at the newspaper with his exaggerated obsequiousness toward the publisher, safe in his knowledge that the publisher will never recognize the compliments as satire. "However good you said he was, it wasn't ever quite so good as he *thought* he was."[46]

In *The Getaway,* Doc McCoy is, in the words of one character, a "prince of men."[47] But this hail-fellow-well-met persona masks the most ruthless killer in Thompson's fiction. In a bit of biographical information it is revealed that Doc inherited his personality from his father, a sheriff in a southern state. An incompetent lawman, Doc's father had been a success because he was the "best-liked man in the county." Thus Doc had been "born popular; into a world where he was instantly liked and constantly reassured of his welcome."[48] As a young man, Doc had moved to New York and found a job. But at work he was a disruptive influence because coworkers tended to gather around him, and supervisors often favored him, hurting workplace morale. Though such skills would have made him an ideal upper-level manager, he was too young for such a position.[49] He therefore turned to a life of crime, where he was his own boss, and his personality skills would be an unambiguous boon.[50]

Roy Dillon in *The Grifters* (1963) is not a ruthless killer like Doc McCoy, but a small-time con man. But he too has developed a winning personality, allowing him to successfully manipulate others. "People were his business, knowing them was."[51] Dillon's cover job is as a salesman, and he realizes that the skills needed for selling and conning are essentially the same. "He had made personality a profession, created a career out of selling himself."[52] Eventually he realizes the fundamental insecurity of building his career on this ethic of personality. "What a way to live, he thought resentfully. Always watching every word he said, carefully scrutinizing every word that was said to him. And never making a move that wasn't studiously examined in advance. Figuratively, he walked through life on a high wire, and he could turn his mind from it only at his own peril."[53]

In postwar culture the family provided a much-needed counterbalance to the insecurity of the other-direction of public life. Bunkered down in its suburban tract housing, the family offered well-defined social roles, the means for acculturation, and a center for consumption, all of which ideally created the stability lacking in the outside world. As Elaine Tyler May has argued, traditional family values also served as a stabilizing force in the face of the Cold War and its attendant insecurities.[54] In Thompson's worldview, the family provides none of this equilibrium. He portrayed the American family as beset by a generational, Freudian crisis, more often than not the source of the ravaged psyches of his protagonists. In *A Swell-Looking Babe,* Dusty Rhodes has never forgiven his father for insisting that Dusty stop sleeping with his mother at the age of ten.[55] As Thompson described her, Dusty's mother is primarily responsible for his sexual deformation, a view that reflected common contemporary thought. In his influential 1942 bestseller, *Generation of Vipers,* Philip Wylie had warned against mothers who foster an unhealthy attachment in their sons, rendering them incapable of developing romantic relationships with other women.[56] As Thompson says of Dusty, "Through the years, he had been so formed that he could accept only one woman," and for this reason he completes the Oedipal story by causing the death of his father.[57]

Biting and Ironic Parables

Perhaps most fundamentally, Thompson stood in contrast to the dominant culture in his view of theology. His vision of an absurd universe, of individuals powerless to effect change in the face of vast economic and political forces that deform human nature and society, reflected the existential despair that was a dominant theme of postwar modernism. But Thompson made his criticism of American culture more pointed by suffusing his worldview with savagely ironic Christian symbolism. For in his emphasis on hell, a vengeful, wrathful, and inscrutable god, and the lack of any moral center, Thompson placed himself firmly in opposition to the preferred inscribed reading of Christianity, which in the postwar period stood as a staunch defender of the American economic and political system. Popular religious figures like Billy Graham and Francis Spellman externalized evil, seeing it in the international communist conspiracy, while believing God had particularly blessed the United States, naming it defender of the faith. Theology had been largely reduced in popular culture to the banalities of Norman Vincent Peale's "positive thinking" and President Eisenhower's proclamation, "Our government makes no sense unless it is founded on a deeply felt religious faith—and I don't care what it is."[58] Thompson, then, sought to insert into the public discourse a dark vision of religion at odds with the increasingly vapid, one-dimensional dominant view.

Repeatedly, Thompson indicated that his characters already lived in hell. Jim Dillon in *Now and on Earth* feels he has merely "slipped deeper" into hell. Clinton Brown in *The Nothing Man* is intent on "extract[ing] payment from the world for the hell I dwelt in."[59] Several times Thompson the author repeated the words of Thompson the character, who, in his drunken rant in *Savage Night* announces, "There is a hell . . . and you do not have to dig for it."[60]

Though Thompson's writing was often graphically realistic, his stories frequently end with a surrealistic descent into hell. At the conclusion of *Savage Night,* when Carl Bigelow and Ruthie escape to the farm of the howling goats, the imagery becomes more hallucinatory, the pace of writing more frenetic, and the chapters shorter (seven chapters in six pages), though the characters themselves settle into an immobility of thought and action, neither eating nor talking, doing nothing but watching and listening to the goats. Knowing Ruthie is trying to kill him, Bigelow hides in the basement. When he comes out, she attacks him with an axe, chopping off various body parts, and what is left of Bigelow descends back into the basement. In the conclusion of the penultimate chapter, Bigelow says, "And he was there, of course. Death was there." The final chapter reads, in its entirety, "And he smelled good."[61] In the final two pages of *A Hell of a Woman,* Dolly Dillon's first-person narration literally fractures in two, with alternate lines relating two different versions of his sordid affair in a cheap hotel, sniffing cocaine and shooting heroin. In one narrative, Dillon's lover castrates him, while in the other he commits suicide by leaping out the window.[62]

The conclusion of *The Getaway* is Thompson's most fully realized description of his protagonists' descent into hell. After making a harrowing cross-country escape and committing several cold-blooded murders, forced to hide out in a coffin-sized underwater cave and a manure pile, Doc and Carol McCoy finally slip across the border to the kingdom of El Rey, a near-mythic hideout for criminals under the dominion of its namesake, El Rey. In this kingdom, all accommodations are first class. Residents are forced to pay for first-class services and penalized if they do not spend their bank accounts quickly enough.[63] Eventually, Doc discovers what becomes of those who live long enough to run out of money. Walking out of the main city, he finds a small, peaceful village and asks a policeman where the people get their food before being struck by the horrifying realization that the scent he smells is roasting human flesh. The policeman smiles, saying, "Quite fitting, eh, señor? And such an easy transition. One need only live literally as he has always done figuratively."[64]

Though in many ways Thompson's is, as Barry Gifford has termed it, a "godless world,"[65] it is filled with godlike figures who act as ultimate powers, playing with people's lives for arbitrary reasons, a world in which guilt and innocence are utterly meaningless. These figures are almost never given names, only titles (always capitalized). They usually appear only remotely and vaguely, though they wield tremendous influence. In *The Criminal,* The Captain is a newspaper publisher who, since he is out of town, appears only as a disembodied voice over the phone. Calling the editor, The Captain demands that a rather minor story concerning a rape-murder case be made into a front-page story. Absolutely indifferent to the fact that the weight of evidence indicates the teenage boy accused of the crime is innocent, The Captain insists that the paper work convicts the boy.[66]

In *Savage Night,* The Man plays a similar role. Carl Bigelow had retired as a hit man and thought he had found a perfect hiding place. But the seemingly omnipotent Man had no trouble finding Bigelow and forcing him out of retirement to carry out an assassination. Bigelow says:

> You've heard of The Man. Everyone has. There's hardly a month passes that the papers don't have a story about him or you don't see his picture. One month he's up before some government investigating committee. The next he's attending a big political dinner—laughing and talking to some of the very same people who were putting him through the wringer the month before. . . .
>
> No one has ever pinned anything on him.
>
> He's too big, too powerful, too covered up. You try to pin something on him, and you lose it along the way.[67]

After failing his assignment, Bigelow realizes he is a victim of The Man's peculiar sense of justice. "Excuses didn't cut any ice with The Man. He picked you because you were stupid; he *made* you stupid, you might say. But if you slipped up, *you* did it. And you got what The Man gave people who slipped."[68]

El Rey in *The Getaway* rules his kingdom with the appearance of solicitousness, offering only the best services. When people complain to him, though, he responds with "biting and ironic parables." "People curse him. They call him the devil, and accuse him of thinking he is God. And El Rey will nod to either charge.

'But is there a difference, señor? Where the difference between the punishment and reward when one gets only what he asks for?'"[69] As Doc and Carol soon learn, El Rey "delight[s] in irony, in symbolism; in constantly holding a mirror up to you so that you must see yourself as you are."[70]

The strangest of Thompson's "divine" figures is Nick Corey in *Pop. 1280.* Over the course of the novel, Corey gradually becomes convinced he is God's avenger, that the murders he has committed and any he might commit in the future are divinely sanctioned. In Corey's view, the world is so dominated by sin, both personal and social, that humans deserve to die, that being murdered is, in fact, a relief. At one point, he thinks of the evil growing out of poverty and cruelty:

> The kind of thinkin' that when you ain't doing nothing else but that, why you're better off dead. Because that's the emptiness thinkin' and you're already dead inside, and all you'll do is spread the stink and the terror, the weepin' and wailin', the torture, the starvation, the shame of your deadness. Your emptiness.
>
> I shuddered, thinking how wonderful was our Creator to create such downright hideous things in the world, so that something like murder didn't seem at all bad by comparison.[71]

Losing Every Game but the Last One

Thompson's universe was built on paradox, on the breaking down of binary oppositions. As he portrayed it, there existed a fine line between order and chaos, law and criminality, sanity and insanity. As Carl Bigelow says in *Savage Night,* "A lie and a truth aren't too far apart; you have to start with one to arrive at the other, and the two have a way of overlapping."[72] Thus, for instance, El Rey does not mind being called either God or devil. Similarly, many of Thompson's protagonist/murderers are lawmen—including Lou Ford, Nick Corey, Uncle Bud in *After Dark, My Sweet,* and Doc McCoy in *The Getaway,* who is the son of a sheriff.[73]

In this world of ambiguity and paradox, of moral chaos and confusion, few characters emerge as sympathetic. Occasionally Thompson showed a soft spot for such relatively innocent naïfs as Bob Talbert in *The Criminal,* Patrick Cosgrove in *Recoil,* Toddy Kent in *The Golden Gizmo* (1954), or Tommy Burwell in *South of Heaven,* allowing them to survive their ordeals with some degree of success. But the only people who could be considered at all heroic are those with a general vision of good, but a ruthless and amoral approach to achieving it. All these characters realize they are fighting a losing battle against an absurd system in which even the concept of success is problematic; and yet, like Sisyphus, they keep rolling the stone back up the hill.

One of the best drawn of these characters is Dr. Peter Murphy, head of El Healtho Sanitarium in *The Alcoholics*. Plagued with self-doubt, constantly belittling himself, in the book's opening pages Murphy swims far out in the ocean and seriously contemplates letting himself drown. As Albert Camus commented, the first question modern humans must ask themselves is whether life is worth living, and Murphy reluctantly decides that, at least for one more day, it is.[74] Murphy realizes he inhabits an absurd world. He wonders, for instance, why the patients come to the sanitarium for help and then spend all their time figuring out ways to drink surreptitiously.[75] He feels he is making no progress in finding answers to his or his patients' problems,[76] and yet he continues to believe in his job.[77] Because of that belief, the alcoholics have great respect for him.[78] For this reason, Murphy threatens to blackmail a wealthy family and its rich, successful physician to prevent El Healtho from being closed down.

Like Murphy, attorney Irving Kossmeyer understands the absurdity of the system in which he is mired. A recurring character, Kossmeyer appears in *The Criminal, Cropper's Cabin, A Swell-Looking Babe,* and *The Kill-Off.* Barely five feet tall, with little formal education and sensitive to anti-Semitic slights, Kossmeyer possesses a brilliant legal mind and a great talent for mimicry.[79] He is a "friendly, helpful and terrifying little man."[80] Kossmeyer has no illusions about the nature of the legal system. As he describes Justice, "That gal isn't blind. . . . She's a cross-eyed drunk with d.t.s and a hearing aid and she doesn't know Shinola unless you shove it under her nose."[81] But he has his own, internal sense of justice, and if he believes a person innocent he will do anything to gain an acquittal. In *The Criminal,* for instance, he bribes witnesses in order to help his client.[82] On the other hand, when convinced of someone's guilt, he pursues any means necessary to win a conviction, as in his relentless hounding of Dusty Rhodes in *A Swell-Looking Babe,* whom Kossmeyer believes responsible for Rhodes's father's death. In the end, Rhodes realizes the fact he has convinced everyone else of his innocence is meaningless if Kossmeyer thinks him guilty. "Kossmeyer. He was retribution. He was justice, losing every game but the last one," because he understood that "the game had no rules."[83]

Finally, and most ironically, the character who emerges as heroic in Thompson's universe is Lou Ford—not the cold-blooded, psychopathic Lou Ford of *The Killer inside Me,* but the slightly different Ford in *Wild Town* (1957). The two Fords bear a strong resemblance to each other. Both are lawmen in small

Texas towns, dating schoolteachers named Amy Stanton. On the surface, both are ruthless, corrupt good old boys, but beneath their exterior masks, they are much more intelligent than almost anyone realizes. As Amy explains in *Wild Town,* Ford is actually a brilliant, scholarly man who had been forced to fit in with those around him, and had done so with a vengeance.[84] Throughout most of *Wild Town,* this Lou Ford seems to be the Ford of *The Killer inside Me.* He is cruel to Amy and appears intent on harming the story's protagonist, Bugs McKenna. But in rewriting the character, Thompson gave Ford a chance to redeem himself, making clear the author's thesis that good and evil are not opposites, but matters of nuance. In the end, Ford captures the villain and makes a match between Amy and McKenna, realizing she will be happier with McKenna than with him. Having done so, Ford knows he will forever be stuck in his present situation and that he has lost the woman he loves. He responds in typical Thompson fashion, "laughing at himself, jeering at himself. Laughing away the unbearable."[85]

After Dark, My Sweet

That a pulp writer like Thompson inherited the mantle of modernism should not be surprising. Modernism had developed in the early twentieth century in reaction to the rigid dualisms of the nineteenth-century paradigm. The earlier, Victorian culture had viewed as polar opposites such concepts as morality and immorality, civilization and primitivism, conscious and unconscious, rationality and irrationality. But at a variety of levels, modernist culture worked to deconstruct such oppositions. In the prewar period, noir authors like Dashiell Hammett, Raymond Chandler, James M. Cain, and Horace McCoy created a godless, claustrophobic world where humans struggled in vain to find meaning. But in the postwar era, as modernism increasingly found itself a servant of the state and a weapon in the Cold War, much of its critical spirit was lost. Many intellectuals, simultaneously seeking to preserve serious modernist art and guard against the implicit dangers in mass culture, constructed an edifice around modernist culture to protect it from the incursions of masscult. Thus developed the concept of "high modernism," a culture removed from popular forms.

Despite the best intentions of elite critics, modernism did not disappear from popular culture. In fact, as it became increasingly entrenched in museums and the academy, the original, oppositional impulse of modernism, with its intention of breaking down binary oppositions, was assumed by popular artists like Thompson. The Cold War worldview rested on a series of stark dichotomies—

communisms/democracy, totalitarianism/freedom, morality/immorality—and high modernism, as a servant of the state, rarely challenged such dualisms. But Thompson specialized in shattering such oppositions. His world of ambiguity and paradox grew out of the assumption that such seeming opposites as sanity and insanity, order and chaos, success and failure, god and devil, were merely differences of shading.

2

"It's Always for Nothing"

The Paperback Worldview of Charles Willeford

About halfway through Charles Willeford's debut novel, *High Priest of California* (1953), the narrator, Russell Haxby, a successful though amoral used-car salesman, drops off his date, Alyce. Unsuccessful in his first attempt to seduce her, Haxby has nonetheless begun formulating a long-term strategy toward achieving his goal. Before returning home, he walks into a tavern and orders a drink. Sitting at the bar, he surveys the other customers and notices that the man next to him is approximately his size. Then, without warning or provocation, Haxby attacks. "I put my drink down, raised my elbow level with my shoulder, and spun on my heel. My elbow caught him just below the eye. He raised a beer bottle over his head and my fist caught him flush on the jaw. He dropped to the floor and lay still. I threw a half-dollar on the bar and left. No one looked in my direction as I closed the door." At home, Haxby puts the "Romeo and Juliet Overture" on the turntable. "I poured a glass full of gin and played the overture several times while I finished the drink. After this emotional bath I felt wonderful. I went to bed and slept soundly all night. Like a child."[1]

With this one indelible scene, Willeford presented his vision of the quintessential postwar American man. Beneath the pleasant exterior of a successful used-car salesman lies a soul equally capable of lashing out in meaningless, anonymous violence or appreciating the beauty of Tchaikovsky. While at this point in the novel the events do not come as a complete surprise—earlier Haxby had kneed a parking attendant in the groin for pointing out that he had parked in the wrong spot—the realization that at the core of his soul Haxby is utterly without conscience prepares the reader for the ultimate revelation that he will treat the people in his life with the same cavalier disdain he shows toward his customers at the car lot.

Haxby is merely the first in a series of Willeford protagonists who outline the darker soul of postwar American culture beneath the dominant consensus. In a string of pulp paperbacks published in the fifties and sixties, Willeford created a world in which the predatory cannibalism of American capitalism provides the model for all human relations, in which the American success ethic mercilessly casts aside all who are unable or unwilling to compete, and in which the innate human appreciation of artistic beauty is cruelly distorted by the exigencies of mass culture. If his main characters are not as psychotic as those of Jim Thompson, they are in some ways even more disturbing because of their appearance of normality.

You Realize That You're the Next One to Die

Willeford's bleak vision derived largely from his own childhood experiences. Born in Little Rock, Arkansas, in 1919, he and his mother moved to Los Angeles while he was still an infant, following the death of his father. After his mother died when he was eight, Willeford was raised by his grandmother. As he would later remember, "When you're an orphan at the age of eight, you realize that you're the next one to die. Your vision of life is colored by reality rather than pipe dreams."[2] At fifteen, seeing his grandmother struggling to survive the Depression, Willeford figured they would both be better off if he left home. For a year and a half he wandered the country with an army of Depression-era tramps. "There were hundreds of us riding those box cars," he would later recall, "looking for food wherever we could get it. I developed a wonderful begging technique. I was a sweet blond-haired kid with blue eyes. I'd say, 'I'm hungry' in sort of a pitiful way and housewives would feed me. Then there were transient camps that had soup kitchens and you could always sing a hymn or two in the missions and they'd give you a meal."[3]

After returning home briefly, Willeford joined the army at the age of sixteen, spending two years in the air corps stationed in the Philippines before reenlisting in the cavalry.[4] During World War II, he served as a tank commander with the Third Army and was highly decorated, earning a Silver Star, Bronze Star, Purple Heart, and Luxembourg Croix de Guerre. In public and in his art, Willeford was always relatively reticent about his war experiences. The two volumes of his autobiography cover only his childhood and young adulthood up to the eve of war. When asked about his medals in a 1987 interview, he said dismissively, "In wartime the opportunities to become a hero come every day."[5]

Willeford dealt less explicitly with his war experiences in his work than such other underground artists as Samuel Fuller and Rod Serling, but his military service significantly colored his worldview. His characters are frequently veterans and often apply wartime morals to their lives. As Dover, the Civil War veteran, says in Willeford's self-described "existential Western," *The Hombre from Sonora* (1971, written under the pen name Will Charles), "In four years of fighting . . . I learned two important things about men. First, men are more like animals than gods." He goes on to say that, like sheep, men will stay close together in battle, even when they know spreading out will save their lives. "And two, I learned something about victory and defeat. The only men who win in a war are those who are still alive when it's all over. . . . The cause—the right and wrong of the war—is a notion that don't mean anything, no matter how many fancy words are embroidered around it."[6] Like Dover, Willeford's experiences made him wary of the abstract causes used to justify wars. "Like most everybody else at the time, I bought the whole bill of goods," he would later remember. "Now I know better; there are no such things as 'good' wars. Nothing ever changes because of them, 'cept some people make money and lots of good young boys are killed for nothing. It's always for nothing."[7]

Willeford's military service also provided source material for the terrifying psychopathic figures that populate his fictive world as he pondered how the skills necessary for survival in wartime would translate to postwar society. As he would later say, "A good half of the men you deal with in the Army are psychopaths." Having witnessed instances in which soldiers cold-bloodedly murdered unarmed prisoners, Willeford said, "I used to wonder, 'What's going to happen to these guys when they go back into civilian life? How are they going to act?' You can't just turn it off and go to work in a 7-11. . . . These guys learned to do all sorts of things in the Army that just weren't considered *normal* by civilian standards."[8]

An aspiring poet since his youth, Willeford gained voluminous, if varied, writing experience in the army, penning everything from soap operas for Armed Forces Radio to press releases to generals' speeches.[9] After the war, while completing his twenty years of military service, he published a collection of poetry, *Proletarian Laughter,* in 1948.[10] Beginning with *High Priest of California* in 1953, he also published three novels before retiring from the army in 1956. Returning to civilian life, Willeford continued to write paperbacks while studying at the University of Miami. While his paperbacks earned him a cult following, he was unable to support himself solely by writing fiction, and from the mid-sixties until his death in 1988, he supplemented his income by reviewing mystery and suspense fiction for the *Miami Herald* and teaching in the Miami community college system. But large-scale success eluded him until the eighties when, on the basis of his series of extremely dark and pessimistic (even by American crime novel standards) mysteries set in Miami[11] and tributes from a younger generation of noir authors like Elmore Leonard and Lawrence Block, Willeford finally broke through to a wider audience.

Willeford's dark and twisted vision and perverse sense of humor were the dominant characteristics of his fiction from the beginning. His novels, which appeared during the rapid increase in paperback publishing in the postwar period, feature a high ratio of sex and action written in a laconic style bearing the strong influence of the prewar magazine *Black Mask,* a pulp that had introduced the writings of such hard-boiled crime novelists as Dashiell Hammett and Raymond Chandler.[12] In Willeford, the influence of the *Black Mask* school can be seen in both the violence and pared-down style of passages such as this one from *Wild Wives* (1955): "I smashed my right fist into his face. His nose crushed noisily and blood spattered and smeared against his skin. His nose would never be termed aristocratic again. I hit him again in the face several times. After each blow he tried to scream, but before he could get it out I would hit him again. I didn't try to knock him out. I wanted him conscious; I wanted him to feel it."[13]

Willeford's style fit perfectly the needs of the burgeoning postwar paperback industry. His first five novels were issued by Beacon Books, a paperback publisher since 1951 specializing in novels with titles like *Hitch-Hike Hussy.* Most of Willeford's own titles were changed to give them more appeal on the paperback market: *Until I Am Dead* became *Wild Wives, The Black Mask of Brother Springer* became *Honey Gal, Made in Miami* became *Lust Is a Woman,* and *The Director* became *The Woman Chaser.*[14] All were given appropriately salacious covers; for instance, Beacon's reissue of *High Priest of California,* released as a double novel with *Wild Wives* in 1956, features on the cover a blonde in a low-cut evening dress fending off a partly visible man. A blurb proclaims in large print, "No woman could resist his strange cult of lechery," a line that has nothing whatsoever to do with the book.[15]

As cultural critic Geoffrey O'Brien has said, the same elements that helped foster the widespread popularity of paperbacks in the postwar period frequently made an implicit criticism of the era's dominant culture. While a broad range of media proffered the official inscribed reading of an American culture of affluence, social and political quiescence, and well-adjusted family life, the pulps focused on a seamier world on the margins of society, one marked by passion, greed, and alienation.[16] Because the paperback industry as a whole abjured any seriousness of purpose—these were, after all, merely passing entertainments written in a style accessible to the less educated and available for thirty-five cents at any drugstore—this emergent, counterhegemonic worldview went largely unnoticed by guardians of the dominant culture, who were usually content to dismiss the whole paperback field as unredeemably masscult.

Within this milieu, Willeford succeeded quite well. As he would later say of Beacon's publication of *High Priest of California,* "It had two editions of 100,000 each and sold out, so I knew I had readers from the first."[17] From the beginning Willeford's writing was unusual, even by the standards of pulp crime novels. The "crimes" that form the basis of the books often are not all that serious, and sometimes it is difficult to tell exactly what the crime is. In *High Priest,* for instance, Haxby, working to have Alyce's feeble-minded husband committed to an asylum, often skirts the edges of legality but never does anything seriously criminal.[18] In other novels, the criminal actions range from a failed mutual suicide pact *(Pickup)* to embezzlement *(The Black Mass of Brother Springer)* to arson and assault *(The Woman Chaser).* Though illegal, these are a far cry from the behavior of Jim Thompson's mass murderers and the other psychotics who populated the noir world of the hard-boiled paperbacks. But Willeford's novels often seem more violent than they are because the personal relations in them are based on a kind of emotional violence in which characters warily size each other up like fighters, feinting and then striking with unexpected jabs of cruelty. Sex especially, in Willeford's world, is as hard and fast as a blow to the solar plexus. For instance, Jake Blake, narrator of *Wild Wives,* steps out on a balcony with a woman for a quick tryst and describes the encounter as follows: "I gathered the heavy tweed of her skirt in my fingers, and lifted. The heat of her body reached out for my hands. The flesh of her was firm and yet oddly relaxed. She wasn't wearing much beneath the skirt. In an instant it was all over. Fiercely and abruptly."[19]

Willeford's work was also unusual in its use of the first person. First-person narrators were common in hard-boiled fiction because they gave immediacy to the genre's action and violence. Such narrators, from Raymond Chandler's Philip Marlowe to Mickey Spillane's Mike Hammer, usually fight on the side of law and the social order, no matter how skewed those concepts become in their respective universes. Willeford, however, employed the first person (which he used in all his novels through the fifties and sixties) more in the style of James Cain or Jim Thompson, who allowed the reader to view the world from the twisted perspective of a sociopath. But Willeford differed from writers like Cain and Thompson in that his narrators are seldom murderers and never commit premeditated murder (as do Frank Chambers in *The Postman Always Rings Twice,* Walter Huff in *Double Indemnity,* or any number of Thompson's narrators). Willeford went out of his way to create some sympathetic characteristics for his protagonists—they are almost all artists of one type or another, many have served with distinction in the military, and others are seeking to escape meaningless and degrading jobs. Finally, as Lou Stathis has pointed out, Willeford's narrative style demonstrates a "complete lack of sentimentality and melodrama" and thus differs from that of most hardboiled writers by creating an emotional distance from both the narrator and the events he relates. "Willeford's prose is as flat-toned and evenly cadenced—as emotionally *neutral*—as the blank visages of his feigned-human socio/psychopaths. The narratives are not dramatized, hyped up, played out, or affected as one would a literary gesture— they're just plain *told,* the careful accretion of detail adding up to an incontrovertible truth of insight.[20]

Most of Willeford's protagonists have adjusted successfully to postwar American society, which, given the psychotic nature of these characters, serves as a damning indictment of the dominant culture. In two novels, *High Priest of California* and *The Woman Chaser* (1960), the narrators are used-car salesmen, an occupation that Willeford saw as an appropriate symbol for postwar American culture. The phrase "high priest of California," in fact, came from a *Life* magazine article about used-car salesmen.[21] While the automobile symbolized mobility (as well as rootlessness, as in the writings of Jack Kerouac), consumption, and planned obsolescence, the salesman represented surface charm and bonhomie, together with the predatory and manipulative practices of American-style capitalism. As a coworker says to Russell Haxby as he prepares to cheat a customer, "Mr. Haxby, I sometimes think you ain't got a conscience."[22]

Of course, Willeford made clear that Haxby has not got a conscience, which is seen as an asset rather than a liability in capitalist culture. To prosper in the struggle for success, it is necessary to couple this lack of a moral sensibility with the pleasant, polished exterior of a Dale Carnegie graduate. As one Willeford character says, "To achieve success in the United States a man must be able to do two things well. First he must be able to speak and think on his feet with conviction, and secondly, he must be able to write a good letter."[23]

As Willeford understood, the amoral and predatory vision of his protagonists cannot be confined to their business practices but must also spill over into their personal relations. Used-car salesmen Haxby and Richard Hudson, in *The Woman Chaser,* view the people in their social lives in the same way they see their customers, as marks to be charmed first, then conquered, and finally cast aside. Haxby is intrigued by Alyce, especially her refusal to submit to his attempts at seduction. When he discovers that she is married to a much older man who has grown feebleminded from the ravages of syphilis, and that she feels constrained by a sense of loyalty to him, Haxby gets him fired from his job and makes it look as if he attempted suicide. At this point, Haxby convinces Alyce to have her husband committed, after which she willingly submits to his seduction. The next morning, he drops her off and informs her he is not interested in seeing her again.

> "That's all you wanted then, just to sleep with me and that's all. Now it's over, isn't it?"
> I'd hoped to avoid all this, but she asked for it. "That's right. You catch on quick. . . ."
> "This is pretty hard to take, Russell."
> "I guess it is. Well, Alyce, I won't say it's been nice because it hasn't. See you. . . ."
> "Just like that." She was staring at me like she couldn't believe it.
> "Just like that."[24]

The novel ends with Haxby going to work and trying to seduce the secretary at the lot.

Richard Hudson is even more callously brutal than Russell Haxby. When Hudson quits his job at the used-car lot to become a movie director, he employs Laura as a temporary secretary. After working with her for several days, he seduces her. The next morning he calls the agency and demands a new secretary, saying Laura is inadequate.[25] He ignores Laura's efforts to contact him. When she tracks him down and tells him she is pregnant, he tells her to get an abortion. When she responds that she does not have enough money and begins to cry, Hudson says: "As I straightened up, I brought my fist up hard. My fist caught Laura squarely in the soft part of her rounded belly and sank in wrist deep. . . . She bent over forward, almost falling, took two short backward steps and then sat down hard on the floor. . . . 'You'll be all right now, kid. That ought to do it for you. There'll be a couple of bad days, I suppose, but they can't be helped. The next time you get layed, you'd better use some kind of precautions. I may not be around to help you.'"[26]

And yet existing within these characters, side by side with their calculating and ruthless business and social personalities, is a keen artistic sensibility and overwhelming desire to create works of art of their own. Willeford's narrators are constantly reading Eliot, Kafka, Joyce, Sartre, and Henry Miller or listening to Bartok, Tchaikovsky, and Moussorgsky. All have a knowledge of art that seems to far surpass whatever formal education they have. Jake Blake, for instance, the none-too-bright private investigator who narrates *Wild Wives,* recognizes the make of furniture, the Noh masks, and the Degas in the living room of a mansion.[27]

Willeford sympathetically portrayed the artistic urge to create as a logical outgrowth of the tedium and banality of the work culture of modern America. In *The Black Mask of Brother Springer* (1958), aspiring writer Sam Springer works as an accountant. "Ten years hunched over a desk clutching a No. 2 pencil in my fingers, adding and subtracting, multiplying and dividing, and writing reports had driven me to the brink of madness. I so detested my job I was willing to do anything to escape from it."[28] Springer further understands that far from providing security, his job creates ever-increasing insecurity. "Like all salaried Americans I had the deeply instilled fear of being fired, and the very real knowledge that I could be fired at any moment. This fear is not ever-present, but it lurks in the subconscious, leaping out when a mistake of some kind is made in your work, or when you realize how long you have been working at the same place without any advancement. The longer a man works for one firm, and the older he gets, the greater the fear."[29]

Similarly, Hudson in *The Woman Chaser* decides to become a film director after being struck by the vacuity of the lives of the striving young businessmen he meets. "These men were prisoners! And yet they were unaware of their plight because they were also their own jailers! A feeling of revulsion and terror swept through me. . . . It was the waste, I thought, the foolish waste, the dullness of their lives, the daily repetition of meaningless tasks, the stupidity of such an existence, and underlying everything—all of my thoughts were jumbled together—they didn't *know!*"[30] Out of this realization comes Hudson's determination to create some work of art. "One creative accomplishment could wipe away the useless days and tie up in a single package our reason for being here, our reason for existence."[31]

All of Willeford's aspiring-artist protagonists discover the difficulty of creating art in the context of American consumer culture, where, as one character says, "People . . . buy [art] the same place they get their furniture."[32] As Hudson comments, "With all of the stumbling blocks in the way, it is a wonder that any art at all is ever produced in the United States."[33] In Willeford's universe, the critical sensibility of modernist art must vie with the functional consumerism of tract housing and used cars. As Irving Howe has said, it is difficult to find a vantage point from which to criticize the comfortably amorphous American culture of postwar affluence.[34] In an appropriate image for the relationship between modern art and American culture, in *Wild Wives* Willeford portrayed a San Francisco art gallery owner living in a run-down hotel, where he has decorated the walls with his collection of original Paul Klees in order to brighten his room.[35]

Moreover, Willeford argued, serious artists are forced to compete for the public's attention with the vast amount of dross that comprises American mass culture. In *The Woman Chaser,* Hudson describes his ex-stepfather, Harry Blake, an aspiring popular composer, whose one hit song, "Lumpy Grits," became a standard on the Grand Ole Opry. As Hudson says, "The melody, without the lyrics, isn't too bad. How could it be? Harry stole the tune from a dozen New Orleans blues numbers, a measure at a time, and blended them beautifully." But Blake never penned another hit and finally committed suicide, Hudson says, "probably because he could never again scale the heights reached by the epic 'Lumpy Grits.'"[36]

Despite the aggressive banality of American popular culture, Willeford's protagonists seek to create serious art, which sometimes provides an opportunity for Willeford to satirize the pretensions of midcult sensibilities. In *High Priest of California,* for instance, Haxby's hobby is rewriting Joyce's *Ulysses* in more accessible language by "taking archaic words from the text and converting them to words in current usage. After changing the words in a paragraph, I would rewrite the paragraph in simple terms. . . . Someday I planned to write a book describing the system I worked by, and would utilize my converted text as an appendix. It was a brilliant idea and it would pay off some day, plus bringing a great book to a simple-minded audience."[37] The idea of simplifying the language in Joyce—rather like rearranging the parts of a Picasso portrait so it looks more like a face—captures perfectly Dwight Macdonald's criticism of midcult, in which the original, critical, and disturbing elements of high culture are excised to make the works less threatening and more palatable to a wider audience.

Even those characters who escape the entrapments of the midcult sensibility and genuinely try to create art with a serious purpose face enormous difficulties. One is the paucity of original ideas. In *The Black Mask of Brother Springer* one character describes Springer's novel: "You don't have anything to say. You don't know anything about people and you don't want to learn. . . . I found that out when I read your novel. A clever little book. Why not? You're a well-read man, and the characters said brittle and clever things, the surface brilliance of a thousand books you've read, and not an original idea of your own on a single page."[38]

Finally, even if an artist has something original to say, he must confront the strictures of American commercial culture. When Richard Hudson leaves the used-car lot, he sets out to make a film about the emptiness and banality at the heart of the American dream. He writes and directs a low-budget movie about a truck driver living a drab existence—wife, kids, house payments, and life on the road—who accidentally hits and kills a child as he is driving and decides to make a run for the Mexican border. He quickly becomes the target of a manhunt, and a chase ensues. Police and citizens erect a blockade, and the truck driver, trying to run it, crashes and burns.[39] Hudson completes his film, which everyone at the studio agrees is brilliant. But it is only sixty-three minutes long, and the studio demands that all movies be ninety minutes. Thus, the studio executives decide to add twenty-seven minutes of stock footage to flesh out the film.[40] Believing this will ruin his movie, Hudson is appalled at the cavalier disdain the studio has shown for his masterpiece as well as at his own naïveté. "The realization that I was as much a Feeb as any used car buyer I had ever dealt with did nothing for my morale," he says. "I had been taken just like any clown who believes in the basic goodness of his fellow men."[41]

Nothing Matters to Me

Not all of Willeford's characters are as well integrated into the dominant culture as used-car salesmen Russell Haxby or Richard Hudson. *Pickup* (1954) focuses on Harry Jordan, a figure inhabiting the margins of the culture of affluence. Jordan lives in a perpetual cycle of working menial jobs long enough to get paid, quitting, and spending his money on booze. He meets Helen, a down-and-out woman from a wealthy family, and the two begin living together, exacerbating each other's self-destructive lifestyles. As Jordan says shortly after they first meet, "I'm pretty much of a failure in life, Helen. Does it matter to you?" "No," she responds. "Nothing matters to me."[42]

As the novel proceeds, it becomes apparent that Jordan was not always a failure. He had once been an artist training at the Art Institute of Chicago and had taught at a private prep school. But at the beginning of the novel, he has not painted in three years because, as he says, he could not capture the essence of the paintings as he pictured them in his head. As a teacher he had also failed because he refused to give encouragement to the "many art students who should have been mechanics."[43]

Without art, he has lost his raison d'être. "All my life I had only wanted to paint. There isn't any substitute for painting. Coming to a sudden, brutal stop left me without anything to look forward to."[44] He began eking out a marginal living, passively waiting for death to come. In Helen he finds a kindred soul, telling her, "This isn't our kind of world, Helen. And we don't have the answer to it either. We aren't going to beat it by drinking and yet, the only way we can possibly face it is by drinking!"[45] The two make a suicide pact, but Helen says she is not strong enough to kill herself. Jordan agrees to help, strangles her, and lies down beside her with the gas turned on. But he is discovered before he dies and revives. "Printed in large, wavering letters on the surface of my returning consciousness was the word for Harry Jordan: FAILURE. Somehow, I wasn't surprised. Harry Jordan was a failure in everything he tried. Even suicide."[46]

Jordan makes a full confession to the police and contents himself with the thought that the state will now complete what he was unable to. But to his amazement he is informed that Helen died of a bad heart, not from strangulation. Without warning and with little explanation, he is released from prison. Standing in a pouring rain, Jordan wonders what to do with the rest of his life. Then, on the final page, Willeford delivers the novel's punch line. "I left the shelter of the awning and walked up the hill in the rain. Just a tall, lonely Negro. Walking in the rain."[47]

Until this point there has been no hint that Jordan is black, and Willeford's two concluding lines transform the reader's entire understanding of the novel. Suddenly Jordan's acute alienation is given a sociopolitical basis; his marginality and inability to express himself artistically are given broader symbolic meaning. With its conclusion, *Pickup* becomes a kind of retelling of the major prewar African American novel, Richard Wright's *Native Son* (1940).[48] Like Wright's Bigger Thomas, Jordan strangles the daughter of a socially prominent white family. But the thematic differences between the two novels indicate the way in which sensibilities changed between the Depression era, in which Wright wrote, and the postwar period. Jordan is not the victim of overt racial hatred and discrimination, like Bigger, but suffers from inarticulateness—an inability to express the meaning of his life and thus the conviction that his life has no meaning. His oppression comes not from being denied jobs and forced to live in ghettos, but from the therapeutic state in the guise of psychiatrists trying to make him fit comfortably into a social order he believes is fundamentally meaningless. After being jailed for the murder of a white woman, Jordan is not subjected to the howls of racist mobs demanding his execution, but to a public titillated by a case of interracial love and murder, as seen when a reporter from *He-Man* magazine visits Jordan's cell and offers to buy the rights to his story.

Pickup also resembles a later novel, Dorothy Hughes's *The Expendable Man* (1963), a murder mystery in which it is not revealed until one-fourth of the way through the story that the protagonist is black. As Frankie Bailey has said in her study of images of African Americans in crime fiction, this approach allows the reader to be introduced to the main character independent of the "mythology of race" that is a fundamental part of American culture.[49] But there are crucial differences between Willeford's and Hughes's books. Writing at the peak of the civil rights movement, Hughes created a respectable black character whom no rational person would want to deny integration into mainstream society. He is a successful intern at the U.C.L.A. Medical Center, the product of a middle-class upbringing, unfailingly clean and well-mannered, who could only be suspected of the crime of which he stands accused because of the unreasoning racist mentality of provincial Americans. In the end he is absolved of the crime and reintegrated into the dominant culture.[50]

Willeford rejected the liberal vision that integration would proceed smoothly as soon as blind prejudice was defeated. His view was much more like that of Chester Himes (whom Willeford greatly admired),[51] who felt that society had severely deformed black culture and personality to the point that integration was problematic. Willeford understood this process but saw it as having even broader implications, for in his alienation, Harry Jordan represents Willeford's vision of the quintessential modern man. In response to Camus's fundamental modern question—"Judging whether life is or is not worth living"[52]—Jordan answers resoundingly that it is not. Similarly, he keeps finding himself confronted by the reality of his own freedom. After being kicked out of prison at the end of the novel, he thinks, "The ugly word, 'Freedom' overlapped and crowded out any nearly rational thoughts that tried to cope with it."[53] Just as Erich Fromm described the modern human condition, Jordan seeks to escape the responsibilities of that freedom.[54]

For most intellectuals in the late forties and early fifties, as Morris Dickstein has argued, Jews, especially "secular Jewish intellectuals," were symbols of modern humanity. Alienated both from the immigrant culture of their parents and the dominant WASP culture, Jewish intellectuals sought to find an appropriate balance between personal identity and social acceptance.[55] Willeford tapped into an emergent postwar cultural view that instead found its symbols in the social underclass, the racial minorities and the superfluous people inhabiting the space around the margins of the affluent society. Over the course of the next decade, this vision would be gradually politicized until, ten years after the publication of *Pickup,* Herbert Marcuse could identify such people as the radical contradiction of American capitalist culture: "Underneath the conservative popular base is the substratum of the outcasts and outsiders, the exploited and persecuted of other races and other colors, the unemployed and the unemployable. They exist outside the democratic process; their life is the most immediate and the most real need for ending intolerable conditions and institutions. Thus their opposition is revolutionary even if their consciousness is not."[56]

Willeford focused specifically on African American opposition to dominant social institutions in *The Black Mask of Brother Springer* (1958), one of the first novels to deal with the post–Brown decision civil rights movement. After quitting his job in Ohio, Samuel Springer moves to Florida where, through a set of convoluted circumstances, he becomes a minister in the all-black Church of God's Flock in Jacksonville, Florida, despite the fact that he is white and has no religious beliefs of his own. But the abbot who ordains him assures Springer that all ministers are frauds and rechristens him the Right Reverend Deuteronomy Springer.[57]

Springer is accepted by his congregation and quickly becomes a popular minister. He envies his parishioners' "blind, unreasoning belief,"[58] but he soon discovers their faith contains depths that, in his cynicism, he never imagined. When a black woman is arrested for refusing to give up her seat on a city bus, the local black ministers invite Springer to join them in formulating a response. Springer proposes they openly violate the law, willingly go to jail, and, in the meantime, organize a citywide bus boycott. Certain the other clergy are as fraudulent as he is, he is amazed when they quickly agree to his plan.[59] He describes the attitude of the black ministers in Sisyphean terms: "The Negro ministers were men with a painful, incurable disease. They had tried cure after cure only to find that their disease persisted; and they felt in their hearts that not even death would wipe out the cause of their illness. . . . Another skirmish, another brush with the law might bring a light concession or gain to their never ending fight to gain equality. Most likely, they would lose. They fully expected to lose, but they were still willing to go through the motions."[60]

The bus boycott is extremely successful, and Springer increasingly comes under attack by the local white community, which alternately denounces him as a meddling northerner and seeks to bribe him into selling out the movement. Because he is a typical Willeford protagonist, Springer does eventually sell out, taking the bribe money as well as raiding the local movement's coffers and absconding with the beautiful wife of his wealthiest parishioner. Going through Atlanta on his way to New York, he sees a newspaper headline, "Race Riot in Jax—4 Killed," but he does not bother to read the story, saying, "I thought, I don't want to read about it. That is a chapter in my life that is over and done with, and I must only look ahead."[61]

Even though Springer ultimately betrays the cause (at the novel's end, he changes his first name to Judas), Willeford's portrait of the civil rights movement was both sympathetic and complex. He showed the struggle rife with conflicts between middle- and working-class blacks, leaders and followers, advocates of violence and nonviolence, and the movement at the national and local levels. Fundamentally, he portrayed it as a grass-roots, democratic movement. Within his bleak worldview of vacuity and viciousness, absurdity and alienation, he allowed for a glimmer of hope in the existential struggle of southern African Americans to gain equal rights. In a world in which human relationships are based on cold calculation and ruthless manipulation, the example of a community of people standing together and demanding equality offered a model for all. As Marcuse wrote, "When [minority groups] get together and go out into the streets, without arms, without protection, in order to ask for the most primitive civil rights, they know that they face dogs, stones, and bombs, jail, concentration camps, even death. Their force is behind every political demonstration for the victims of law and order. The fact that they start refusing to play the game may be the fact which marks the beginning of the end of a period."[62]

Part Two

Progress
and Its
Discontents

Science Fiction and
Fantasy Authors

"I'm Being Ironic"

Imperialism, Mass Culture, and the Fantastic World of Ray Bradbury

Over lunch one day, a friend asked Ray Bradbury where he got the ideas for his stories. "Anywhere," the author replied, looking at the mushrooms on his plate. "There's a story in mushrooms." To prove his point, Bradbury went home and wrote a frightening tale of extraterrestrial invaders coming to Earth in the form of mushrooms, taking over the bodies of those who eat them. The story appeared as a brilliant episode of the television show "Alfred Hitchcock Presents" entitled "Special Delivery" (1959) and was later published as a short story, "Come into My Cellar" (1962).[1]

Few artists in the postwar period maintained so childlike a sense of wonder as did Bradbury. Fascinated with the possibilities created by the scientific and technological revolutions of the twentieth century, Bradbury created a fictive universe where travel to Mars and beyond (even to the sun itself), totally automated houses, and a society that satisfies every physical pleasure are commonplace. Despite his fascination with the possibilities created by technology, Bradbury's work expressed a profound ambivalence. His sense of wonder also contained a strong element of terror and made possible such nightmarish visions as invading mushrooms. In Bradbury's world, complete paranoia is complete awareness, as people constantly find themselves under siege by such forces as totalitarian governments, alien invaders, newborn infants, and the natural elements. To some extent, this theme reflected the official paranoia of American Cold War policy, but Bradbury complicated this reductionist reading of his work by occasionally making his invaders benign sojourners who fall victim to the lynch-mob mentality of paranoid Americans and also, in several stories, by turning the tables and making Americans the aliens invading distant lands.

Moreover, Bradbury feared the effects of technology on society and the human spirit. He saw social forces at work actively seeking to crush humans' ability to think critically, both through political suppression of dissent and by means of a culture that satiated less cerebral, more physical desires. In such works as *Fahrenheit 451* (1953), Bradbury penned a critique of mass culture that reflected the elite cultural view of the postwar period. The supreme irony, though, is that Bradbury made this criticism in the guise of a science fiction novel, one of the most debased forms of mass culture and the literary establishment's equivalent of exile to Siberia.

Bradbury was an outspoken liberal, and several of his early stories and nonfiction writings were self-consciously designed as polemics. After the 1952 election, for instance, he published a full-page advertisement in *Variety* deploring the Republican practice of tarring Democrats like himself as left-wing or unAmerican. "I have seen too much fear in a country that has no right to be afraid," he complained. "I have seen too many campaigns . . . won on the issue of fear itself, and not on the facts." Finally, Bradbury pleaded, "in the name of all that is right and good and fair, let us send McCarthy and his friends back to Salem and the seventeenth century."[2] At the same time, though, many of Bradbury's stories undermine the efficacy of liberal reformism, arguing that where such reforms are not oppressive attacks on the imagination, they often tend to vastly underestimate such unpleasant realities as evil and death.

Despite his avowed liberalism, as an artist Bradbury was not really interested in politics in any traditional sense. Rather, his focus was always on the individual. With Dwight Macdonald, Bradbury could easily have complained, "The trouble is everything is too big. There are too many people, for example, in the city I live in. In walking along the street, one passes scores of other people every minute; any response to them as human beings is impossible. . . . A style of behavior which refuses to recognize the human existence of the others has grown up of necessity."[3] In his art, Bradbury resisted this modern tendency. He always avoided the abstract level of political language, which, as George Orwell said, is primarily "the defense of the indefensible . . . [and thus] has to consist largely of euphemism, question-begging and sheer cloudy vagueness."[4] Therefore, for instance, while Bradbury's stories are filled with images of nuclear holocaust, he never discussed the wars that caused the apocalypse. Bradbury insisted on viewing the world on a human scale. In this way he was able to articulate a wide-ranging critique of American society, from its totalitarian characteristics and cultural pressure for conformity to its imperialist foreign policy, while escaping the censure encountered by many more explicitly political artists.

"Bradbury," wrote Kingsley Amis in *New Maps of Hell,* his 1960 study of science fiction, "is the Louis Armstrong of science fiction, not in the sense of age or self-repetition but that he is the one practitioner well-known by name to those who know nothing whatever about his field."[5] Primarily on the basis of *The Martian Chronicles* (1950) and *Fahrenheit 451,* Bradbury was the first of those who began writing for the science fiction pulps to attain mainstream commercial and critical success. By the sixties, his books were emblazoned with the unattributed quote, "The World's Greatest Living Science Fiction Writer." But classifying Bradbury as a science fiction writer is problematic. As science fiction author and critic Damon Knight commented, "Although he has a large following among science fiction readers, there is at least an equally large contingent of people who cannot stomach his work at all; they say he has no respect for the medium; that he does not even trouble to make his scientific double-talk convincing; that—worst crime of all—he fears and distrusts science."[6] Despite being without honor among many science fiction purists, Bradbury has gained a great deal of respect from artists and intellectuals across the cultural and political spectrum. John Huston asked Bradbury to write the screenplay for his 1953 movie, *Moby Dick,* and François Truffaut made a film of *Fahrenheit 451* (1967). Christopher Isherwood, Nelson Algren, Kurt Vonnegut, and Ingmar Bergman all proclaimed themselves fans, and the enthusiasm of Federico Fellini and Bernard Berenson led to personal friendships with Bradbury. Russell Kirk, the leading intellectual light of postwar conservatism, has stated, "like C. S. Lewis, like J. R. R. Tolkien, Ray Bradbury has drawn the sword against the dreary and corrupting materialism of this century: against society as producer-and-consumer equation, against the hideousness in modern life, against the mindless power, against sexual obsession, against sham intellectuality, against the perversion of right reason into the mentality of the TV viewer."[7] Harlan Ellison, doyen of the American New Wave science fiction authors of the sixties, wrote in response to criticism of Bradbury: "Ray Bradbury is very probably better than we ever imagined him to be in our wildest dreams. . . . Let's face it, fellow readers, we've been living off Ray Bradbury's success for twenty years. Every time we try to hype some non-believer into accepting sf and fantasy as legitimate *literature,* we refer him or her to the words of Ray Bradbury. Who the hell else have we produced who has approached the level of Bradbury for general acceptance?"[8]

Part of the problem is that, as many science fiction fans have argued, Bradbury is not really a science fiction writer at all. Unlike Isaac Asimov, for instance, Bradbury is not a scientist and knows little about physics, chemistry, or the other fields that form the basis for science fiction. Other attempts to label Bradbury, such as "fantasist" or "futurist," are similarly inadequate. Though he built his reputation on the science fiction, horror, and fantasy stories he published in the forties and early fifties in such pulp magazines as *Weird Tales, Planet Stories, Amazing Stories,* and *Galaxy,* he also published crime and mystery stories in *Dime Mystery, Detective Tales,* and *New Detective Magazine* as well as straight fiction in such mass-circulation journals as the *American Mercury,* the *New Yorker, Collier's, Playboy,* and the *Saturday Evening Post.* Like most artists in the underground culture, Bradbury not only openly flouted arbitrary categorization, he consciously sought to break down the rigid definitions he thought limited artists.

Bradbury was born in 1920 in Waukegan, Illinois, a small town on Lake Michigan forty miles north of downtown Chicago. Waukegan would eventually play a major role in Bradbury's fiction as the embodiment of the idyllic, slow-paced life and community values of premodern America. In 1932 the family moved to Tucson and, in 1934, to Los Angeles, where Bradbury has lived ever since. His formal education ended after graduating from high school, but in the late thirties he joined the Los Angeles Science Fantasy society, where he formed friendships with such established writers as Robert Heinlein, Henry Kuttner, and Leigh Brackett, all of whom played major roles in the Golden Age of science fiction.[9] While Bradbury was deeply influenced by these early friendships, he largely forged his own literary path. The dominant figure in science fiction's Golden Age was Robert Campbell, editor of such pulp journals as *Astounding Science Fiction,* who nourished nearly every major writer in the field in the postwar period.[10] But Bradbury had little luck selling his stories to Campbell and thus became, as Asimov commented, "the only great writer of the Golden Age to remain outside the Campbell stable."[11]

To understand Bradbury's career, one must recognize the paradoxes inherent in his worldview. At times a savage critic of mass culture, he was also an unabashed product of American popular culture, listing among his formative influences carnivals, movies, radio, and comic strips, as well as the writings of Poe, Bierce, L. Frank Baum, H. P. Lovecraft, and Edgar Rice Burroughs. The artist, he has stated, needs to be well versed in both popular and high culture. "From an ever-roaming curiosity in all the arts, from bad radio to good theater, from nursery rhyme to symphony, from jungle compound to Kafka's *Castle,* there is basic excellence to be winnowed out, truths found, kept, savored and used on some later day. To be a child of one's time is to do all these things."[12] Bradbury was both fascinated with the prospects of the future and anchored in nostalgia for the small-town past of his youth. He was simultaneously obsessed with and wary of technological progress. For instance, while his stories are filled with rocket and time travel, the author himself never learned to drive and, until relatively late in life, refused to fly.[13] Such contradictions form the ideological basis of Bradbury's oeuvre. Like his character in *Dandelion Wine* (1957), "He was a man who did not suffer but pleasured in sleepless nights of brooding on the great clock of the universe running down or winding itself up, who could tell? But many nights listening, he decided first one way and then the other."[14]

A Silly, Mad Plot

In his short story "Pillar of Fire" (1948), Bradbury told the story of a twentieth-century man, William Lantry, who rises from the dead in the year 2349 to find a world in which all fantasy has been eradicated. Children are not afraid of the dark, and people do not understand such concepts as dishonesty and criminality. Lantry declares a one-man war on this sterile world, and, as he goes around murdering people, he is convinced he can continue doing so indefinitely. After all, he thinks, "Paranoids were nonexistent in this civilization."[15]

Within Bradbury's universe, an absence of paranoia is an unhealthy sign, because it reflects a dangerous naïveté. Throughout his stories, people are constantly under attack by forces not only beyond their power to resist, but even beyond their power to comprehend. In "The Small Assassin" (1946), a mother insists her infant son is trying to kill her. Her husband thinks she is losing her mind, and the kindly Dr. Jeffers insists she is suffering from normal postpartum depression. Only too late does her husband come to believe her. When he tries to convince Jeffers the baby murdered its mother, the doctor says, "If what you say is true, then every mother in the world would have to look on her baby as something to dread, something to wonder about." The husband responds, "And why not? Hasn't the child a perfect alibi? A thousand years of accepted medical belief protects him. By all natural accounts he is helpless, not responsible.

The child is born hating. . . . In later years it would be too late to express its hatred. *Now* would be the time to strike."[16] Similarly, in "The Wind" (1943), a man is being pursued by the world's winds, which are an intelligent force, because he has discovered the remote valley in the Himalayas where the winds gather and plot destruction.[17]

It would be a mistake, however, to reduce Bradbury's paranoid vision to a mere reflection of the Cold War mentality. In the first place, his paranoia is evident from his writings in the early and mid-forties, before the Cold War. Moreover, it is multifaceted, serving a variety of allegorical purposes. Sometimes he used it to comment on the potentially threatening anonymity of modern life. In "The Crowd" (1943), a man wonders who the people are who immediately show up at automobile accidents. Investigating, he realizes that the same people make up the crowd of onlookers at all disasters, and whether the victim lives or dies depends on the actions of these mysterious people. "It was all a silly, mad plot. Like every accident. . . . And that's the way it's been since time began, when crowds gather. You murder much easier, this way. Your alibi is very simple; you didn't mean to hurt him." With evidence in hand, the man heads to the police, only to find himself in an accident, surrounded by the mysterious, omnipresent crowd.[18]

Whatever its origins, Bradbury's vision dovetailed smoothly with the emergence of paranoia as the dominant cultural sensibility in the Cold War period, and in several stories he made this connection explicit. In "Zero Hour" (1947), the world has grown complacent because people believe perfect peace has been obtained through a balance of weapons. Mrs. Morris is amused when the children in the neighborhood begin playing a game called "invasion." As her seven-year-old daughter tells her, they are being aided by an alien only the younger children can see, because only they have the imagination to see into the fourth dimension. The alien tells the children they will be a fifth column, paving the way for the invasion. Only too late does Mrs. Morris realize it is not a game.[19] In "Come into My Cellar," Bradbury played on common Cold War science fiction imagery, in which invaders take over the bodies of humans. Arriving in the form of mushrooms, the aliens assume control of the bodies of those who ingest them. Interestingly, as in "Zero Hour," the aliens conduct their invasion by means of children, spreading across the country through an advertisement on the back of *Popular Mechanics* encouraging kids to grow mushrooms in their own cellars.[20]

Elsewhere Bradbury undermined the straightforward anticommunist reading of such invasion stories. In his story "It Came from Outer Space," the basis of the 1953 movie, an alien craft lands on Earth, and the extraterrestrials begin taking over the bodies of humans. When one man figures out what is happening, the aliens inform him they mean no harm and are only borrowing the human bodies until they can repair their ship. They cannot appear in their true form, they say, because humans, who are such xenophobes, would find them too ugly and attack them. Sure enough, upon discovering the aliens, the townspeople form a posse to lynch them. As film critic Peter Biskind has argued, "*It Came from Outer Space* begins like a radical-right film, but it is gradually transformed into a left-wing film as it becomes clear that the aliens mean us no harm. . . . 'Don't be afraid,' they [say] in a disconcerting monotone. 'We don't want to hurt you. We have souls and minds, and we are good.' Not only are we relieved, we feel sorry for them. . . . They had struggled thousands of years to reach the stars, only to end up in the middle of a godforsaken desert someplace on Earth harassed by a bunch of dumb yokels."[21]

Bradbury also deconstructed the Cold War trope of anticommunist invasion films by frequently presenting humans—and specifically Americans—as the alien invaders. In "The City" (1950), a deserted city on a distant planet has waited 20,000 years for its revenge on humans, who had wiped out the original inhabitants by infecting them with a human disease. Highly mechanized, the city has been programmed to murder the crew of an arriving ship, replace them with robot duplicates, and send them back to Earth carrying a deadly virus.[22]

In fact, several of Bradbury's works form a sustained critique of American imperialism, both historical and contemporary. In "Perhaps We Are Going Away" (1964), two Indians, an elderly man and a boy, sense something in the air telling them their world has suddenly changed forever. They go looking for the cause of this feeling and find it in a lonely-looking encampment of white men along the seashore, the first Europeans they have ever seen.[23] And in *The Martian Chronicles,* a Cherokee astronaut specifically links human destruction of the ancient Martian civilization with the devastating effects of white policy toward the Native American population.[24]

Bradbury continued his discussion of American imperialism in his Martian stories. Space exploration and the settlement of other planets gave him an opportunity to discuss the continuing importance of the frontier in American mythology. As usual, he was ambivalent about the frontier tradition. "The Wilderness" (1952) focused on a group of women preparing to join their husbands as some of the first settlers on Mars. One thinks: "Is this how it was over a century ago

. . . when the women, the night before, lay ready for sleep, or not ready, in the small towns of the East, and heard the sound of horses in the night and the creak of the Conastoga wagons ready to go? . . . Is this, then, how it was so long ago? On the rim of the precipice, on the edge of the cliff of stars. In their time the smell of buffalo, and in our time the smell of the Rocket."[25]

In linking the future colonization of space with America's history of expansion, Bradbury was critical of U.S. policy and its impact on foreign lands and peoples. Significantly, these stories were written in the late forties and fifties, at the height of the Cold War. At a time when dissent regarding foreign policy had been largely driven out of public discourse, Bradbury used these allegorical tales to raise troubling questions about America's role in foreign affairs.

As he made clear in *The Martian Chronicles,* when Bradbury talked about humans settling other planets, he specifically meant Americans.[26] The Americans are definitely not welcome, and the Martians kill the visitors at the end of the first three landings. Just as they destroyed the Indians, the Americans end up conquering the planet anyway, inadvertently wiping out the native population by importing alien diseases.

After decimating the population, the Americans begin a policy of desecrating the Martian landscape. One character reflects on the human capacity to destroy nature, specifically blaming "commercial interests."[27] The destruction of the Martian culture ushers in a new attitude toward the land, signaled by the names given the natural and man-made features. "The old Martian names were names of water and air and hills. They were the names of snows that emptied south in stone canals to fill the empty seas." But the human names are ugly and functional: Iron Town, Aluminum City, Corn Town, Detroit II.[28] Bradbury further developed his indictment of the eco-destruction engendered by American imperialism in his story "Here There Be Tygers" (1951). An expedition to a lush planet is financed by a mining company, whose representative, Chatterton, openly proclaims his desire to mine the planet with no concern for the long-term effects. But the planet has the self-protective ability to mete out rewards or punishments to the settlers, and while the rest of the crew, who love the planet, are granted their every desire, Chatterton sees his expensive drill swallowed up by the earth and is devoured by tigers.[29]

In addition to his broader critique of American imperialism, Bradbury wrote several antiwar stories in the early fifties, when the Cold War heated up in Korea. "A Piece of Wood" (1952) is the story of a soldier who invents a device that turns all weapons to rust. He is hunted by the military brass, who fear "mass panic." "Each nation would think itself the only unarmed nation in the world, and would blame its enemies for the disaster. There'd be waves of suicide, stocks collapsing, a million tragedies."[30] "There Will Come Soft Rains" (1950) is a haunting story of an automated house that goes on working for years after its inhabitants are vaporized in a nuclear war.[31] In "The Garbage Collector" (1953), the title character tells his wife he is quitting the job he has worked for many years because it has totally changed. Garbage trucks were being equipped with radios so that, in case of nuclear war, they could be dispatched to pick up bodies. His wife encourages him to think his decision over, but he says, "I'm afraid if I think it over, about my truck and my new work, I'll get used to it. And, oh Christ, it just doesn't seem right a man, a human being, should ever let himself get used to any idea like that."[32]

The Other Foot

Despite his obsession with death and the genuinely terrifying nature of some of his horror stories, Bradbury has been frequently dismissed as possessing a sentimentalized vision, especially of childhood and small-town life. As Damon Knight correctly pointed out, with success Bradbury increasingly elected to forego straight horror stories in favor of romanticized slices of Americana.[33] But beneath his Norman Rockwell–like nostalgia stories there frequently lies a dark underside threatening to subsume the atmosphere of security and quietude. For example, in *Dandelion Wine,* Bradbury's collection of fictionalized reminiscences of his childhood in Waukegan, the town's geography is dominated by the ravine, a black and threatening abyss that frightens even the adults who have to cross it after dark. Moreover, lurking around the town is the Lonely One, a rapist and strangler who has been preying on young women and is closely associated in townspeople's minds with the ravine.[34] Also, Bradbury consistently used his vision of a halcyon age as a critique of American modernization. Faced with the onslaught of industrialization, mechanization, urbanization, and mass culture, he repeatedly emphasized the world we have lost.

To further his criticism of modern society, Bradbury frequently presented romanticized views of foreign cultures or subcultures that he found charming— and sometimes threatening—because of their premodern value system. In a series of stories about Ireland, Bradbury portrayed a society filled with eccentrics that respected its art and music and was centered around the community and camaraderie symbolized by the local pub.[35] Another series of stories was set in the village of Guanajuato, Mexico, a culture that Bradbury both admired and feared for its integration of death into the daily existence of the town's inhabitants.[36] Bradbury also wrote several stories set in monasteries, showing admiration for the slow-paced, contemplative, and communal lives of priests.[37]

Throughout his work, Bradbury expressed strong sympathy for those living on the margins of society—minorities, outcasts, and grotesques. Frequently these outsiders are carnival people, witches, warlocks, vampires, or some other type of monster. In "The Dwarf" (1953), the title character goes alone into a fun house every night to stare at himself in a mirror that makes him appear tall and thin.[38] "Uncle Einer" (1947) is a vampire who, while flying one night, crashes into a high-tension tower and loses his sense of direction, thus becoming another of Bradbury's victims of technology.[39] "The Fog Horn" (1951) tells the story of a lovesick dinosaur, last of an extinct breed, who mistakes the sound of a foghorn for the mating cry of another dinosaur.[40]

This sympathy for outcasts prompted Bradbury to write several interesting stories focusing on racial and ethnic minorities. "The Big Black and White Game" (1945), for example, concerns a baseball game between the blacks and whites in a small midwestern town. The game degenerates into a riot after a white player spikes the black first baseman. The story portrays the anger, ready to explode in violence, lurking just beneath the surface of black consciousness, which few whites were willing to recognize in the mid-forties.[41] In a pair of Martian stories published in the early fifties, Bradbury extended his vision of black resistance. "Way in the Middle of the Air" (1950) opens with all the blacks in the South packing up one morning and boarding rockets to fly to Mars. The whites are stunned and hurt. One white woman moans that she will be lost without her maid. Another white man says, "I can't figure why they left *now*. With things lookin' up. I mean every day they got more rights. What they *want*, anyway? Here's the poll tax gone, and more and more states passin' anti-lynchin' bills and all kinds of equal rights. What *more* they want?"[42] In a sequel, "The Other Foot" (1951), Mars, populated solely by African Americans, is visited by white astronauts for the first time after twenty years. Several blacks prepare to lynch the intruders. But the white astronauts tell them Earth's civilization has been destroyed in World War III, and the Earthlings desperately need their help. At first the black Martians refuse, but when the visitors begin listing the cities destroyed in the war, including many of their hometowns, their hearts soften, and they agree to help.[43] In these stories Bradbury countered the optimism of white liberals concerning the willingness of African Americans to patiently seek integration into white society.

Elsewhere Bradbury painted sympathetic portraits of other minorities. "The Long Night" (1944) is set in Los Angeles during the zoot suit riots. The story is narrated by a Mexican-American pachuco who discovers the riots are being instigated by a Nazi agent provocateur seeking to stir up racial animosity. But when he tries to warn people, he is set upon by a gang of whites and badly beaten. "Sometimes," he thinks, "they won't let you change sides in a war."[44] "I See You Never" (1947) is a touching story, also set in Bradbury's native Los Angeles, about an illegal immigrant, about to be deported, who comes to bid a tearful farewell to his landlady.[45] While these two stories present sympathetic Hispanic characters victimized by white society, Bradbury also used Latinos to represent such values as community, which he found lacking in modern culture. In "The Wonderful Ice Cream Suit" (1958), he painted a romanticized portrait of a group of young, unemployed Latinos who find six men about the same size, each of whom contributes ten dollars to buy a fancy suit. The first night they own it, each one gets to wear the suit for a half hour, and during that time, each has some long-held fantasy fulfilled. In the end, one laments that success will eventually destroy their sense of mutuality. "If we ever get rich, it'll be kind of sad. Then we'll all have suits. And there won't be no more nights like tonight. It'll break up the old gang. It'll never be the same after that."[46] In "Sun and Shadow" (1953), Bradbury marvelously satirized a bizarre example of American cultural imperialism. As he would comment, the story grew out of his righteous indignation over a photo spread in *Harper's Bazaar.* "I came across an issue where the *Bazaar* photographers, with their perverted sense of equality once again utilized natives in a Puerto Rican back-street as props in front of which their starved-looking mannikens postured for the benefit of yet more emaciated half-women in the best salons in the country."[47] In his story, Ricardo, a native villager, keeps following the photographer and models around, standing in the background and exposing himself to ruin the pictures. After the frustrated photographer departs, Ricardo thinks that now he will return to his house and family. "We shall sit eating and talking, not photographs, not backdrops, not paintings, not stage furniture, any of us. But actors, all of us, very fine actors indeed."[48]

The Concrete Mixer

In condemning a mass-circulation magazine like *Harper's Bazaar* for reducing the vastness of human experience to a quaint backdrop for a fashion spread, Bradbury articulated a critique of American mass culture similar to that of contemporary elite critics.[49] A dominant theme of Bradbury's work was the effect of mass society and technology on people. In "The Concrete Mixer" (1949), for instance, Bradbury parodied the narcotizing and assimilative nature of America's consumer capitalist culture. Set in 1966, the story begins with a Martian invasion of Earth. The Earthlings surrender immediately and warmly welcome the invaders. While most Martians are pleased with this response, the angst-ridden Ettil wonders if it is all part of a plot to "inundate us with banality [and] destroy our sensibilities."[50] Meeting a friendly woman, Ettil asks if there is more to life than going to movies and buying things. "You know what you talk like, mister?" she asks. "A Communist! Yes, sir, that's the kind of talk nobody stands for, by gosh."[51] In a letter to his wife, Ettil describes "the entire civilization into which we have been dropped like a shovelful of seeds into a large concrete mixer. Nothing of us will survive. We will be killed not by the gun but by the glad-hand."[52] When Ettil asks one man why humans have been so nice to their invaders, the man responds in terms of the ersatz populism of mass culture. "This is the century of the Common Man . . . and we're proud we're small. . . . You're looking at a planet full of Saroyans—everybody loving everybody." He also points out that Mars is a huge potential market for Earth's consumer goods. When he finds out that Martians do not wear shoes, for instance, he sees an enormous potential market as soon as advertisers "shame everyone into wearing shoes. Then we sell them the polish!" As Ettil concludes, "War is a bad thing, but peace can be a living horror."[53]

Bradbury most fully confronted the dehumanizing nature of mass society in *Fahrenheit 451*. A dystopian tale of a futuristic society in which reading is prohibited and a fireman's job is to burn contraband books, *Fahrenheit 451* is usually read as an anti-McCarthy tract. Though it is that, the novel is more fundamentally a criticism of American consumer culture. Guy Montag, a fireman who starts to wonder what is in the books he burns, begins reading secretly, thereby setting in motion a process that will make him an outlaw and enemy of the state. Montag begins to wonder about his job after meeting Clarisse, an eccentric teenage neighbor, who tells him she has been forced to see a psychiatrist who "wants to know why I go out and hike around in the forests and watch the birds and collect butterflies."[54] School too is an enormous machine designed to produce conformity. Clarisse has been kicked out, she says, because she is considered antisocial. "I don't mix. It's so strange. I'm very social indeed. It all depends on what you mean by social doesn't it? Social to me means talking to you about things like this."[55] Like elite critics of mass culture, Bradbury connected the culture of leisure with the exhausting but mentally unstimulating routine of work or school. As Clarisse says, "They run us so ragged by the end of the day we can't do anything but go to bed or head for a Fun Park to bully people around, break windowpanes in the window smasher place or wreck cars in the car wrecker place with the big steel ball."[56]

Clarisse stands in contrast to Montag's wife, Mildred, who stays home watching the "parlor walls," which cover three of the walls in her living room. Her chief goal in life is to save enough money to buy a screen for the fourth wall. When not watching television, Mildred has small radios in her ears. When she takes an overdose of sleeping pills, paramedics arrive with two nasty-looking machines to purge her blood. Such overdoses are so common—"We get these cases nine or ten a night," one paramedic tells Montag—that there is no need to send a physician.[57] A decade before Betty Friedan characterized the suburban home as a "comfortable concentration camp," Bradbury portrayed housewives as narcotized into a false sense of meaning and pleasure in their highly mechanized homes, desperately fending off bouts of suicidal depression.

In his clearest denunciation of masscult, Montag's boss, Captain Beatty, tells Montag that mass culture began with the development of photography in the nineteenth century, followed by motion pictures, radio, and television. "Things began to have *mass*. . . . And because they had mass, they became simpler. . . . Once, books appealed to a few people, here, there, everywhere. They could afford to be different. The world was roomy. But then the world got full of eyes and elbows and mouths. . . . Films and radios, magazines, books, leveled down to a sort of paste-pudding norm."[58] Mass culture, then, serves the interest of the state by eliminating differences of opinion and imposing conformity. The chief goal of society, according to Beatty, is to keep people happy. "Well, aren't they? Don't we keep them moving, don't we give them fun? That's all we live for, isn't it? For pleasure, for titillation? And you must admit our culture provides plenty of those."[59]

Bradbury's dystopian vision anticipated many of the issues that would be raised a decade later by Herbert Marcuse in *One-Dimensional Man.* The culture in *Fahrenheit 451* is based on what Marcuse labeled "institutionalized desublimation" and the triumph of the "happy consciousness."[60] Society's "supreme promise," Marcuse claimed, "is an ever-more-comfortable life for an ever-growing number of people who, in a strict sense, cannot imagine a qualitatively different universe of discourse and action."[61] At one point, Montag wonders why no one has ever questioned the permanently militarized economy and the country's relationship to the rest of the world. "I've heard rumors; the world is starving but we're well fed. Is it true, the world works hard and we play? Is that why we're hated so much?"[62] As he realizes, such questions have never been asked because the ability to imagine a different state of being has been systematically crushed. Furthermore, Marcuse argued, modern culture is pervasive, invading even humans' "inner freedom"—that is, "the private space in which man may become and remain himself."[63] Similarly, while riding on the subway, Montag tries to remember what he has read, but his thoughts are constantly scattered by the piped-in Muzak ad for toothpaste, a catchy jingle that permeates his subconscious and sets the other riders' toes tapping.[64]

Throughout *Fahrenheit 451* and several of his other stories, Bradbury viewed modern culture as a concerted war on the imagination.[65] The image of book burning recurs in several stories. In "Usher II" (1950), Bradbury specifically mentioned the anti–comic-book crusade of the postwar period as the starting point of the movement toward censorship of fantastic literature, culminating in the Great Fire of 1975, when all the works of Poe, Hawthorne, Baum, Lovecraft, Bierce, and other imaginative writers had been burned.[66] In this story, Stendahl builds a house on Mars patterned after the one in Poe's "House of Usher." When Garrett, the investigator of Moral Climates, appears to examine the house, Stendahl explains that he is tired of realism and film versions of Hemingway. "My God, how many times have I seen *For Whom the Bell Tolls* done!" Stendahl is told he will have to tear down his house, because it violates the Moral Climates law. Before doing so, he invites the members of the Society for the Prevention of Fantasy to a party, where he murders them all in Poe-like fashion, finally chaining Garrett to a wall in the basement and bricking him in. "For God's sake, what are you doing?" cries Garrett, to which Stendahl replies, "I'm being ironic."[67]

In "The Pedestrian" (1951), Bradbury also argued that America's technological society was an assault on authentic experience in favor of pseudo-experiences. A man living in the year 2053 is pulled over by an automated police car and questioned for his suspicious activities, which include walking alone at night. When he explains that he is out to enjoy the air and look at the sights, the car's computer voice asks whether he has television to watch and conditioned air to breathe at his house. For his inexplicable behavior, the man is taken in for psychiatric examination.[68]

Like Stendahl and the pedestrian, the heroes of Bradbury's stories tend to be cranky, eccentric intellectuals who distrust the modern world. A humorous example is "The Murderer" (1953), in which a man undergoes psychiatric evaluation for having cold-bloodedly killed all the electrical appliances in his house.[69] In "To the Chicago Abyss" (1963), an old man in a postapocalyptic future remembers trivia from the prewar era and recites lists of brand names and descriptions of everyday items that no longer exist. For his trouble he is beaten up by people who do not want to be reminded of what has been lost and pursued by the special police. Eventually he is contacted by members of an underground organization, which provides him with a means of escape, warning him, though, to keep quiet. Even then, he cannot refrain from talking about the past. "What did I have to offer a world that was forgetting?" he asks. "My memory! How could this help? By offering a standard of comparison. By telling the young *what once was,* by considering our losses."[70]

On occasion, Bradbury's intellectual heroes turn violent in the face of society's institutionalized evil. And each character who strikes out in violence against an antihumanist society gains the reader's sympathy, at least to some extent. Stendahl, in "Usher II," is much more charming than the bureaucratic drones he murders. Similarly, Montag in *Fahrenheit 451* turns his flame thrower on Captain Beatty in order to escape.[71] Lantry, the living dead man in "Pillar of Fire," carries out his series of murders to reintroduce terror into a world that has lost its imagination.[72] And in "—And the Moon Still Be as Bright" (1948), Spender, a member of the first landing team on Mars after disease has killed all the original inhabitants, begins researching Martian culture and develops a deep fascination with it. Convinced that humans will destroy the planet, Spender goes native, proclaims himself a Martian, and begins murdering the other astronauts. He is ultimately killed by the surviving crew members, but his predictions about how humans will treat the planet are borne out.[73]

Who Wields Me, Wields the World

Though Bradbury remained an outspoken liberal in politics, many of his stories emphasized the deleterious consequences of reformist liberalism. "Usher II," for example, locates the origins of the censorship movement in the campaign to ban comic books, which was led by such prominent liberals as Frederick Wertham. Furthermore, like such intellectuals as Reinhold Niebuhr and Arthur Schlesinger Jr., Bradbury insisted that liberalism must recognize such unpleasant realities as sin, evil, and death. When it does not, he argued, the results could be catastrophic. "The Scythe" (1947) is the story of a man who inherits a farm with a scythe bearing the inscription "Who Wields Me—Wields the World." He discovers on his farm a very curious wheat field, in which, each day, no more wheat ripens than he can cut. Gradually he realizes that he is, in fact, the grim reaper and that every stalk of wheat represents a thousand lives. When he recognizes the wheat that includes his family, he puts the scythe away and vows to cut no more. That night—May 30, 1938—his house burns down, and his wife and children are trapped in a nether world between life and death. No one in the world dies until the farmer, in a rage, goes into the field and begins chopping wheat indiscriminately.

> Slicing out huge scars in green wheat and ripe wheat, with no selection and no care, cursing, over and over, swearing, laughing, the blade swinging up in the sun and falling in the sun with a singing whistle! Down!
> Bombs shattered London, Moscow, Tokyo.
> The blade swung insanely.
> And the kilns of Belsen and Buchenwald took fire.
> The blade sang, crimson wet.
> And mushrooms vomited out blind suns at White Sands, Hiroshima, Bikini, and up, through, and in continental Siberian skies.[74]

Similarly, in "A Sound of Thunder" (1952), Bradbury scrutinized Cold War liberal ideology, which viewed freedom and totalitarianism as polar opposites. The story, about a group of men who travel back millions of years in time to hunt a *Tyrannosaurus rex,* is also a political parable about the thin line between democracy and dictatorship.

The group enters an office bearing the sign:

TIME SAFARI, INC.
SAFARIS TO ANY YEAR IN THE PAST.
YOU NAME THE ANIMAL.
WE TAKE YOU THERE.
YOU SHOOT IT.

They discuss the recent presidential election, in which the liberal candidate, Keith, narrowly defeated the crypto-fascist, McCarthyesque Deutscher, whom one describes by saying, "There's an anti-everything man for you, a militarist, anti-Christ, anti-human, anti-intellectual."[75] As the hunters travel back in time, the guide explains that all steps have been taken to ensure that the past will not be changed. The only dinosaurs hunted are those that would have died within a few minutes anyway. The hunters must stay on a special path floating six inches above ground, for if one strays off the path and crushes even a single mouse, it could have disastrous effects. The guide explains: "For want of ten mice, a fox dies. For want of ten foxes, a lion starves. . . . Infinite billions of life forms are thrown into chaos and destruction. Eventually it all boils down to this: fifty-nine million years later, a cave man . . . goes hunting wild boar or saber-tooth tiger for food. But you, friend, have stepped on all the tigers in that region. By stepping on *one* single mouse. So the cave man starves. And the cave man, please note, is not just any expendable man, no! He is an *entire future nation*."[76]

When the *Tyrannosaurus rex* appears, one of the hunters panics and leaves the path, inadvertently crushing a butterfly. Returning to the present, they enter the office, where the sign now reads:

TYME SEFARI INC.
SEFARIS TU ANY YEER EN THE PAST.
YU NAIM THE ANIMALL.
WEE TAEK YU THAIR.
YU SHOOT ITT.

To their horror, the hunters discover that Deutscher and not Keith won the recent election. "Killing one butterfly couldn't be *that* important!" the distraught hunter thinks. "Could it?"[77]

In this story, Bradbury expressed a worldview that mathematicians and physicists would gradually formulate only in the sixties and seventies and label "chaos theory." The basis of chaos theory is that, in a system with a large number of variables—such as weather forecasting or economics—infinitesimal changes at one point can make vast differences later. A favorite example cited by chaos theorists is that a butterfly flapping its wings in China today can cause gales in New York next month.[78] In the same way, Bradbury's butterfly symbolized the tenuous nature of American freedom in a chaotic and unpredictable universe.

Bradbury, then, can be understood as a tragic liberal, caught in the fundamental paradox confronting liberal intellectuals in the postwar period. As Irving Howe had pointed out, liberals viewed the world as marked by chaos and a terrifying freedom that, in the words of Arthur Schlesinger Jr., had made anxiety "the official emotion of our time."[79] And yet, Howe continued, liberals sought to deal with these problems by proposing a modest reform program, woefully inadequate to cope with the world they described.[80] Throughout his career, Bradbury skated along this fissure. Sometimes he expressed optimism about the prospects for reform. Other times, his underlying vision of a universe built on chaos, absurdity, anxiety, and alienation emerged, subverting his own professed belief in liberal reform. If Bradbury failed to successfully reconcile the contradictory impulses of his worldview, it reflected the broader failure of postwar liberalism.

4 The Devil and Charles Beaumont

In his 1960 short story, "Gentlemen, Be Seated," Charles Beaumont worked a variation on Ray Bradbury's *Fahrenheit 451*. Beaumont's dystopia lies in the not-too-distant future, a world scientifically designed to stress functionalism, which rewards steady, unimaginative labor in large, bureaucratic organizations. Whereas Bradbury's totalitarian society forbade thinking, Beaumont's has outlawed laughter. But in the midst of this drab and conformist world, a vibrant humor underground celebrates irreverence, spontaneity, and inspired chaos.[1]

"Gentlemen, Be Seated" addresses some of the major themes of Beaumont's brief career. From the early fifties until his incapacitation due to illness in the mid-sixties, Beaumont used a wide range of genres in several media—short stories, novels, essays, film, and television—to cast a critical eye on a variety of issues in postwar culture. In Beaumont's vision, American mass society, with its emphasis on homogenization and commodification, was destroying the authenticity of popular-cultural experience, and its totalitarian tendencies threatened to extirpate individuality in the name of a bland conformity. Furthermore, Beaumont portrayed Americans as obsessed with an ultra-rational paradigm, which, denying the irrational and supernatural, left them ill prepared to understand the universe and human nature. Frequently, Beaumont suffused his universe with religious underpinnings—though his theology placed much greater emphasis on the devil than god—and argued that Americans' belief in progress and science obscured the reality of evil. From this point of view, he frequently attacked specific targets in postwar American culture—racism, sexual oppression, imperialism, and environmental destruction—but more generally, he created a vision that emphasized the irrational and absurd, often portraying life as a vast cosmic joke.

Beaumont was born Charles Leroy Nutt in Chicago in 1929. Because his mother suffered serious health problems, he lived much of his childhood with five widowed aunts who ran a boarding house in Washington state. "Each night we had a ritual," he would remember years later, "of gathering around the stove and there I'd hear stories about the strange death of each of their husbands." As a child, Beaumont was deeply influenced by the writings of Poe, Baum, and Edgar Rice Burroughs, as well as numerous pulp science fiction magazines. After dropping out of high school in the tenth grade, he served a short stint in the military and worked a variety of jobs, including artist for the science fiction pulps, piano player, disc jockey, and editor for a comic-book company, while trying to break in as a writer. He changed his name to Beaumont along the way.

Unable to sell his first seventy-two stories, Beaumont's maiden publishing success was "The Devil, You Say?" which appeared in *Amazing Stories* in 1951. Throughout his career, Beaumont published his work in such pulps as *Venture, Infinity Science Fiction, Orbit, If,* and *Gamma.* Beginning in the mid-fifties, his work also began appearing in such mainstream publications as *Playboy* (which placed him on a monthly retainer of five hundred dollars for first-refusal rights to his stories) and its imitator, *Rogue.*[2] By the late fifties, Beaumont also moved into film and television, contributing regularly to *The Twilight Zone* (he eventually wrote or was credited with twenty-two scripts, second only to Rod Serling) and authoring four screenplays for Roger Corman.[3] As his career reached its height, Beaumont suffered increasing health problems, later diagnosed as an extremely premature case of Alzheimer's disease. Unable to maintain the frenetic pace of his early career, Beaumont farmed out increasing amounts of work to various young protégés. Several of the later *Twilight Zone* episodes credited to him were coauthored or written entirely by others. Beaumont died in 1967 at the age of thirty-eight.[4]

Remember? Remember?

Underlying Beaumont's view of American society was a critique of the effects of mass culture that, in many respects, echoed that of elite critics. In his 1963 collection of nostalgic essays, *Remember? Remember?* Beaumont portrayed the dominant postwar culture as a concerted assault on genius, imagination, creativity, authenticity, sexuality, and genuine leisure, and the triumph of commercialism, ignorance, and bad taste. Unlike such elite critics as Dwight Macdonald, Beaumont's attack on mass culture did not look to some unadulterated high culture as an alternative. Rather, Beaumont upheld an earlier version of popular culture as the standard by which to judge the decline of postwar culture. In the period before World War II, he argued, Americans appreciated the genius of an artist like Charlie Chaplin for his personification of pure joy. But in the postwar era, with its political blacklists and resurgent Victorian morality, Chaplin became the target of small-minded zealots. Beaumont commented, "People have a way of resenting great artists. A man may travel to the searing center of his soul and come out with a new vision, and the world will ask him why he hasn't changed his shirt."[5]

The attack on Chaplin, Beaumont claimed, was also symptomatic of Americans' loss of the joyous exuberance that previously marked their popular culture. "We are grown sophisticated—willing to chuckle but afraid to laugh."[6] Contrasting the belly laughs provoked by earlier clowns—from Fatty Arbuckle and Buster Keaton to the Marx Brothers—to the cerebral chuckles elicited by such contemporary comedians as Mort Sahl and Lenny Bruce, Beaumont argued only half-jokingly that the decline of Americans' international prestige reflected the decline of American humor. In the prewar period, "mirth was one of our principal products . . . creating thereby an image of the United States as the capital of joy and merriment." As Beaumont admitted, "It was not a very dignified image, to be sure." At the same time, Americans were genuinely liked, and the United States was widely respected throughout the world. In the context of the Cold War: "Now that we take ourselves seriously, as the hard-hitting, no-nonsense leaders of the Free World, our prestige has plummeted almost to the vanishing point. . . . Now we are among the least liked and least respected of countries, scorned, vilified, resented, ridiculed. And, whether or not there is a connection, it all started when we forgot how to laugh."[7] In such an atmosphere there is not room for a genius like Keaton, who was left to languish unappreciated for the last several decades of his life.[8]

In identifying villains in this war on anarchic laughter, Beaumont pointed at McCarthyite conservatives, neo-Victorian bluenoses, and earnest liberals alike. In "Gentlemen, Be Seated," one character explains that most humor is based on cruelty. In a reference to such liberal censors as Frederick Wertham, he says that with the growing influence of psychologists, this kind of humor was deemed unhealthy.[9] Of the effort by white and black liberals to cancel the television show *Amos 'n' Andy,* the character bemoans the fact that all racial humor has been driven out of mainstream culture to protect people's sensibilities. "When television was born, censors started cracking down. Any humor that might offend—that's to say, all real humor—was banished. A new humor sprang up. It didn't offend anyone, but it didn't amuse anyone either."[10]

Why, Beaumont wondered, is postwar American culture built on the repression of spontaneity, exuberance, and authenticity in favor of the ersatz? "Is it that we have mistaken the point of civilization and assumed it to mean the suppression of all natural tendencies?"[11] In several cases, Beaumont portrayed this suppression as a war carried out by adults against children. Contemporary holidays, for example, lack the mystery and excitement they used to have. "Having created the safe and sane Fourth, the Lifetime Aluminum Christmas tree, the trick-or-treat bag, we now sit about drinking Martinis and sighing bitterly about Kids Nowadays. . . . The guilt is entirely ours. We are the they who commercialized the holidays, who cheapened them, who tamed them."[12] With store-bought Halloween candy, he continued, "we have bribed the children into submissiveness," thus depriving them of the creative pranksterism that marked earlier Halloween celebrations.[13] Similarly, mass-produced Valentine's Day cards served to thwart the nascent sexual stirrings the holiday had previously encouraged.[14]

Ironically, for someone who made his reputation largely through television writing, Beaumont viewed the triumph of television as a further attack on the creative world of children. Unlike radio, he complained, television leaves nothing to the imagination, featuring, as Macdonald would say, the built-in reaction: "Television makes no demands, except upon our patience. It presents its stories ready to wear. All the work is done. There is nothing we can contribute. For this reason, television is an impersonal form of entertainment. Radio was something else again. . . . Through the use of sound effects, music, a very special form of writing, and acting which bore scant relationship to other modes of acting, radio created a world which had to be believed to be seen. Radio provided a sketch, but it was up to the listener to make the finished picture. The greater reality was his to create."[15]

Television also helped kill the old-fashioned movie serials, ironically, by raising children's "level of sophistication." In the minds of children, remote geographical regions had once been populated by exotic and mysterious people and thus were arenas for endless adventure. "Today," wrote Beaumont, "Darkest

Africa is a strife-torn group of emerging nations; Transylvania, ancestral home of unmentionable horrors, is part of a country which has fallen under Red domination; China is a gray land of Communes—and we'd better not call them fiends or they might blow us to hell."[16] In his short story "The Magic Man" (1960), Beaumont similarly blamed a rising level of sophistication for destroying children's sense of wonder and enjoyment. A touring magician succumbs to children's repeated requests that he tell them how he performs his tricks, only to find they have lost all interest in his show and respect for him once he does so.[17]

For Beaumont, killjoys like Wertham had seriously harmed children's imaginative capacities in the name of saving them.[18] In order to protect children, American culture had been purged of all sense of fear. While Beaumont conceded the value of protecting kids from physical danger, he questioned "the wisdom of protecting them from nightmares."[19] In the new therapeutic culture, children had to be spared the experience of terror. For instance, older-style amusement parks, with their genuinely scary roller coasters and wax museum murderers' gallery, had been supplanted by Disneyland. "It is a splendidly imaginative park, full of wonders to behold, but it offers no terrors to the young. Walt Disney, who always made sure there was at least one spine-chilling sequence in his films, has turned Pollyanna, perhaps in response to the letters of worried parents. His films are all sunlight and fun, now, and so is his park."[20]

Beaumont extended his critique of mass culture in several short stories. In "The Monster Show" (1956), a futuristic comedy in which aliens conquer Earth through the medium of television, he raised standard concerns of elite critics about the totalitarian potential of mass culture, but he did so in such exaggerated form that the story can be seen as a parody both of masscult and its discontents.[21] In "The Beautiful People" (1952), he depicted a future society in which everyone, at age eighteen, undergoes "the Transformation," a surgical process that makes them beautiful. Mary, a girl about to turn eighteen, does not want to be transformed, a heresy unimaginable to everyone else. "But you're so ugly, dear!" her mother says.[22] Mary, however, continues to resist the world of "handsome model men and . . . beautiful, perfect women, perfect, all perfect, all looking alike. Looking exactly alike."[23] In Beaumont's vision, this dystopian society is the reductio ad absurdum of postwar mass culture with its emphasis on what Herbert Marcuse termed the "happy consciousness." The story was made into an episode of *The Twilight Zone,* "Number Twelve Looks Just Like You," in which people are constantly encouraged to drink a cup of Instant Smile whenever they feel depressed.[24] Unlike Kurt Vonnegut's short story "Harrison

Bergeron" (1957), in which everyone has been leveled by being made equally ugly, "The Beautiful People" followed the logic of consumer culture by making people equally beautiful. The point, of course, is that the concept of beauty loses all meaning when there is no standard of comparison. In the end, confronted with a petition signed by thousands demanding that she undergo the Transformation, Mary stands trial, and the judge orders her to conform. As she is taken away to surgery, she helplessly wonders, "What will happen to *me?*"[25]

It Was All Personality

For Beaumont, the fear of the loss of identity also grew out of a work culture that stressed role-playing and manipulation of one's own image and of others. As one Beaumont character realizes, the modern success ethic consists of "playing forces against each other, getting in with the bosses, doing little extra things— these were the deciding factors in any business. It was all personality. Sheer talent alone couldn't get you anywhere these days."[26] A crucial part of this ethic is the ability and willingness to ruthlessly manipulate others, and in several stories Beaumont portrayed the viciousness underlying the strategy of manipulation. "The Trigger" (1958) is a mystery revolving around the suicides of several prominent, successful members of an exclusive country club. Eventually the detective discovers that the club's bartender, under the pretense of listening to the members' troubles, has learned to pierce their image of success and uncover their most fundamental insecurities. Fueled by a pathological jealousy, he then convinces the men they are failures, prompting them to kill themselves.[27] Similarly, in "Night Ride" (1957), Max Bailey, the leader of a jazz band, brings into the group musicians who are suffering from some kind of personal problem, from drug addiction to guilt at having accidentally killed a child while driving drunk. Bailey takes the musicians under his wing, setting himself up as one to whom they can pour out their troubles. Only slowly does the narrator realize that Bailey is using his role as father confessor to make everyone continue suffering for their past mistakes because he is convinced that it will make them play better. Another band member explains, "You thought you were in a band. But you weren't. You were in a travelling morgue. . . . You might have pulled out of your wing-ding years ago, only [Bailey] kept the knife in."[28]

Beaumont sympathized with those who lacked the requisite social and "personality" skills to fit into modern society. Charlie Parks, protagonist of Beaumont's screenplay for *The Twilight Zone* episode "Miniature," is a middle-aged man, still living with his mother, who infantilizes him by tucking him into bed and serving him hot cocoa. Parks works a boring desk job, and when he is late getting back from lunch one day, his boss tells him, "This is the first sign of humanity you've show in almost four years."[29] Nevertheless, he must fire Parks because an office is "a team, a platoon." Since Parks is not a team player, he does not "fit in."[30] In "The Vanishing American" (1955), Beaumont again examined the endemic loss of identity in modern American society. A nondescript man working an office job realizes he has become utterly invisible. Nobody sees him, not his boss or fellow workers, not the people in the bar or store he stops by after work, not even his wife and son, but because no one had ever paid much attention to him, it takes him a while to realize it. As he thinks back over his lifetime and all the dreams he has never realized, it occurs to him that "he had not just suddenly vanished, like that, after all. No; he had been vanishing gradually for a long while."[31]

Black Country

In several stories, Beaumont narrowed his focus to specific political issues, articulating a left-liberal critique of postwar society. And while some of these stories exhibited a liberal reformism that fell within the Cold War consensus, Beaumont's vision transcended its limits. Like Ray Bradbury, Beaumont believed Americans were unprepared to accept the reality of evil and the persistence of the irrational in modern life. Just as George Orwell once said that H. G. Wells was "too sane to understand the modern world,"[32] so Beaumont thought the same of Americans. Because of this limitation, their well-meaning reforms would frequently have disastrous consequences.

When he attempted to write polemical stories, Beaumont occasionally succumbed to bathetic liberal pieties. In "The Neighbors" (1960), he wrote a morality tale expressing faith in the fundamental decency of people. Having recently moved into a new house, possessed of some unnamed fear, Miles Cartier, the husband and father, keeps thinking, "What am I afraid of? This isn't fifty years ago. This is today. The 1960s." Then a rock comes crashing through the window with a note attached to it, reading, "WE WARNED YOU COON NOW WERE [sic] THROUGH PLAYING AROUND."[33] Only at this point do we learn that the Cartiers are a black family moving into a white neighborhood. Unlike in Charles Willeford's *Pickup,* the strategy of belatedly revealing their race is not used to deepen the social critique, but to establish the family's normality, thus gaining the reader's sympathy. Before the threats Cartier had always believed in the innate goodness of humans, but no longer.[34] At this point a crowd of white neighbors marches up to Cartier's door. When he steps out to confront them, the group's leader surprises him by apologizing. "I'm afraid we didn't give you much of a welcome. I don't know exactly why, but I guess, well, I think it was just that we didn't know exactly how to go about it. And every day, it got a little harder." The neighbors then announce that they have apprehended the person who has been making the threats and are turning him over to the police. Some of the men invite Cartier over to play poker.[35]

In his 1959 novel *The Intruder,* Beaumont expanded on his belief that even though only a handful of people are vicious racists, when decent people hold back from the conflict, then the racists have the floor and dominate debate. Adam Cramer, a young man from Los Angeles, comes into the small southern town of Caxton in 1956 to arouse opposition to court-ordered school desegregation. Beaumont sketched a broad cast of characters, successfully portraying not only the struggle between the races but also intraracial arguments and the conflicts raging within individuals. Unlike many whites at the time, Beaumont recognized divisions within the African American community. In the novel, many blacks argue that token integration will serve little useful purpose. But as the local black minister tells Joey, the leader of the black students, "None of that makes any difference now. Because the tiger's loose, boy, and it's running."[36] Beaumont also avoided the glum earnestness with which many white liberals viewed black culture, recognizing the crucial role humor played in confronting white oppression. At one point, a group of blacks, watching a parade of Klansmen drive by, begins wondering aloud what would happen if one of them got a flat tire. Would the driver leave his sheet on and get it dirty changing the flat, or would he remove it? If he took it off, everybody would see he was "the little bookkeeper over at the Mill who's afraid of his boss."[37]

In portraying Cramer, Beaumont drew together several common postwar theories of the origins of fanaticism. A reporter digging into Cramer's background discovers he had a sickly childhood and a mother who pampered him. "I was the best friend he ever had; the only friend, really," says the mother, "and I *tried* to make him see this. 'I've given up my life for you,' I told him, 'and you're all I have. You're my own baby.'"[38] According to Philip Wylie's influential bestseller, *Generation of Vipers* (1942), American men were victimized by domineering mothers who prevented their sons from developing into independent adults, capable of thinking for themselves and developing healthy romantic relationships with other women.[39] True to form, Cramer is impotent with respectable girls, but when he hears rumors about the questionable past of a friend's wife, he immediately seduces her.[40]

Similarly, Beaumont portrayed Cramer as a "true believer" in the sense popularized by Eric Hoffer, in which fanatics, uncomfortable with the freedom of modern existence, must believe in some cause, though it makes little difference what it is.[41] For Cramer, the cause is not opposition to integration per se. Rather, he has fallen under the sway of a charismatic philosophy professor, Max Blake, whom one character describes as a "leftist fascist." At a time when left- and right-wing totalitarianism were frequently fused in the concept of "red fascism,"[42] Beaumont created an intellectual armchair revolutionary preaching the need for a political strongman. According to Blake, this strongman needs to seize on an area of unrest and build on the tension. Above all, he must be absolutely ruthless; both Hitler and Mussolini had ultimately failed, in Blake's view, because "they had too much regard for humanity."[43] Cramer, then, neither antiblack nor against integration, uses the issue to put his (and Blake's) intellectual theories into practice.[44] He regularly writes Blake, apprising him of his progress. But Blake lacks the courage of his convictions, eventually arriving in Caxton to demand that Cramer cease his activities, screaming that his life is being ruined by the notoriety Cramer has caused, "all because you chose to take some innocent theorizing literally."[45] Though Cramer is crushed—feeling rejected by his "father"—he refuses to quit.

Most of the middle- and upper-class white citizens of Caxton remain on the fence, though over time they gradually lean toward the anti-integrationist view. The great exception is Tom McDaniel, the publisher of Caxton's newspaper, who had originally editorialized against integration but, appalled by his friends' reaction, slowly grows to understand its necessity. When the town's black church is dynamited and the minister killed, McDaniel assumes the role of leader, marching with the black students across town to the school.[46] Joey, falsely accused of rape and locked in the principal's office with a lynch mob waiting outside, explains that he has belatedly come to accept the logic of integration because of the decency of so many people he has met, especially McDaniel. Pointing to the mob, he tells the principal, "I used to think *they* were the white people, but I found out that wasn't true. How many are there outside now? Thirty? Forty? Forty people in a town of sixteen thousand. You see what I mean? I was prejudiced . . . because I judged the whole white race by *them*—a sick little bunch of hateful people."[47] While such pious faith in human nature may have been Beaumont's intended point, he had let the reader into the minds of too many characters who belie Joey's optimism. Thus Beaumont the artist subverted Beaumont the polemicist.

In two other stories, "Black Country" (1954) and "Night Ride," Beaumont focused on race in a different context—the postwar jazz subculture. Beaumont's fascination with jazz grew out of his belief that it maintained the playfulness and willingness to take risks that authentic popular culture should express. Based on improvisation, jazz could not be replicated; its experience was, by definition, transitory. In short, it was unable to be commodified. In both stories, Beaumont focused on white jazz musicians totally immersed in African American culture and thereby articulated a theme similar to that of Norman Mailer's "White Negro." For Mailer, the "hipster" stood as the most authentic rebel in the postwar period, his "psychopathic brilliance" representing an affront to the staid conservatism of the dominant culture. "A totalitarian society makes enormous demands on the courage of men, and a partially totalitarian society makes even greater demands, for the general anxiety is greater. . . . So it is no accident that the source of Hip is the Negro for he has been living on the margin between totalitarianism and democracy for two centuries. . . . Any Negro who wishes to live must live with danger from the first day, and no experience can ever be casual to him."[48] In Mailer's view, Hip owed its spread to the influence of jazz, and white jazz musicians exemplified the Hip ethic, having absorbed the "existential synapses of the Negro."[49]

Beaumont's stories, both narrated by black musicians, concern young white musicians who are symbols of "white Negroism." The narrator of "Black Country" says of Sonny Holmes, "He was white, but he didn't play white."[50] The story traces the relationship between Sonny and bandleader Spoof Collins, a Miles Davis–type trumpeter, who takes his young protégé under wing and teaches him to play the trumpet. Eventually the two fight over the band's female lead singer, and Spoof, dying of cancer, commits suicide. Sonny begins adopting more and more of Spoof's mannerisms. At times he seems possessed on the bandstand and lets loose a phenomenal, Spoof-style solo. One night, playing in the town where Spoof died, Sonny shows up with Spoof's old horn, which had been buried with him, and begins playing. "Everything got lost, then, while that horn flew. It . . . was the heart of jazz, and the insides, pulled out with the roots and held up for everybody to see; it was blues that told the story of all the lonely cats and all the ugly whores who ever lived, . . . a blues that spoke for all the lonely, sad and anxious downers who could never speak for themselves. . . . And he laid back his head . . . and blew some more. Not sad, now, not blues—but not anything else you could call by a name. Except . . . jazz. It was jazz."[51]

Similarly, in "Night Ride" Beaumont commented that jazz offered new perspectives on the American experience, perspectives borne of its African American origins. In describing the audition of a white pianist for Max Bailey's band, the narrator says, "The kid swung into some chestnuts, like 'St. James Infirmary' and 'Bill Bailey,' but what he did to them was vicious. St. James came out a place full of spiders and snakes and screaming broads, and Bailey was a dirty bastard who left his woman when she needed him most."[52]

Beaumont celebrated the influence of jazz in the emerging underground culture, but he did so without the romantic racism of many whites. In the works of Mailer and Jack Kerouac, for example, jazz symbolized the instinctual spontaneity marking black culture, an outgrowth of African Americans' oppressed status.[53] As jazz critic Nat Hentoff has argued, Mailer's portrait of jazz musicians is one-dimensional and ignores the hard work necessary to master the art form. "As the music has become an object in itself," Hentoff commented, "a discipline and responsibility is required of the jazzman which the 'authentic' hipster cannot regard as worth that much time and trouble if the only values are right now."[54] Beaumont's portrait of jazz musicians reflected the importance of this discipline, making clear the amount of work and effort they put into their music. While Beaumont recognized the music as a cultural form growing out of African Americans' oppressed status, he did not see it as a simple expression of anger, but as anger mixed with a host of other emotions, including joyous exuberance. As Max Bailey explains, jazz "is a vocabulary. A way of saying something. You can have a small vocabulary or a large one. We have a large one, because we have a lot on our minds."[55]

They Had to Be Destroyed

In *One-Dimensional Man,* Herbert Marcuse argued that advanced technological society "finds its ideology in the rigid orientation of thought and behavior to the given universe of facts," continuing that "the capacity to contain and manipulate subversive imagination and effort is an integral part of the given society."[56] Fantasy and science fiction, by nature, transcend the given universe of facts. Thus there is something implicitly subversive in these forms. This is not to say that the genres are necessarily radical, as the popularity of conservative authors like Robert Heinlein attests, but that they encourage readers to escape one-dimensional patterns of thought.

In his fantasy stories, Beaumont encouraged this transcendence by positing a variety of alternative futures, which, in several cases, allowed him to raise topics that would become political issues over the next two decades. As Raymond Williams has commented, literature often signals the development of a new emergent culture by voicing concerns long before they find political articulation, when they exist as little more than "an unease, a stress, a displacement, a latency."[57] Beaumont identified several tensions within the dominant consensus, and in such areas as imperialism, gay rights, and environmental destruction, his dystopian warnings served as a harbinger of things to come.

With "The Jungle" (1956), one of the most outspoken attacks on American imperialism to emerge out of the postwar period, Beaumont deconstructed the contemporary political science theories of modernization and the Cold War image of the United States as the world's savior. Set in the twenty-second century, the story takes place in Mbarara, a domed, air-conditioned city, complete with "cultured Grant Wood trees" and moving sidewalks, carved out of the African jungle.[58] Designed "to pamper five hundred thousand people," Mbarara now sits empty except for its designer, Richard Austin, and his deathly ill wife.[59] All other westerners have either left or died of a mysterious disease that causes its victims to suffer delirium as their skin decomposes. As Austin travels through the deserted city, he remembers the history of Mbarara. Suffering overpopulation, the Western nations had announced their plan to build a city in the jungles of Kenya. The natives protested to the "Five-Power governments." "No explanation had satisfied them. They saw it as the destruction of their world and so they fought. With guns and spears and arrows and darts, with every resource at their disposal, refusing to capitulate, hunting like an army of mad ants scattered over the land. And since they could not be controlled, they had to be destroyed."[60]

Accompanying this genocide had been a policy of eco-destruction in which the land was "leveled, smoothed as a highway is smoothed, its centuries choked beneath millions of tons of hardened stone."[61] In a pointed criticism of the Western ethnocentrism underlying imperialism, Beaumont portrayed Austin's patronizing attitude toward the natives: "Let them wallow in their backward filth? In their disease and corruption—merely because their culture had failed to absorb scientific progress? No."[62] Though their superstitions would be crushed, Austin believes, eventually they will be grateful. Austin journeys to the outlying village to talk with the medicine man who put the curse on the westerners. The medicine man explains that his people fought the foreign invaders just as the whites would have fought if the Africans had come to their land and built a city. Until it was too late, Austin had refused to believe that Western science and rationality could be defeated by native superstition.[63]

In "The Crooked Man" (1955), Beaumont envisioned a future society marked by sexual decadence. Jesse enters a club called The Phallus just before the nightly "orgy time." Jesse hates orgy time, but only inside can he escape notice: "Outside . . . every inch of pavement was patrolled electronically, every word of conversation, every movement recorded, catalogued, filed." From the beginning, it is apparent that Jesse is considered some kind of sexual deviant, and the reader is tempted to assume he is a homosexual. In the current political climate, Jesse is the object of persecution. "Before it wasn't so bad," he thinks, "not this bad, anyway. You were laughed at and shunned and fired from your job, sometimes kids lobbed stones at you, but at least you weren't hunted. Now—it was a crime."[64] The witch hunt is led by the McCarthyesque Senator Knudson, who proclaims, in a speech filled with red-baiting and antigay imagery common to the era, "The perverts who infest our land must be flushed out, eliminated *completely* as a threat not only to public morals, but to society at large."[65] Only at this point is it made clear that Jesse is a heterosexual in an exclusively homosexual world. In the bar, he meets his lover Mina, who sneaks in disguised as a man. When Mina cries in frustration over being a "queer," Jesse explains that in the long-forgotten past, heterosexuality had been considered normal. Mina has come to tell Jesse that, despite her love for him, she is going to submit to "the Cure." Before she can do so, the two are arrested by the vice squad, and Jesse is taken away and surgically "cured." By reversing the power relationship between homosexuality and heterosexuality, Beaumont exposed normality and deviance as largely social constructs. Moreover, he did so long before there existed any gay rights movement to support such a notion, when homosexuality was classified as a mental illness and closely linked in popular culture with political deviance. And, in the supreme irony, he did so in a story published in *Playboy,* the postwar bastion of swinging heterosexuality.

Having raised the subject of environmental destruction in "The Jungle," Beaumont confronted the issue more directly in "Something in the Earth" (1963), again portraying American hubris—a result of scientific rationalism—as an inability to comprehend irrational forces that can lay waste all the nation's technological marvels. The story is a futuristic tale about the caretaker of the last forest on earth, which has been set aside as a park, the rest of the world having been turned into a vast city. When U.S. Rockets needs a site to construct its new subsidiary, the president orders the forest leveled. The caretaker protests: "In all the world there will not be a blade of grass nor a single tree! And children will be born and raised who will never know the robin's song, whose hands will know only the feel of cold metal."[66] When workers come to tear down the forest, they find the trees have mysteriously become petrified, rendering them impervious to all attempts to fell them. "It must be something in the earth," the president says. "The F-Bomb—that's it. Polluted the earth or something last war."[67] Eventually the president orders the forest bombed, but with the destruction of the last forest, the earth exacts its own revenge. "[The caretaker] stared at the cities as they broke and crumbled. As the air grew fat with screams of many people. As the roots of giant trees, greater than he had ever seen, came up from the stone and spread and toppled the mighty buildings. As the water came flooding in through the steel canyons. As the mountains pulled the earth apart and rose and made room for the fields and forests."[68]

Worse Things than Confusion

In such stories, Beaumont's vision stretched far beyond the boundaries of the Cold War consensus. But in an even more fundamental way, he subverted the consensus paradigm with his absurd, antirational worldview. His stories are marked by a grim, black humor and the sort of ironic twists that made him an effective writer for *The Twilight Zone*. In "Place of Meeting" (1953), a group of survivors of a nuclear holocaust search in vain for any signs of life. In the end they are revealed as a group of vampires who need the blood of the living to survive as the undead.[69] Frequently, Beaumont's humor took the form of parodies of popular genres similar to those found in *Mad* magazine in the early and mid-fifties.[70] "The Last Caper" (1954), for instance, satirized pulp science fiction and crime writing. Narrated by Mike Mallet, a futuristic private eye, the story contains several amusing parodies of Mickey Spillane. As Mallet seduces a beautiful alien, he says, "She threw a vicious kick at my groin but I dodged and grabbed her leg. Then I grabbed her other leg. Then I grabbed her other leg."[71] Regarding a Venusian, Mallet comments, "I hated him right away because I didn't understand him and I always hate what I don't understand. Sometimes I hate what I *do* understand."[72] And Beaumont also reprised the classic final scene of Spillane's *I, the Jury*. "I let her have it in the gut. She sprawled. I grabbed the blaster and pretty soon there was some jam on the floor instead of a dame. 'I'm sorry, baby,' I whispered to the sticky heap, 'really sorry.'"[73]

Much of Beaumont's work represented a sustained critique of Western rationalism. "The Jungle," for instance, revolves around a conflict between a modern, rational, scientific paradigm and a primitive, savage, magical one, with the latter triumphing. Similarly, in his screenplay for the 1962 movie *Burn, Witch, Burn* (coauthored with Richard Matheson), a teacher at a British university refuses to believe his rapid rise to success is the result of his wife's witchcraft.

His disbelief in the irrational and magical threatens his wife's life when it is revealed that one of the other faculty members is also a witch intent on sabotaging his career.

As he argued in *Remember? Remember?* Beaumont saw modern society as built on the constant repression of natural instincts.[74] Much of the irrational element in his fiction came about through the return of the repressed. Characters are often afraid to go to sleep because the dream world has invaded reality, threatening to subsume it. In "Perchance to Dream," a mysterious woman pursues a man throughout his dreams, driving him closer and closer to what he knows will be a fatal shock.[75] In "Traumeri" (1955), a death-row inmate insists that no one really exists except in his dream, and that if they execute him he will wake up and they will all die.[76] And in "The Dark Music," a repressed high school teacher wanders at night in a dreamlike state into the forest, where she is seduced by a Pan-like satyr/spirit.[77]

Beaumont believed Americans were ill-equipped to understand the persistence of evil in the modern world because they were blinded by their belief in progress and rationality. In "The New People" (1958), he laid bare what he saw as the potential for evil inherent in the banality and conformity of suburbia. As in "The Neighbors," a family has just moved into a neighborhood and wonders if they will fit in. "The Neighbors" reaffirms the basic goodness of human nature, but "The New People" undermines that confidence. As one character says, "You're only on the outskirts of confusion, my friend. But there are worse things than confusion. Believe me."[78] When a neighbor invites them to the neighborhood's weekly "group activity," explaining that it is based on the supposition that anything is better than boredom, the new people are sucked into and eventually victimized by these activities, which begin with card-playing and progress to spouse-swapping, bank robbing, terrorist acts, and, finally, human sacrifice.[79]

To symbolize this evil, Beaumont occasionally included the devil himself among his cast of characters. In "The Howling Man" (1960), American David Ellington undertakes a walking tour of Europe in the early twenties. Falling ill, he stumbles to the door of a remote German abbey, where the monks reluctantly take him in. Upon recovering, he discovers a filthy, naked man imprisoned in a small, dirty cell. The abbot, Father Jerome, tells Ellington that the man is the devil, whom the members of the brotherhood had captured shortly after the war. "We chant his chains each day," Jerome says, explaining that Satan's imprisonment has brought peace to Germany in the aftermath of World War I.[80] Convinced he is dealing with an insane fanatic, Ellington surreptitiously releases the prisoner, who laughs malevolently as he flees into the night. Ellington says,

"When the pictures of the carpenter from Branau-am-Inn began to appear in all the papers, I grew uneasy; for I felt I'd seen this man before. When the carpenter invaded Poland, I was sure." In the end, after World War II, Ellington receives a postcard from a brother at the abbey saying, "Rest now, my son. We have him back with us again."[81]

In "The Devil, You Say?" Dick Lewis, a small-town editor/publisher, complains that nothing newsworthy ever happens in his community when a small, elderly man arrives and introduces himself as Mr. Jones. But unlike Dylan's Mr. Jones, this one knows exactly what is happening. He tells Lewis he will create newsworthy events and promptly moves into the paper's press room, where he modifies the printing press and chases the other employees out with a pitchfork. Soon, absurd events become commonplace in town, all immediately covered by the paper with headlines like "Mayor's Wife Gives Birth to Baby Hippopotamus" and "Farmer Burl Illing Complains of Mysterious Appearance of Dragons in Back Yard."[82] Subscriptions begin to pour in, though Lewis worries, "We're going to be jailed, sure as the devil."[83] Eventually Jones reveals that he is the prince of darkness, and anything he prints on the modified press will come true. The devil proposes a Faustian bargain, offering to make the paper successful in exchange for Lewis's soul. Jones appreciates the challenge that Lewis offers. "What with wars and crime and politicians and the like, I scarcely have anything to do these days. No fun in merely shoveling 'em in."[84] When he realizes Jones is not joking, Lewis says, "Before he's done he'll send the whole world off its rocker, just so I can get subscriptions."[85]

In his revised version of "The Devil, You Say?," written as the 1963 *Twilight Zone* episode "Printer's Devil," Beaumont emphasized even more the conflict between twentieth-century rationalism and the supernatural. In this version, the devil (renamed Smith) taunts the publisher (renamed Winter) to get him to sign the contract. "Mr. Winter," the devil says, "as a sophisticated, intelligent, twentieth-century man, you *know* the devil does not exist. True?" A bit later, he says, "Fancy that, a grown-up man who believes in the devil."[86] For Beaumont, this progressive, scientific disbelief leaves humans unprepared to comprehend the extent and nature of modern evil, and without this understanding, attempts at reform can backfire. David Ellington, for instance, acts with the best humanitarian motives in freeing the howling man, and in the process unleashes the most destructive war in human history. In Beaumont's universe, then, no paradigm is complete unless it leaves plenty of room for irrationality, absurdity, and evil.

Part Three

Outside Looking In

Minority Artists

"So Much Nonsense Must Make Sense"

The Black Vision of Chester Himes

In the penultimate chapter of Chester Himes's 1969 crime novel *Blind Man with a Pistol*—the last in his series of stories set in Harlem—the title character makes his first appearance, shooting craps in a small gambling house on a hot summer afternoon. After losing all his money, he walks to the subway station and boards a train. An eccentric pride precludes the man from admitting his blindness to anyone, including himself, and his naturally surly temperament is exacerbated by his gambling losses. On a crowded subway car he sits across from Fat Sam, an embittered black laborer carrying on a loud and intense argument with himself. Fat Sam mistakes the blind man's unseeing gaze for a mocking stare and begins belligerently shouting at him. Unaware that he is the object of Sam's anger, the blind man pays no attention, which further infuriates Sam. When a female passenger sticks up for the blind man, he unleashes his anger at both her and Sam, saying all he wants is the money that has been taken from him. A neighboring black minister, reading the *New York Times,* puts down his paper and attempts to maintain peace, pleading, "Brothers! Brothers! You can settle your differences without resorting to violence." A nearby white passenger retorts, "Violence hell! What these niggers need is discipline," to which the blind man responds, "Beware, mother-raper! Beware!" The white man and Fat Sam take offense at the warning, and the white man knocks the blind man down. Getting up, the blind man says, "If'n you hit me again, white folks, I'll blow you away." As the minister begs, "Peace, man, God don't know no color," the blind man pulls a .45 from beneath his coat and fires, accidentally striking the minister in the heart. A woman begins screaming "BLIND MAN WITH A PISTOL," and pandemonium ensues as the blind man fires two more shots. "The second blasts were too much," Himes wrote. "Everyone reacted immediately. Some thought the world was coming to an end; others that the Venusians were coming. A number of the white passengers thought the niggers were taking over; the majority of soul people thought their time was up." Fat Sam escapes by shattering the subway's glass doors just as the train pulls into the 125th Street station. Others follow as the station landing becomes strewn with bodies, cut by glass, screaming in panic. As the woman continues yelling "BLIND MAN WITH A PISTOL," the title character stumbles over the bodies lying about the floor, waving his gun, asking, "Where? Where?"

Meanwhile, on the street above the subway station, a group of angry Harlem residents is watching the demolition of condemned slum buildings, part of an urban renewal program that has succeeded primarily in displacing the ghetto's inhabitants without providing new housing. The famous black New York city detectives, Coffin Ed Johnson and Grave Digger Jones—heroes of eight Himes novels—are standing at the intersection of Lenox Avenue and 125th Street using their signature long-barreled, nickel-plated .38-caliber pistols on .44-caliber frames to shoot rats fleeing the condemned buildings, while several white policemen stand by watching. Having long since been pulled off the case that provided the original plot for the novel—a case everyone, including the author, seems to have lost sight of—Johnson and Jones vent their fury on Harlem's literal, rather than figurative, rats. Fat Sam bursts out of the nearby subway, followed by a crowd of running, hysterical people covered in blood. As the white policemen pull their pistols, the blind man comes stumbling up the stairs and fires his gun, hitting a white cop in the middle of the forehead, before being gunned down by the other officers. The denizens of Harlem immediately begin crying that white cops have killed an innocent black man. Rumors spread rapidly, and Harlem is quickly engulfed in a full-scale riot. Grave Digger's commanding officer, Lieutenant Anderson, asks, "Can't you men stop that riot?"

> "It's out of hand, boss," Grave Digger said.
> "All right, I'll call for reinforcements. What started it?"

"A blind man with a pistol."
"What's that?"
"You heard me, boss."
"That don't make any sense."
"Sure don't."[1]

With this incredible scene—simultaneously violent, disordered, grotesque, and humorous—Himes drew his series of Harlem crime novels to its logical conclusion, as the chaos that had permeated his fictive world explodes in racial apocalypse. Coming in 1969, the scene contained numerous references to recent events and to tensions between the races in general. A year after the assassination of Martin Luther King Jr., Himes portrayed an ineffectual black minister pleading nonviolence and reconciliation, who, ironically, is the gunman's first victim. At a time when each political party sought to outdo the other in calling for "law and order"—a racially charged code term for cracking down on urban violence—Himes had a white bystander scornfully declare, "What these niggers need is discipline." Fat Sam, a handyman for a white family, embittered by his low pay, demeaning work, and degrading contacts with his white employers, pathetically seeks to exert what power he can by forcing others to listen to his tirade. Himes depicted the impotent anger of Harlem's black population confronting a distant, bureaucratic city government that cavalierly destroys their homes. Protesters carry pickets that whites do not read and most blacks ignore or mock. Tensions with white police, the only immediate and tangible representatives of the imperious city government, have reached the breaking point. The title character symbolizes the blind rage of African Americans, who, denying the existence of their handicap, eventually lash out in violence, usually making other blacks their first victims. As Himes wrote in the preface, the novel's central metaphor derived from a true incident a friend had told him about. "I thought, damn right, sounds like today's news, riots in the ghettos, war in Vietnam, masochistic doings in the Middle East. And then I thought of some of our loudmouthed leaders urging our vulnerable soul brothers on to getting themselves killed, and thought further that all unorganized violence is like a blind man with a pistol."[2]

Introducing Absurdity into the Human Condition

Though relatively few, minority artists played a special role in the development of the underground culture, since, as George Lipsitz said, "their exclusion from political power and cultural recognition has allowed aggrieved populations to cultivate sophisticated capacities for ambiguity, juxtaposition and irony."[3] Himes employed these artistic strategies in an effort to unmask the cultural contradictions of America in the postwar period. He ironically subverted many of the basic principles of the dominant Cold War consensus by accepting them and then carrying them to their logical extreme. In a period when race relations were being recognized as "an American dilemma," the great exception to America's democratic egalitarianism, Himes went further in saying that racism had severe pathological effects on both blacks and whites, undermining the very nature of American democracy and, as he argued in his later works, threatening the future of the nation itself.

Himes's paradigm differed in significant ways from the traditional African American worldview. As Lawrence Levine has said, historically blacks have had little understanding of and appreciation for absurdity.[4] Normally, only those fully integrated into a system of beliefs have the luxury of being able to see it as absurd. With their history of exclusion from and struggle to gain admission into the dominant culture, black Americans have seldom viewed the social order as fundamentally meaningless, because that would similarly render their struggle meaningless. In the Cold War period, one never finds the dark and absurdist core in the humor of Dick Gregory that one finds in Lenny Bruce's. Similarly, when white northern college students preparing to work in the Student Nonviolent Coordinating Committee's Mississippi Freedom Summer project met with black southern civil rights veterans for a training session in June 1964 and watched a television report featuring interviews with vitriolic segregationists, the white students began to laugh. The black workers were infuriated and walked out of the room, later telling the whites, "Maybe you won't laugh when you meet these guys and hear them talk, and know they are doing it every day."[5] The white students were able to view the logic underlying segregation as absurd, while blacks could see it as nothing other than tragic.

Himes, though, viewed absurdity as a concept central to an understanding of race. As an expatriate living in Europe during the height of the civil rights struggle, he gained enough distance from the American situation to formulate a concept of race relations that contrasted sharply with most African Americans' understanding of the issue. Himes saw race as a dialectical relationship that progressed toward increasing absurdity. As he wrote in the second volume of his autobiography, "Racism introduces absurdity into the human condition. Not only does racism express the absurdity of the racists, but it generates absurdity in the victims. And the absurdity of the victims intensifies the absurdity of the racists, ad infinitum. If one lives in a country where racism is held valid and practiced in all ways of life, eventually, no matter whether one is a racist or a victim, one comes to feel the absurdity of life. Racism generating from whites is first of all absurd. Racism creates absurdity among blacks as a defense mechanism. Absurdity to combat absurdity."[6]

White Men with Black Skins

Within the formulation of the Cold War consensus, African Americans served a crucial function. Official policies of racism were becoming increasingly embarrassing in light of the United States' new role as self-proclaimed defender of the free world. Having just completed a war against the racist philosophy of Nazism while civil rights advocates decried the hypocrisy of carrying on that fight with a Jim Crow army, Americans now faced an even stickier dilemma. The Cold War pitted the United States and Soviets in a struggle for the hearts and minds of the world. Much of this campaign would be carried on throughout the Third World, with its largely colored population. In this light, American policy makers began a gradual effort to abolish official segregation, and this effort became, in their eyes, a bright and shining symbol of democracy, inclusiveness, and American willingness to reform.

Accompanying this change in official policy, black Americans assumed a new importance in the vision of liberals who viewed segregation as a perfect outlet for their penchant for reform. The period after World War II saw a new interest in what Swedish sociologist Gunnar Myrdal termed the "American dilemma" in his influential 1944 study. Liberals began agitating for integration in a variety of areas. But in an effort to achieve reform, many liberals, both black and white, sought to reassure Americans that integration would not substantially alter their way of life, that blacks were really no different from whites. The classic statement of this view came in historian Kenneth Stampp's 1956 study of slavery, which he began with the assumption that "slaves were white men with black skins, nothing more, nothing less."[7]

Pioneers in breaking the color barrier were often handpicked to ensure they would be dignified and nonthreatening representatives of typical American values. They had to prove their loyalty, and, symbolically, the loyalty of all African Americans by denouncing threats to the American system. In the liberal paradigm, if blacks, with their legacy of suppression, publicly proclaimed their loyalty to the United States, their patriotism would make an extremely effective rejection of communism. Thus, Jackie Robinson was called before HUAC to refute the procommunist views of Paul Robeson.[8] On the other hand, when the young, handsome, and talented black actor James Edwards refused to testify before HUAC, his promising career went into a sustained decline from which it never recovered.[9] In the liberal imagination, integration was spearheaded by figures who posed no threat to standard American values. By the time of John Ball's 1965 detective novel *In the Heat of the Night,* the hero, Virgil Tibbs, could literally be described as a "white man with black skin." "His face lacked the broad nose and thick, heavy lips that characterized so many southern laborers. His nose was almost like a white man's and the line of his mouth was straight and disciplined. If he had been a little lighter, Sam would have seen white blood in him, but his skin was too black for that."[10]

The Effect of Oppression on the Human Personality

Himes never accepted the vision of successful integration into the Cold War consensus because his personal experiences precluded optimism about the possibilities for blacks to share in the American dream.[11] Born in 1909 in Jefferson City, Missouri, Himes spent his early years in several southern and border states, where his father taught blacksmithing and wheelwrighting at a number of black state colleges. Within the insular community of a black college, Himes's father was a man of esteem. But the history of Himes's childhood was one of downward mobility as the family fell victim to a combination of personal and professional misfortunes. Part of the problem, according to Himes, was that his light-skinned mother—who could pass for white—resented his dark-skinned father, hated living in all-black communities, and constantly created problems that caused the family to be shunned by the rest of the community. The family moved to St. Louis in 1922, where Himes's father found work as a waiter, and he never worked as anything other than a manual laborer the rest of his life.

In 1925 the family moved to Cleveland, where Himes graduated from high school the next year. After graduation, while working as a waiter in a local hotel, Himes was severely injured when he fell down an empty elevator shaft, leaving him hospitalized for an extended period and forcing him to wear a back brace for several years. With a disability pension, Himes entered Ohio State University in the fall of 1926, where he encountered the hypocrisy of northern-style Jim Crow. "Black students could star in any of the school athletic activities, but they could not live in the school dormitories on the campus, nor attend the movie theaters, nor visit or become a member of the white fraternity houses. Yet this was Columbus, Ohio, where all forms of racial discrimination were pro-hibited by state laws."[12]

Himes was expelled from school after taking a group of black students with him to a local whorehouse and speakeasy.[13] Upon returning to Cleveland, he began consorting with members of the city's criminal underworld. In 1928 he held up the house of a rich, white couple at gunpoint, stealing money, jewels, and a car. Arrested in Chicago, he was badly beaten by two detectives who cuffed his feet together and his hands behind his back, hung him upside down from an open door, and beat him with the butts of their guns around his ribs and testicles. Extradited to Cleveland, he was sentenced to twenty-five years in the Ohio State penitentiary.

For seven and a half years, before being paroled in 1936, Himes perfected the skills necessary for survival in prison, a violent and absurd world that would, in many ways, be mirrored in his fictive portrait of Harlem. In a line reprised almost word for word in one of his crime novels, he said, "Convicts stabbed, cut, slashed, brained, maimed, and killed each other almost every day for the most nonsensical reasons. Two black convicts cut each other to death over a dispute as to whether Paris was in France or France was in Paris."[14] Similarly, Himes learned about the capriciousness and arbitrariness of life and the finality of death when, on April 21, 1930, a fire swept through the prison, killing 317 con-victs in their cells in less than an hour and sparking a series of riots that lasted over a week.[15] In his 1934 short story, "To What Red Hell," his fictionalized ac-count of the fire, he wrote of the rows of dead bodies, "Wherever they had been, or had ever dreamed of being; whatever they had done or failed to do; whatever their race or their nationality or their background—that foot of greenish vomit hanging from their teeth made them all alike."[16]

Deciding it was his best alternative to a life of crime, Himes began his writ-ing career in prison, publishing short stories in such black journals as *Abbot's Monthly* and the *Atlanta Daily World* in 1933. He achieved mainstream success the next year when his stories of prison life, "Crazy in Stir" and "To What Red Hell," were printed in the August and October issues of *Esquire,* which published several of his stories over the next twelve years. After his parole, Himes returned to Cleveland, where he married and began working for the Works Progress Ad-ministration as a laborer, library research assistant, and, finally, a member of the Ohio Writer's Project. In 1940 he moved to southern California and worked at a variety of jobs—virtually all unskilled—in the booming war industries. Later, he wrote of this period of his life, "Up to the age of thirty-one I had been hurt emotionally, spiritually, and physically as much as thirty-one years can bear . . . and still I was entire, complete, functional . . . and I was not bitter. But under the mental corrosion of race prejudice in Los Angeles I had become bitter and saturated with hate. And finding myself unable to support my black wife, whom I loved desperately, I had become afraid. . . . I was thirty-one and whole when I went to Los Angeles and thirty-five and shattered when I left."[17] With this understanding, Himes saw through one of the fundamental beliefs of the emerging liberal consensus view regarding race—that racism was primarily a southern phenomenon resulting from a peculiarly regional social pathology. In this view, propounded by Myrdal, racism resulted from the South's inferior education system and archaic social structure.[18] But Himes discovered that in the North, "Black people were treated much the same as they were in an industrial city of the South. The difference was that the white people of Los Angeles seemed to be saying, 'Nigger, ain't we good to you?'"[19]

Wartime Los Angeles provided the setting for Himes's first two novels, *If He Hollers Let Him Go* (1945) and *Lonely Crusade* (1947), both focusing on the racial and class tensions among workers in the war industries.[20] These protest novels examine both the blatant and the subtle and invidious ways that racism permeates society and its debilitating effects on white and black consciousness. They are written in a style showing the influence of the *Black Mask* school of Tough Guy writing—which would also serve Himes well in his later detective series—and a tone of unabashed bravado.[21] The moderate success of *If He Hollers* spurred Himes into a more explicit exploration of the political alternatives blacks faced in *Lonely Crusade.* The novel's protagonist, union organizer Lee Gordon, rejects the duplicitous philosophy of the Communist party, which is all too willing to sell out the black workers in the name of the coming workers' state. In the end, Gordon discovers meaning only in the greater cause of interracial unionism and, in good proletarian-novel fashion, willingly becomes a martyr to the cause.

Perhaps only Himes could have written an anticommunist novel in 1947 that was as roundly hated as *Lonely Crusade.* As he would later remember, "Everyone hated the book. . . . The left hated it, the right hated it, Jews hated it, blacks hated it."[22] Even the book's explicit rejection of communism could not allow critics to overlook Himes's unflattering portraits of a wide variety of other social groups. The book's failure, in significant ways, set the course for the rest of Himes's career. Henceforth, he would reject politics and focus much more on personal issues, or later, on his crime series. Politics largely escaped his thinking from this point on, to the extent that in the two volumes of his autobiography such massive racial cataclysms as the Algerian war, the various independence movements in Africa, and the civil rights movement in the United States were scarcely mentioned, while he spent several chapters detailing his experience with an especially obstreperous Volkswagen he owned in France. The novel's failure also affected his future actions in another way, as he remembered later: "It was then that I decided to leave the United States forever if I got the chance. I could not be a communist because I am not a joiner. I could not be a reactionary, even if I had wanted to, because they wouldn't have me. The whites rejected me, the blacks didn't want me. I felt like a man without a country, which in fact I was."[23] When he had enough money, Himes left the United States and settled in Europe, where, except for a few brief periods, he spent the rest of his life.

Embittered by the failure of *Lonely Crusade,* Himes issued a salvo against the contradictions of the emerging Cold War racial consensus. Invited to give a talk at the University of Chicago in 1948 called "The Dilemma of the Negro Novelist in the United States," he used the forum to explore the psychic ravages of racism on black consciousness. In searching for a true understanding of African American existence, he said, the black novelist faces many pitfalls, not least of which is the temptation to become a spokesman for the dominant white culture. "The oppressor pays, and sometimes well, for the submission of the oppressed." Rejecting this option, he said, the black author must be prepared to be rejected by white culture, and much of black culture too, because an honest look at African Americans will reveal a psychologically damaged people and indict the society that has caused the damage.

In an interesting variation on W. E. B. DuBois's conception of the dual nature of black consciousness—in which blacks are constantly mediating their African and American selves—Himes said, "The American Negro, we must remember, is an American; the face may be the face of Africa, but the heart has the beat of Wall Street." Himes, however, did not believe the Americanism of blacks would allow for easy integration, for the history of racial antagonism had left deep scars. "To hate white people," he said, "is one of the first emotions an American Negro develops when he becomes old enough to learn what his status is in American society. . . . At some time in the lives of every American Negro there has been this hatred for white people; there are no exceptions. It could not possibly be otherwise." This hatred wreaks considerable psychic damage. First, blacks hate whites, then, living in constant fear their hatred will be discovered, they hate themselves because of their fear. The results of this vicious circle must be the subject of inquiry for the black author, Himes said. "If this plumbing for the truth reveals within the Negro personality, homicidal mania, lust for white women, a pathetic sense of inferiority, paradoxical anti-Semitism, arrogance, uncle tomism, hate and fear and self-hate, this then is the effect of oppression on the human personality. These are the horrors, the daily realities, the daily experiences of an oppressed minority."[24] This speech, like *Lonely Crusade,* drew a decidedly hostile response. As Fred Pfeil has said, "The reaction to such total honesty was utter silence, in response to which Himes stayed drunk for the better part of five years."[25]

At this point in his career, at least in part, Himes echoed many of the dominant trends in the Cold War consensus. His insistence on the fundamental Americanness of African Americans reflected the mainstream view, which, for instance, countered Robeson's claim that black Americans would not take up arms against the Soviet Union. Similarly, his rejection of politics, specifically the politics of communism and black nationalism, in favor of personal issues reflected a major theme of such authors as Philip Rahv, Lionel Trilling, and Ralph Ellison. Himes shared with such liberal modernists a view that political literature tended toward propaganda and thus an obliteration of much of life's ironies and ambiguities. This separation of politics and "art" in the Cold War period had special relevance for black artists, according to Thomas Hill Schaub. "Today this position seems at once naive and reactionary, but once relocated within the discursive context from which it emerged, the separating of art and politics becomes a more complex event, and regains some of its original plausibility. More than that: within the African American community that distinction participates in a strategy of withdrawal from centers of power, both democratic and communist, that was provoked by a crisis in black American leadership during World War II."[26]

Unlike other repentant radicals, Himes's apostasy did not make him welcome within the consensus. If his views reflected the dominant consensus, it was the distorted reflection of a fun-house mirror. For coupled with his insistence that blacks were first and foremost Americans was a disquisition on the pathological effects of racism on both blacks and whites. At a time when black and white integrationists sought to reassure white America that blacks were a benign people and integration could proceed smoothly, Himes insisted that the legacy of racism had severely deformed black culture and consciousness, leaving African Americans a potentially dangerous people and making integration problematic. Later, he wrote of blacks living in ghettos, "They had been forced to live there, in all the filth and degradation, until their lives had been warped to fit."[27] Further, unlike Myrdal and his minions, Himes refused to consider racism as a largely regional aberration to the American mainstream; to him, racism *was* the mainstream. He felt driven from his homeland and, in 1953, emigrated to Europe, becoming one of a substantial group of black American expatriate artists.

During his European sojourn Himes was always a stranger in a strange land, his soul seldom finding refuge. Though he lived in France for nearly two decades, he never bothered to learn the language. His relations with the community of black American artists in Paris were always strained, especially his on-again, off-again friendship with Richard Wright. He was as appalled by French racism as by the American variety, and his book *A Case of Rape* (1963) is an attack on both.[28] He ran through a series of difficult, occasionally violent, relationships with white women, both American and European. Despite his eventual success in France, he was as unable to earn an adequate living from his writing in Europe as he had been in America, and for nearly a decade and a half, he lived a hand-to-mouth existence.

I Got the Handle, by Some Miracle

It was during one of these many periods of dire financial straits that Himes's friend Marcel Duhamel (who had translated *If He Hollers Let Him Go*), editor of Gallimard's La Serie Noire, urged him to write a crime story for the series. In retrospect, the suggestion seems much more natural than it did to Himes at the time. Not only did Himes claim not to know how to write detective stories, but virtually no black American authors had ever used the mystery story genre.[29] But as Duhamel remarked, Himes's prose already bore a strong resemblance to American Tough Guy detective stories. "Write like you did in the novel I translated," he told Himes. "All action. Perfect style for a detective story."[30] Beyond Himes's personal style, the genre itself is in many ways ideally suited for minority writers. As John Reilly has written: "Tough-Guy fiction in viewpoint or setting reflects conditions produced by the class and caste system. In the manner of Naturalism it depicts character as the product of social conditions, and from the standpoint of an outsider it provides a guide to the disorder of American civilization, making clear that the cause of it all is eventually located in the practices of the dominant class."[31]

Himes's adoption of the hard-boiled crime genre allowed him to escape the standard categorization of black writers, which fit all writing by blacks under the heading of "protest." Like Ralph Ellison's Invisible Man, black authors in the postwar period were invisible because of the dominant white culture's determination to force them into a predetermined, stereotyped mold of protest writer, a problem Himes had faced repeatedly. In the shadow of Richard Wright, black writers were expected to portray, with naturalistic despair, the effects of racism. At the same time that blacks were given only this one creative outlet, the public was growing weary of black protest novels. Himes too was dissatisfied with the form. In his autobiography, he wrote, "I had the creative urge but the old, used forms for the black American writer did not fit my creations. . . . I knew the life of an American black needed another image than just the victim of racism. We were more than just victims. We did not suffer, we were extroverts. We were unique individuals, funny but not clowns, solemn but not serious, hurt but not suffering, sexualists but not whores in the usual sense of the word; we had a tremendous love of life, a love of sex, a love of ourselves. We were absurd."[32] Ironically, only by allowing himself to be typecast as a writer within another fictional genre—one relegated to second-class citizenship in the field of literature—could Himes escape the confines of being a black writer.

The universe of Himes's Harlem crime stories is marked by chaos, ambiguity, absurdity, and violence, and his description of it is filled with "that bitter self-corroding irony which white people call 'Negro humor.'"[33] Harlem's residents were so accustomed to the disorder and violence of their surroundings that they felt comfortable in it. "It was all so crazy," he wrote, "it was reassuring."[34] Or as Grave Digger says at one point, "So much nonsense must make sense."[35] Even the elements contribute to this sense of chaos and violence. All of Himes's stories take place in the oppressive heat of summer or the bitter cold of winter. In the Harlem of his crime stories, Himes found a perfect metaphor for his worldview, which he described in his autobiography: "Some time before, I didn't know when, my mind had rejected all reality as I had known it and I had begun to see the world as a cesspool of buffoonery. Even the violence was funny. A man gets his throat cut. He shakes his head to say you missed me and it falls off. Damn reality, I thought. All of reality was absurd, contradictory, violent and hurting. It was funny, really, if I could just get the joke. And I got the handle, by some miracle."[36]

The atmosphere of violence pervading this world is immediately apparent in that virtually all of the stories open with a scene mixing chaotic and graphic violence with slapstick comedy. *The Real Cool Killers* (1965), for example, begins with a diminutive patron in a crowded bar accosting the only white man in the establishment. When Big Smiley, the bartender, comes to the aid of the white man, the small man cuts his arm with a knife. Big Smiley reaches beneath the bar, pulls out a fireman's axe, and cuts off the attacker's arm. "The severed arm in its coat sleeve, still clutching the knife, sailed through the air, sprinkling the nearby spectators with drops of blood, landed on the linoleum tile floor, and skidded beneath the table of a booth." Big Smiley continues to advance on the small man, who yells, "Wait a minute, you big mother-raper, till Ah finds my arm! It got my knife in his hand," before collapsing. When the white manager announces that everyone should remain calm and that the police have been called, the bar's remaining patrons stampede for the door. As soon as they exit, a hophead on the sidewalk accuses the same white patron of messing with his wife and pursues him with a gun. The chase is soon joined by a gang of juvenile delinquents disguised as Arabs—the Real Cool Moslems—and a large crowd of black bystanders. Finally the white man is shot, and the hophead gunman and the gang stand around his body laughing until the police come.[37] Several of the other opening scenes are equally as bizarre.

These wildly absurd introductions foreshadow increasing chaos. Himes contended that he sought to realistically portray the effects of violence. Cultural images of violent death rarely depict the effects guns, knives, and other weapons have on the human body, he said. "Even when they just say 'blown to pieces' that doesn't describe what they look like blown to pieces. When a shell hits a man in a war, bits of him fly around, half of his liver is flying through the air, and his brains are dribbling off. These are actual scenes, no one states them outright."[38] No one except Himes, whose graphic descriptions of violence utilized grotesque metaphors and, often, slapstick comedy. In a typical passage, a gunman opens fire on a parade of policemen, hitting the commissioner. "He wore no hat to catch his brains and fragments of skull, and they exploded through the sunny atmosphere and splattered the spectators with goo, tufts of gray hair and splinters of bone. One skull fragment, larger than the others, struck a tall, well-dressed man on the cheek, cutting the skin and splashing brains against his face like a custard pie in a Mack Sennet comedy."[39]

This juxtaposition of high comedy and graphic violence frequently reached even more extreme lengths. In *All Shot Up* (1960), Grave Digger and Coffin Ed chase a tire thief riding a motorcycle and sidecar on an icy winter night. With the heater in his car broken, Digger can barely see through the ice-covered windshield. Ed leans out the window and tries to shoot out the cyclist's tires. As the thief attempts to pass a truck carrying sheets of metal, a bullet ricochets off a manhole cover and hits the truck's tire, causing a blowout. The truck skids on the icy street, and the sheets of metal fly out, neatly severing the cyclist's head. While the head bounces on the street, the headless cyclist continues at a rapid clip. Seeing the accident, the truck driver passes out, and his truck crashes into a black church with a lighted box bearing the title of the day's sermon, "Beware! Death is closer than you think!" As the headless body on the motorcycle gradually runs out of blood, its muscles go limp, and it crashes into a jewelry store with a sign reading "We Will Give Credit to the Dead."[40]

Self-consciously, Himes sought to place his portrayal of violence in the broader context of American history and culture. "There is no way," he once said in an interview, "that one can evaluate the American scene and avoid violence, because any country that was born in violence and has lived in violence always knows about violence."[41] It is, in fact, the close interrelationship between American culture and violence that forms the basis for the large body of American hard-boiled detective novels. "No one," Himes said, "*no one,* writes about violence the way that Americans do . . . for the simple reason that no one understands violence or experiences violence like the American civilians do. . . . American violence is public life, it's a public way of life, it became a form, a detective form."[42] In *Run Man Run* (1966), Himes directly related the violence of his story to the broader cultural milieu. As a black man hides from a crooked, murderous white cop, he thinks about the murder of three civil rights workers in Mississippi and a crazed sniper in New Jersey who had randomly killed thirteen passers-by. "White cops were always shooting some Negro in Harlem. This was a violent city, these were violent people. Read any newspaper any day."[43]

Himes also played with other icons of American culture in his portrayal of violence. Coffin Ed and Grave Digger are often viewed as fast-on-the-draw sheriffs and Harlem as a dangerous frontier town. As one character says upon seeing Ed and Digger arrive on the scene of a crime, "Now we've got those damned Wild West gunmen here to mess up everything."[44] The two mete out their own brand of frontier justice in an attempt to maintain some semblance of order amidst the daily chaos of Harlem. Their first appearance in the series occurs in *A Rage in Harlem* (1957). They are standing outside the Savoy Ballroom on a sidewalk crowded with people waiting to buy tickets and aim their revolvers down the sidewalk to keep the line straight. "Whenever anyone moved out of line, Grave Digger would shout, 'Straighten up!' and Coffin Ed would echo, 'Count off!' If the offender didn't straighten up the line immediately, one of the detectives would shoot in the air. . . . Folks in Harlem believed that Grave

Digger Jones and Coffin Ed Johnson would shoot a man stone dead for not standing straight in line."[45]

As Himes described Ed and Digger, the people of Harlem are perhaps not far from wrong in this belief. Their first appearance in a book is almost always immediately followed by mayhem. In *The Real Cool Killers,* when one of the defiant Real Cool Moslems throws a bottle of ceremonial perfume at Coffin Ed—who once had a bottle of acid thrown in his face—Ed fires off two shots, killing the perfume-thrower, injuring a woman bystander, and sending the crowd into a panicked stampede, trampling the injured woman and two others.[46]

In this case, first appearances are not deceiving. Beatings, threats, and shootings are the primary means by which Digger and Ed solve their cases. In *A Rage in Harlem,* they take turns slapping one suspect on the cheek. "They slapped him fast, from one to another, like batting a Ping-pong ball. Gus's head began ringing. He lost his sense of balance and his legs began to buckle. They slapped him until he fell to his knees, deaf to the world."[47] Later in the novel, when the beautiful suspect Imabelle tries to seduce Grave Digger to avoid being arrested, Himes writes, "He slapped her with such savage violence it spun her out of the chair to land in a grotesque splay-legged posture on her belly on the floor."[48] Protestations that such acts constitute violations of civil rights have little effect on Ed and Digger. In *The Real Cool Killers,* the two confront a group of teenagers in an attempt to track down the Real Cool Moslems. When Digger grabs two girls to prevent them from leaving, a boy says, "He can't hold you 'less he's got a warrant." Digger slaps the boy out of his seat, grabs him by the lapels, lifts him, slams him back down in his seat and then asks him to repeat what he said. Wisely, the boy remains silent.[49]

Himes's ambiguous attitude toward his protagonists is reflected in *The Crazy Kill,* in which Ed and Digger take the suspect Chink back to police headquarters to elicit information from him. There they beat him in exactly the same manner the young Himes was beaten when arrested for armed robbery. Chink's ankles are cuffed together, and his hands behind his back, and he is hung upside down by his ankles from an open door, then the two put their heels in Chink's armpits and push down.[50] Such practices frequently lead Ed and Digger into trouble with the Harlem community and the police hierarchy, and the two often find themselves reprimanded or suspended by the commissioner or excoriated in the press for excessive use of force. But Ed and Digger believe their brutal tactics are necessary for survival in the violent and bizarre world of Harlem. "They had to be tough to work in Harlem. Colored folks didn't respect colored cops. But they respected big shiny pistols and sudden death. It was said in Harlem that Coffin Ed's pistol would kill a rock and that Grave Digger's would bury it."[51]

With this portrayal of his two detectives, Himes epitomized a major transformation in the late fifties and sixties in popular-cultural images of heroes. In his excellent study of sixties films, Ethan Mordden cites the actor Lee Marvin as an example of the "very relative morality" of the era. During the fifties, Marvin had been typecast as a brutal and violent heavy and then graduated to playing heroes in the sixties, but his heroes were as brutal and violent as his villains. "In Marvin," Mordden said, "we have . . . a figure to centralize the decade's growing belief in violence as an expression not of villainy but of humanity."[52] In his description of Marvin's performance in *Point Blank* (1967), Mordden could easily be describing Coffin Ed and Grave Digger. "There's steel in his mad, even charm in his tense. No regrets. No opinions. When you deal with cheaters and liars and 'the organization,' violence is like breathing: necessary."[53] In the era's popular culture, perhaps only Mickey Spillane's Mike Hammer rivaled Ed and Digger for sheer brutality. But the New York City that Hammer stalks is a Manichean world in which good and bad are easily identifiable. Himes's heroes, on the other hand, inhabit an ambiguous and chaotic universe where values are relative, and the two blunder through, acting on an imperfect knowledge of good and evil. While Hammer never accidentally shoots innocent bystanders, Ed and Digger frequently beat and injure the innocent along with the guilty.

What redeems these two is that they adhere to a strict code of ethics, though one that does not necessarily jibe with the law. In this sense they reflect one of the dominant themes of American mystery stories. From Dashiell Hammett's Sam Spade to Robert Parker's Spenser, detectives have been considered heroic if, in the midst of a chaotic, violent, and morally ambiguous world, they have carved out and maintained a rigorous code of honor. The first principle of Ed and Digger's code is absolute loyalty to each other. The two are constantly together—they live within a block of each other on Long Island—to the point that their personalities are almost interchangeable. Distrusted by the community they serve, frequently at odds with the department hierarchy, the two realize they can absolutely count on no one but each other. When a criminal throws acid in Ed's face in *A Rage in Harlem,* permanently scarring him, Digger is determined to track down the culprit. Similarly, when Digger is shot in *The Heat's On* and a false bulletin released announcing his death, Ed uses whatever tactics are necessary to find those he believes murdered his partner.

In their Sisyphean quest to maintain order in Harlem, Digger and Ed have

formulated a complex code of selective law enforcement. "They took their trib-
ute, like all real cops, from the established underworld catering to the essential
needs of the people—game-keepers, madams, streetwalkers, numbers writers,
numbers bankers. But they were rough on purse snatchers, muggers, burglars,
con men, and all strangers working any racket. And they didn't like rough stuff
from anybody but themselves."[54] As John Reilly has pointed out, Ed and Digger accept organized crime because its very organization lends consistency and
stability to the community. But individual crime is unpredictable and exacer-
bates the normal chaos, so it is intolerable.[55]

The two also have a well-ordered hierarchy of crime in which drug dealing
is the most serious offense. As Digger says of pushers, "I hate this type of criminal worse than God hates sin."[56] When the two are reprimanded for using excessive force in inadvertently killing a drug pusher, the district attorney says,
"You killed a man suspected of a minor crime, and not in self-defense," to which
Digger replies, "You call dope peddling a minor crime? . . . All the crimes committed by addicts—robberies, murders, rapes. . . . All the fucked-up lives. . . .
All the nice kids sent down the drain on a habit. . . . Twenty-one days on heroin
and you're hooked for life. . . . Jesus Christ, mister, that one lousy drug has
murdered more people than Hitler. And you call it *minor!*"[57] At the same time,
accepting the moral ambiguity of their environment, Ed and Digger have an
agreement with Ma, a gray-haired old woman who deals heroin, to keep their
stool pigeons supplied with drugs.[58]

Similarly, the two often reach compromises that, while technical violations
of the law, meet their own moral code and preserve peace and order. At the end
of *The Real Cool Killers,* for example, Grave Digger lets the true murderer go
because the victim was a white pervert who enjoyed whipping young black girls,
and the killer, one of his victims, killed him to prevent the same thing from happening to her friend.[59] In *The Big Gold Dream* (1960), they allow the arrest and
conviction of a technically innocent, but truly evil, man after discovering the actual murderer is dead.[60] And in *Cotton Comes to Harlem,* they force a corrupt
white con man to pay an $87,000 bribe so they can return the money to eighty-
seven families who have invested $1,000 each in a back-to-Africa scam.[61]

Digger and Ed are also admirable because of their inestimable skill as cops
on New York's toughest beat and the envy they inspire in other, mainly white,
policemen. When they break up a potential riot in *Cotton Comes to Harlem,*
Himes comments, "The white cops looked at Grave Digger and Coffin Ed with
the envious awe usually reserved for a lion tamer with a cage of big cats."[62] On

occasion the two have to earn the respect of other policemen. In *All Shot Up,* at the scene of a crime, a white cop twice uses the word "nigger." Ed tells him: "'If you use that word again I'll kick your teeth down your throat.'" The cop bristled. 'Kick whose teeth—.' He never got to finish. Coffin Ed planted a left hook in his stomach and crossed an overhand right to the jaw."[63]

Digger and Ed are also sympathetic characters because, through the exterior of toughness, can sometimes be seen glimpses of educated and sensitive men. Digger demonstrates his learning with occasional references to such literary classics as Gorki's *The Bystander* and Hemingway's *For Whom the Bell Tolls.*[64] Both are avid aficionados of jazz.[65] And both are given to crying when overwhelmed with joy or grief, as Ed does in *The Heat's On* when he discovers Digger is not really dead.[66]

Himes once said that "the characters in my detective stories, in order to remain credible, had to grow with the passage of time and as they did so, they developed a greater race consciousness."[67] The major difference between Ed and Digger and the rest of the police department had always been their direct connection with the community. Both had been born and raised in Harlem and knew many of the residents by name.[68] At one point Coffin Ed explains the difference in attitude between them and others in the department: "Brody is a homicide man and solving murders is his business. He goes at it in a routine way like the law prescribes, and if some more people get killed while he's going about it, that's just too bad for the victims. But me and Digger are two country Harlem dicks who live in this village and don't like to see anybody get killed. It might be a friend of ours."[69]

Over the course of the series, their affinity for the people of Harlem takes on a more specifically racial feeling. In *Cotton Comes to Harlem,* the next-to-last book in the series, Grave Digger exclaims, "All I wish is that I was God for one mother-raping second," to which Ed replies, "I know. You'd concrete the face of the mother-raping earth and turn white folks into hogs."[70] In this novel, Digger and Ed are deeply moved by the plight of the black families who have put up their hard-earned money to return to Africa. Himes wrote, "Everyone has to believe in something; and the white people of America had left them nothing to believe in."[71] The two detectives sympathize with the people taken in by the back-to-Africa movement while rejecting the movement itself, a sentiment that paralleled Himes's own. In the early sixties, Himes, who had become a friend of Malcolm X's, said, "He did not have to indoctrinate me into distrusting white people; I had mistrusted them all along."[72] He went on to say, "I agreed with everything about his program except his religion. I tried . . . to tell him that the Moslems were the first people to go into black Africa and collect the blacks whom they took to the African coasts and sold to the European slave-traders, but Malcolm saw the Moslems as the saviors of the blacks. I had been in Egypt and had seen the blacks in Cairo and Alexandria still treated as slaves, and I didn't agree with him at all. But I was all in favor of his politics."[73]

In *Blind Man with a Pistol,* Digger and Ed specifically discuss Malcolm X.

> "You know one thing, Digger. [Malcolm] was safe as long as he kept hating white folks—they wouldn't have hurt him, probably have made him rich; it wasn't until he began including them in the human race they killed him. That ought to tell you something."
>
> "It does. It tells me that white people don't want to be included in a human race with black people."[74]

As Long as There Are Jungles

The Harlem that Grave Digger and Coffin Ed patrol is as stylized as the Bedford-Stuyvesant of Spike Lee's 1989 film *Do the Right Thing.* As Himes wrote in his autobiography, he had only lived in Harlem a brief time and so, while he knew the geography of the area, he "didn't really know what it was like to be a citizen of Harlem. . . . *The Harlem of my books was never meant to be real; I never called it real; I just wanted to take it away from the white man if only in my books.*"[75] Similarly, he said that, not having lived among American blacks for many years, his urban patois was anachronistic.[76] By lifting Harlem out of the realm of realism and into the symbolic, Himes could portray it, in Edward Margolies' words, "as the intensification, the logical absurdity, the comic horror of the black experience of America."[77] In a typical passage, Himes captured the contradictions of black life in Harlem, wherein widespread poverty fosters serious social problems, while, at the same time, the community offers black people their only refuge from whites. "It was a street of paradox: unwed young mothers, suckling their infants, living on a prayer; fat black racketeers coasting past in big bright-colored convertibles with their solid gold babes, carrying huge sums of money on their persons; hardworking men . . . talking in loud voices up there in Harlem where the white bosses couldn't hear them; teen-age gangsters grouping for a gang fight, smoking marijuana weed to get up their courage; everybody escaping the hotbox rooms they lived in, seeking respite in a street made hotter by the automobile exhaust and the heat released by the concrete walls and walks."[78]

Violence permeates Himes's Harlem, both the repressive violence of the police and the violence born of frustration that blacks practice on one another. Knifings, shootings, and throat-slashings are an everyday occurrence. At one point, Ed and Digger's lieutenant reads aloud from the daily police reports: "Man kills his wife with an axe for burning his breakfast pork chop . . . man shoots another man demonstrating a recent shooting he had witnessed . . . man stabs another man for spilling beer on his new suit . . . man kills self in a bar playing Russian roulette with a .32 revolver . . . woman stabs man in stomach fourteen times, no reason given . . . woman scalds neighboring woman with pot of boiling water for speaking to her husband . . . man arrested for threatening to blow up subway train because he entered wrong station and couldn't get his token back."[79] Violence even marks Himes's description of Harlem's geography. In describing the distance between two points, he wrote, "It was ten minutes by foot, if you were on your way to church, about two and a half minutes if your old lady was chasing you with a razor."[80]

In Himes's view, the violence of Harlem's residents is a pathological response to their social position. Harlemites prey on each other in wildly absurd ways and often for ridiculous reasons. Frantz Fanon described a similar tendency among colonial peoples, terming it "collective autodestruction." Fanon wrote, "While the settler or the policeman has the right the livelong day to strike the native, to insult him and to make him crawl to them, you will see the native reaching for his knife at the slightest hostile or aggressive glance cast on him by another native; for the last resort of the native is to defend his personality *vis-à-vis* his brother."[81] In Himes's novels whites look at the behavior of the people of Harlem as justification for outside control, as further evidence that they are not reasonable human beings.

Himes's universe is populated with grotesque characters. As Jackson Lears has argued, a recurrent theme of modernist artists is that the commercial image of the sleek, successful twentieth-century American is neither as substantial nor as realistic as the portraits of the pathetic and grotesque denizens of, for instance, Winesburg, Ohio, or Yoknapatawpha County, Mississippi.[82] Similarly, black modernists faced the slick, Sidney Poitier image of the successful black integrationist, one they knew did not convey the reality of their lives. But not in their darkest nightmares could Sherwood Anderson or William Faulkner have conjured up the grotesqueries of Himes's Harlem, peopled as it is with a giant, albino, Negro idiot; a dwarf pusher; an elderly, withered, female faith healer and heroin pusher; a badly scarred exfighter, mute because his tongue

has been cut out by the mob to prevent him from testifying; a transvestite nun/
con man/junkie who sells tickets to heaven; and a ninety-year-old black Mor-
mon with eleven wives and a brood of children who run around naked and eat
from a trough. Even Coffin Ed is a grotesque. His face, badly scarred when a
criminal threw acid in it, is now a patchwork of varicolored skin grafted from
his thigh. "The result was that Coffin Ed's face looked as though it had been
made up in Hollywood for the role of the Frankenstein monster."[83] Minor characters also often have deformities or physical handicaps. In such figures Himes
gave form to his thesis that American racism severely deformed black personality and culture.

Among Himes's contemporaries, perhaps only Nelson Algren consistently
provided as nuanced and sympathetic a portrait of society's losers, its petty criminals and small-time con men. But Himes (like Algren) never romanticized his
subjects. His vision is absent any cloying populist sentimentalism about the no-
bility of the poor. With his naturalistic sensibility, Himes accepted the dehumanizing effects of the environment on people. When Ed and Digger's lieutenant
says of Harlem, "I hate to see people tearing at one another like rapacious animals," Digger responds, "Hell, what do you expect? As long as there are jungles
there'll be rapacious animals."[84] Yet neither Himes nor his two detectives let
cynicism overwhelm their fundamental sympathy. When a white policeman
complains that the numerous witnesses to a crime are "all stone blind," Ed replies
testily, "What do you expect from people who're invisible themselves?"[85]

Just as Lawrence Levine has argued that slave tales were an ongoing and per-
ceptive parody of white slave-owners' society,[86] so Himes's Harlem is a savage
satire of American capitalist culture. As he said in his 1948 speech at the University of Chicago, blacks may have "the face of Africa, but [their] heart has the
beat of Wall Street." Harlem's residents are as avaricious as the big money men
on Wall Street, but the stakes they play for are smaller, and the money-making
schemes they engage in usually do not have the official imprimatur of law. They
also live in an unpromising environment: "Looking eastward from the towers
of Riverside Church, perched among the university buildings on the high banks
of the Hudson River, in a valley far below, waves of gray rooftops distort the
perspective like the surface of a sea. Below the surface, in the murky waters of
fetid tenements, a city of black people who are convulsed in desperate living,
like the voracious churning of millions of hungry cannibal fish. Blind mouths
eating their own guts. Stick in a hand and draw back a nub. That is Harlem."[87]
Within this environment, blacks have developed a vibrant economy with the

materials at hand and the requisite skills for success. As Digger once remarks, "If our people were ever let loose they'd be a sensation in the business world, with the flair they got for crooked organizing," to which Ed replies, "That's what the white folks is scared of."[88]

The predatory nature of this world can be seen in the two dominant character types that populate Himes's Harlem—squares and sharpies, according to Stephen Milliken's fine study of Himes. "The sharpies are always comfortably committed to some kind of lucrative illegal activity," writes Milliken, "and the squares have back-breaking jobs that bring in almost no money, but the essential point of demarcation is the question of gullibility. Squares will believe literally anything, and sharpies are fanatically cynical."[89] Himes's sharpies work a variety of rackets with varying degrees of success, from tire thieves, numbers runners, and small-time con men to organized crime bosses, political bosses, and ministers. They have no sympathy for the hard-working squares who serve as their victims. Sweet Prophet Brown, the crooked preacher in *The Big Gold Dream,* says disdainfully of Alberta Wright, one of his parishioners, "That woman's story can be told in two lines. Born like a fool, and worked like a mule."[90] Brown hypnotizes Wright and has her give him the $29,000 she won playing the numbers. When, at the end of the novel, he is exposed and members of the black press ask him why he took the money, he unrepentantly responds, "I needed it. It takes a lot of money to be a prophet these days. It's the high cost of living."[91] Himes also captured the pathos of the squares when Wright tells the police that Brown need not have tricked her, that if he had asked for the money, she would have given it to him. "Because I believed in him. . . . That's why. If you is a black woman like me, you got to believe in something."[92] Similarly, Digger and Ed sympathize with the working-class families swindled by the back-to-Africa scam in *Cotton Comes to Harlem.* "They didn't consider these victims as squares or suckers. They understood them. These were people seeking a home—just like the Pilgrim Fathers. Harlem is a city of the homeless."[93]

In portraying Harlem as the underside of the American dream, Himes offered a vision of America as violent, chaotic, and absurd. This view captures what Marshall Berman identified as one of the central tenets of modernism, a realization of "the destructive brutalities that bourgeois nihilism brings to life," the logical outgrowth of a world in which, as Marx wrote in *The Communist Manifesto,* "all that is solid melts into air."[94] Just as Coffin Ed and Grave Digger struggle constantly merely to maintain some semblance of order in Harlem, so Himes depicted the "order" of the American capitalist system as a thin veneer masking a dark and nihilistic core. At the end of *Blind Man with a Pistol,* the mask is ripped away, and the chaos that always lay just below the surface is exposed. Similarly, in his short story "Prediction," Himes depicted a lone black gunman hiding in a church watching a parade of white policemen march by. He opens fire, and in the exchange between him and the police department, more than seventy people are killed, the downtown area decimated, and the church leveled. "In the wake of this bloody massacre," Himes wrote, "the structure of capitalism began to crumble. Confidence in the capitalistic system had an almost fatal shock. All over the world millions of capitalists sought means to invest their wealth in the Communist East."[95] In this passage, Himes articulated what had been implicit throughout his crime series, a sensibility that captures, in Berman's words, "the glory of modern energy and dynamism, the ravages of modern disintegration and nihilism, the strange intimacy between them; the sense of being caught in a vortex where all facts and values are whirled, exploded, decomposed, recombined; a basic uncertainty about what is basic, what is valuable, even what is real; a flaring up of the most radical hopes in the midst of their radical negations.[96] Or, in the words of the unnamed Harlem intellectual Himes quoted as an epigraph to *Blind Man with a Pistol,* "Motherfucking right, it's confusing; it's a gas, baby, you dig."[97]

"Some Torture That Perversely Eased"

Patricia Highsmith
and the Everyday
Schizophrenia of
American Life

Vic van Allen, protagonist of Patricia Highsmith's 1957 novel *Deep Water*, re-signedly accepts his status as cuckold, even deriving a perverse pleasure out of his public image of wronged husband tolerating his wife's indiscretions with a Jobian patience. But the cultured and learned Vic wonders why all of Melinda's lovers are such mediocre boors. Why must they all represent "insubstantiality personified"?[1] When one of her companions has the effrontery to approach him at a party and thank him for being so "sporting," Vic decides he has had enough. "'I appreciate your sentiments,' Vic said, with a small smile, 'but I don't waste my time punching people in the nose. If I really don't like somebody, I kill them.'" Referring to an old friend of Melinda's who has recently been murdered by a burglar, he asks, "You remember Malcolm McRae, don't you?" Because of Vic's reputation as the village nonconformist—he drives an old car, runs a small publishing house specializing in obscure books, does not own a television, and tolerates his wife's affairs without outward signs of jealousy—he realizes that his threat is more believable. "People who do not behave in an orthodox manner, Vic thought, are by definition frightening."[2]

The results of Vic's lie are sudden and widespread. The story disseminates quickly, Melinda's current and potential lovers maintain a respectful distance, and Melinda is furious. Those who know Vic well treat the whole incident as a joke, while everyone eyes him with a new respect.[3] Faced with a lack of suitors, Melinda behaves herself, and Vic finds his social relations running much more smoothly. But when McRae's real murderer is captured, Vic realizes his situation has dramatically deteriorated. Melinda will once again begin her philandering, and everyone will know that, Vic's surface calm notwithstanding, he really does care, or else he would not have lied about the murder.[4]

True to form, Melinda quickly acquires a new lover, whom Vic thinks even more boring and puerile than the others. When he finds himself alone with her paramour, Vic makes a spur-of-the-moment decision to kill him. The rest of the community rally around Vic, amazed at his patient tolerance of Melinda's increasingly hysterical accusations against him. Vic feels no guilt and is certain no one will ever be able to prove the murder. When Melinda finds another lover, a confident Vic similarly murders him and hides the body. But Melinda guesses the fate of her missing lover and tricks Vic into revealing the body's location. Furious that he has been discovered, Vic savagely beats Melinda to death. He is arrested and taken to jail, convinced that his defeat signals the triumph of the common herd—"The ugly birds without wings. The mediocre who perpetuated mediocrity, who really fought and died for it."—and the crushing of all that is beautiful, cultured, and refined.[5]

In such novels as *Deep Water,* Highsmith staked her claim as the quintessential chronicler of the postwar underground culture. Her universe both inhabited the comfortable and complacent world of the period's dominant culture and existed beneath it, in the seamy underside of the middle-class ideal, where the image of the happy suburban family masks a murderous hatred, and the charming, successful businessman is a dangerous sociopath. Highsmith's work represented a radical break with the era's dominant cultural narratives. Placed in the context of the Cold War and the suburban ideal, her fiction signaled a sustained critique of the major cultural assumptions of the period, challenging the rigid dichotomies and the vision of America as the savior of the world that marked official foreign policy as well as the dominant gender assumptions and the concept of home and family as a place of salvation that constituted the official domestic ideology.

Was There Ever Anything Logical about It?

The sense of violence and arbitrariness pervading Highsmith's worldview can be traced to before her birth in Fort Worth, Texas, in 1921. Her parents divorced before she was born, and her mother tried to abort her. "Not that I minded," Highsmith said in a 1989 interview. "Suppose my parents had succeeded in having the abortion. They would have waited, and had a baby when they were ready. Not exactly me, but . . . ."[6] Her family moved to New York when she was six. She grew up in Greenwich Village and graduated from Barnard. Her first nationally published short story, "The Heroine," appeared in *Harper's Bazaar* in 1946 and was selected to appear in the *O. Henry Memorial Prize Stories.* In the late forties, with the aid of Truman Capote, Highsmith was invited to attend the Yaddo art colony in Saratoga Springs, New York (where she roomed next door to Chester Himes).[7] While there, she completed her first novel, *Strangers on a Train* (1950), which brought her fame when it was turned into a film by Alfred Hitchcock the next year.[8]

Highsmith eschewed the paperback market that provided the normal venue for writers falling under the rubric "suspense" and frequently published her short stories and serializations of her novels in such mass-circulation magazines as *Woman's Home Companion, Cosmopolitan,* and the *Saturday Evening Post,* as well as such specialist journals as *Ellery Queen's Mystery Magazine.* She quickly established a reputation in both the United States and Europe as one of the best writers in the field of suspense literature, winning the Mystery Writers of America scroll and the Grand Prix de Littérature Policière in France for *The Talented Mr. Ripley* (1955), while *The Two Faces of January* (1964) was recognized as the best foreign crime novel by the Crime Writers Association of England. She gained an avid following in England and on the European continent because of her consistent attempts to expand the boundaries of the category of suspense fiction, and encomiums to her often worked some variation on the patronizing theme, "She is the crime writer who comes closest to giving crime writing a good name."[9]

Working within generic boundaries, Highsmith wrote, leads to both problems and benefits. After *Strangers on a Train,* she found herself labeled a suspense writer, "which means also to find oneself fated to no more than three-inch-long reviews in the newspapers, squeezed in among good and bad books which get the same brief treatment—and by bad books, I mean the books of careless hacks."[10] At the same time, the market for suspense literature had a floor of sales, "meaning that a certain number of any such books will be bought, no matter how bad they are," providing some degree of financial security. "But there is no doubt," according to Highsmith, "that in America the suspense and mystery book has a cheapness hanging about it, a reputation for superficiality, a stigma of inferiority to the straight novel, which is just as automatically assumed to be more serious, important, and worthwhile because it is a straight novel and because the author is assumed to have a serious intent in writing it."[11] Within the genre's confines, however, Highsmith said, the suspense novelist has a great deal of room to raise fundamental questions about the nature of such issues as justice, morality, and courage and, implicitly, to cast a critical eye on the world we live in.[12] After all, such authors are working in a great literary tradition. "I think most of Dostoyevsky's books would be called suspense books, were they being published today for the first time," she said. "But he would be asked to cut, because of production costs."[13]

From 1963 until her death in 1995, Highsmith lived abroad in England, France, and Switzerland. Because of her expatriate status, her European popularity, and the stylistic differences between her writing and that of most American suspense novelists,[14] Highsmith was often mistakenly classified as a European author (one issue of *Contemporary Literary Criticism* even referred to her as "an American-born British mystery writer").[15] But Highsmith's work must be understood as a product of postwar American culture. Nearly all her major characters are American, she said, because she was most comfortable writing about them, and her dominant theme was "showing the American's everyday or garden variety of schizophrenia."[16]

These characters are firmly situated within the context of the dominant images of Cold War culture—the horror of the nuclear age, the anonymous and debasing quality of mass culture, and the banality of the suburban ideal. In *A Game for the Living* (1958), for instance, Highsmith (in a rare instance of self-conscious authorial intrusiveness) described the protagonist, Theodore: "He believed the world had no meaning, no end but nothingness, and that man's achievements were finally all perishable—cosmic jokes, like man himself. . . . Theodore thought he was as happy as anyone logically could be in an age when atomic bombs and annihilation hung over everybody's head, though the word 'logically' troubled him in this context. Could one be logically happy? Was there ever anything logical about it?"[17] In *The Price of Salt* (1952, written under the pen name of Claire Morgan), the main character, Therese, temporarily working in a department store during the Christmas rush, views the store as the intensification of the major elements of American society, marked as it is by wasted chores and ersatz freneticism, which prevent people from making human contact.[18] Many of Highsmith's stories examine the way in which the home, far from providing a retreat from the world, frequently serves as a battleground where love quickly turns to hate, anyone can be a murderer, and the quest for an idyllic family life is, as often as not, a form of psychopathology. Highsmith's postwar America is like the schoolhouse in *The Glass Cell* (1964)—a beautiful, four-story brick building with an American flag on top, but built out of such faulty materials that it is useless as anything but a monument to corruption and incompetence.[19]

Much of Highsmith's work can be understood as a sustained metaphor for the Cold War.[20] In the official Cold War worldview, Americans needed to renounce the traditional isolationism that had marked their relations with the rest of the world. The United States necessarily must involve itself in the affairs of other countries as a democratic and civilizing force, exporting the benefits of American culture. Within this broader sociopolitical context, many of Highsmith's characters are Americans living abroad, involved in their own personal crises in a variety of European and Third World settings. Unlike Daisy Miller, however, Highsmith's Americans are not wide-eyed ingenues, but largely an unsavory lot of con men, insufferable whiners, and cold-blooded murderers who wreak chaos and destruction wherever they go. From Mexico *(A Game for the Living)* to England *(The Story-Teller)* to southern Europe (Italy in *The Talented Mr. Ripley* and *Those Who Walk Away,* Greece in *The Two Faces of January*) to Tunisia *(A Tremor of Forgery),* Highsmith's protagonists belied the preferred inscribed message of the official Cold War vision that Americans came in peace.

The first and most brilliant example of this character type is Tom Ripley in *The Talented Mr. Ripley.*[21] The twenty-five-year-old Tom is living in New York, engaged in a minor scam in which he poses as an Internal Revenue Service agent demanding back taxes from various people. He is more interested in perpetrating the hoax than in profiting from it (he does not even cash the checks) and considers the con nothing more than a practical joke, "good clean sport."[22]

Tom is approached by Herbert Greenleaf, a wealthy shipping magnate whose son, Dickie, is an acquaintance of Tom's (Greenleaf mistakenly believes the two are close friends). Expressing concern that Dickie has no interest in the family business and has moved to a small village in southern Italy to become an artist, Greenleaf asks Tom to convince Dickie to come home. Tom travels to Italy and befriends Dickie. Increasingly fascinated with Dickie's life, he begins mimicking Dickie's way of walking and surreptitiously dressing in his clothes. Further, Tom grows jealous of Dickie's girlfriend Marge and resents her telling Dickie that she thinks Tom is gay.[23] When Dickie begins trying to squeeze Tom out of his life, Tom murders him and assumes Dickie's persona. Eventually, Tom fakes

Dickie's suicide, forges a will leaving all of Dickie's money to himself, and escapes punishment.

As Anthony Hilfer has argued, Tom Ripley is a "protean man," whose character is fundamentally based on his "non-essentiality, his lack of a determinate identity."[24] Like the nameless protagonist of Ralph Ellison's *Invisible Man* (1952), Tom grows to understand that as an individual he is absolutely invisible.[25] His existence is merely a series of roles he must play, and all relations with others are, according to Hilfer, "external and illusory, a matter of surface appearances."[26] At first this realization fills Tom with a sense of dread. But gradually, like Ellison's protagonist, Tom realizes that his invisibility can be liberating, as well. Early in the book, Tom buys a hat and learns that even such a small costume change can create an entirely new role. "A cap was the most versatile of headgears, he thought. He could look like a country gentleman, a thug, an Englishman, a Frenchman, or a plain American eccentric, depending on how he wore it. He had always thought he had the world's dullest face, a thoroughly forgettable face with a look of docility that he could not understand, and a look also of vague fright that he had never been able to erase. A real conformist's face, he thought. The cap changed all that."[27]

Tom realizes that "Dickie Greenleaf" is merely another role and that he is as capable of playing it as Dickie is. Thus, he murders Dickie and becomes "Dickie." Tom trains himself to jump in and out of character, eventually even fooling a policeman by talking to him at one point as Dickie and later as Tom. Like the title character of Herman Melville's *The Confidence Man,* the real identity of Tom Ripley becomes lost in the series of masks he takes off and puts on at will. He becomes nothing more than the roles he plays. As he comes to understand, "If you wanted to be cheerful or melancholic, or wistful, or thoughtful, or courteous, you simply had to act those things with every gesture."[28]

In Tom Ripley, Highsmith portrayed the logical culmination of the American success ethic. As historian Karen Halttenun has argued, in the mid-nineteenth century, the confidence man was a common figure in Victorian culture. Advice manuals warned young men to beware the wiles of this unscrupulous type. But beginning in the late nineteenth century, with the rise of modern corporate capitalism, emphasis gradually shifted away from the Victorian ethic of character toward the development of such traits as personal magnetism and executive management, all of which, in Halttenun's words, "pointed to a growing willingness to regard success as a form of confidence game. In late-nineteenth century success ideology, the manipulation of others through artifice was coming to be accepted as a necessary executive skill."[29] By the twentieth century, the confidence man had largely vanished from American success literature; instead, his tactics of role-playing and personal manipulation were being touted by the likes of Dale Carnegie as the means of "winning friends and influencing people." In his perfection of these skills and the final success of his endeavor, Tom Ripley symbolizes the ultimate triumph of American success ideology. In placing Tom in an international setting and depicting this American success story as based on a completely amoral worldview, which easily rationalizes cold-blooded murder, Highsmith challenged the Cold War paradigm that pronounced America's fitness to dominate the world.

These issues were even more explicitly raised in *The Tremor of Forgery* (1969). Howard Ingham, an American author, has traveled to Tunisia to work on a film script. Early on, Howard loses his reason for remaining in Tunisia when his partner, the film's director, commits suicide. For reasons he cannot articulate, he remains in a small village on the Tunisian coast. American cultural imperialism extends even to this isolated outpost as Howard sees a counterfeit pair of Levis in a store—a good copy, he thinks, except that the label reads, "This is a genuine pair of Louise."[30]

Howard makes friends with Francis Adams, a middle-aged widower, who announces, "I consider myself an unofficial ambassador for America. I spread goodwill—I hope—and the American way of life. Our way of life," which immediately causes the sardonic Howard to think of Vietnam.[31] Adams believes in the twin pillars of democracy and God, "a sort of Billy Graham, all-around God with an old-fashioned moral code thrown in. What the Vietnamese needed, Adams said in appallingly plain words, was the American kind of democracy." What Americans are really exporting to Vietnam, Howard thinks, are "the capitalist system in the form of the brothel industry, and the American class system by making Negroes pay higher for their lays."[32]

Eventually Adams reveals that he works making secret weekly broadcasts that are beamed behind the Iron Curtain—"pro-American, prowestern pep talks," he calls them.[33] Howard finds the broadcasts so absurd he thinks Adams must be paid by the Soviets. Dubbing Adams OWL (Our Way of Life), Howard ponders the amount of damage this one, well-meaning, misguided man can do. "What was the matter with OWL's silly illusions, anyway, if they kept him going, if they made him happy? The harm OWL did (and he might, by his absurdity, and by making nonsense of the Vietnam War, be doing some good) was infinitesimal compared to the harm done by America's foreign policy makers who actually sent people off to kill people. Perhaps it took some illusions to make people happy."[34]

As in most of Highsmith's novels, the plot of *The Tremor of Forgery* is minimal, building its suspense primarily on atmosphere and character.[35] During his stay in Tunisia, Howard wonders whether a person makes his own standards or if he and his standards are merely the creation of his surroundings.[36] Amazed by the cavalier attitude toward such practices as pedophilia, theft, and murder in Tunisia, Howard comments, "Africa does turn things upside down." Adams responds that this fact should make westerners cling ever more tightly to the values of civilization and Christianity.[37] But when a thief breaks into his bungalow and Howard hits him on the head with a typewriter, Howard neither knows nor cares if he has killed the man. Adams urges him to confess in order to keep from sinking to the level of an Arab.[38] But Howard sees no reason to, since no one else seems to take the matter seriously. At a time when the United States was at the height of its involvement in Vietnam, and stories of wartime atrocities were becoming increasingly commonplace, Highsmith conveyed both the vapid banalities that characterized America's defense of its role in world affairs and the rapidity with which Americans could forget their vaunted standards of civilization.

The Cold War metaphor also marked Highsmith's standard plot line, which involved two characters locked in "a dreadful marriage of hate" (to use I. F. Stone's description of the United States and Soviet Union in the Cold War)[39]— a match of wits and emotions, spiraling downward with tragic consequences. Each person in this struggle is committed to the defeat of the other and yet, at the same time, dependent on him, for this other provides the only meaning in the character's life. In *Those Who Walk Away* (1967), for instance, Ray Garrett realizes that his father-in-law, Ed Coleman, who blames Ray for his wife's (and Coleman's daughter's) suicide, derives his raison d'être from his vendetta against Ray. "Ray began to realize that Coleman's anger against him went much deeper. It was the deepest thing in Coleman's existence now. Coleman would obviously risk his own life, or life imprisonment, for it. People did that for love quite often. Coleman was doing it for hatred."[40]

This "marriage of hate" is, occasionally, a literal marriage, as between Vic and Melinda in *Deep Water,* or Sydney and Alicia Bartleby in *The Story-Teller* (1965).[41] Very rarely, it is a struggle between two women, as in the short story "The Cries of Love," in which two elderly women sharing a room in a rest home plot to destroy the other's most valued possessions and yet cannot bear the loneliness of living apart from each other.[42] But typically, what Highsmith describes as her "pattern" focused on "the relationship between two men, usually quite different in make-up, sometimes obviously the good and evil, sometimes merely ill-matched friends."[43] The ensuing struggle between these characters draws out the worst in both, as the conflict gradually subsumes all other interests and motives. And yet the characters often bring to this battle a sense of fair play. In *The Two Faces of January,* Rydal Keener is on the verge of ending his continuing cat-and-mouse conflict with Chester McFarland by leading Chester into a trap set by the police. At the last second, unwilling to bring to a premature conclusion a contest he feels should be settled between the two of them, Rydal tips Chester off, allowing him to escape.[44]

The dualistic struggles that dominate Highsmith's stories reflected the official American ideology, which portrayed the United States engaged in an ongoing conflict with the Soviet Union. For Americans, the Cold War paradigm was built on a series of rigid dichotomies between us and them, good and evil, innocence and guilt. In Highsmith's fiction, such oppositions were consistently broken down. She succeeded marvelously in muddying the distinctions between, for instance, innocence and guilt. In *The Blunderer* (1956), Walter Stackhouse reads in the newspaper about the death of Helen Kimmel and guesses, correctly, that her husband murdered her. Unhappy in his own marriage, Walter begins collecting information about the Kimmel case and even goes to visit Kimmel. When Walter's wife Clara commits suicide, this fascination with the Kimmels is used as evidence that Walter killed her. Eventually Walter realizes his technical innocence is irrelevant in face of the fact that he had plotted Clara's death, whereas Kimmel's actual guilt is similarly irrelevant, since he has succeeded in putting the police off his trail.

In *The Story-Teller,* Sydney—an American writer living in England, working on a television crime series—wonders what it feels like to be a murderer. But when his wife Alicia decides to move out for a while to give their troubled marriage some space, Sydney decides to pretend he has murdered her. He fills his notebook with descriptions of the imaginary murder and the feelings he is "experiencing," and even takes an old, rolled-up carpet out and buries it in the woods to see how difficult it would be to dispose of a body. When the police come to investigate Alicia's disappearance, Sydney delights in the opportunity to find out how it feels to be a suspected criminal, even acting guilty during questioning. When Alicia does not turn up, all of Sydney's playacting is construed as real evidence, and his actual innocence cannot save him. When an elderly neighbor dies of a heart attack because of the strain of living next to a "murderer," Sydney realizes that even the dichotomy between truth and falsity is meaningless. As he understands, Alicia had died because of an "attitude," which, in turn, had been based on his "attitude." "Both things were quite false, yet had important and very real effects." Similarly, another neighbor had an attitude, one of suspicion. "[Her] conventions were attitudes, too, just as false as heathenism and the worship of pagan gods (or as true), yet since hers tended to maintain law and order and family unity, they were the attitudes this society endorsed. Religions were attitudes, too, of course. It made things so much clearer to call these things attitudes rather than convictions, truths or faiths. The whole world wagged by means of attitudes which might as well be called illusions."[45]

Highsmith worked to break down the oppositions between us and them, good and evil, in the way she encouraged the reader to sympathize with her criminal protagonists. As she wrote in her how-to book, *Plotting and Writing Suspense Fiction,* the author needs to create "likable criminals." To do so, she suggested "giving the murderer-hero as many pleasant qualities as possible—generosity, kindness to some people, fondness for painting or music or cooking, for instance."[46] Vic, in *Deep Water,* possesses all these qualities, and, until the end, his capacity for murder is seen as a minor character flaw in an otherwise charmingly eccentric personality. In other works, Highsmith introduced characters who are attractive and successful and have, seemingly, only insignificant flaws— such as David Kelsey's obsession with an old girlfriend in *This Sweet Sickness* (1960) and Robert Forester's voyeurism in *The Cry of the Owl* (1962).[47] Often that character is seriously warped, but the reader only realizes it gradually as the problem slowly drives the character to extremes.

The characters in Highsmith's fictive world often symbolize the interconnectedness of such opposites as good and evil. Nowhere is this more apparent than in *Strangers on a Train,* where the social misfit, Bruno, develops a fawning attachment to a handsome and successful architect, Guy Haines. After a chance meeting on a train, Bruno concocts a plot in which he and Guy would each murder a person who is making the others victim's life miserable. Because Bruno and Guy have no known connection to the deceased, there would be no apparent motive for the murders, and the two would be absolved. Though Guy is horrified by the idea, he is strangely fascinated by Bruno. At one point Guy ponders the closeness, even the wholeness, of opposites. "But love and hate, good and evil, lived side by side in the human heart, and not merely in differing proportions in one man and the next, but all good and all evil. One had merely to look for a little of either to find it all. . . . All things had opposites close by, every decision a reason against it, the male the female, the positive the negative. The splitting of the atom was the only true destruction, the breaking of the universal law of oneness. Nothing could be without its opposite that was bound up with it."[48] Applying this concept to his own situation, Guy realizes that to live, he has only to crush the other half of his self, that is, Bruno. "But there were too many points at which the other self could invade the self he wanted to preserve, and there were too many forms of invasion."[49] Moreover, Guy thinks, if he acknowledges the evil within himself, is there not also a need to express it? "How else," he wonders, "could one really explain in mankind the continued toleration of wars, the perennial enthusiasm for wars when they came, if not for some primal pleasure in killing."[50]

Against the certitude of the dichotomous Cold War paradigm, Highsmith created a world rife with confusion. Guy thinks, "If everything was as ambiguous as he believed, how could he really be sure?"[51] Or, in *A Game for the Living,* Theodore comes to understand that "ambiguity was the secret of life, the very key to the universe."[52] But this understanding enervates and immobilizes him. "It was a curse to be able to see two sides of things, perhaps three."[53] As another character tells Theodore, for all his existential vocabulary about choice, "it's harder for you to make a simple decision than for anybody I know."[54] Only those who have an explanatory "illusion" or "attitude" are capable of decisive action. Thus, in *Those Who Walk Away,* Ray finds something admirable in Coleman's madness—his illusion that Ray had ruined his life by driving his daughter to suicide—because at least Coleman has "conviction," making him capable of action.

A Void So Frightening

Like foreign policy in the postwar era, domestic ideology was built on a series of dichotomies. According to the dominant vision, a family, a house in the suburbs, and a successful job equaled mental health and happiness, whereas the absence of these things led to sickness. Highsmith consistently worked to break down these oppositions. Especially in her view of American men, Highsmith subverted many of the ideological bases of the suburban ideal.

Highsmith's stories deal primarily with men, but women are very much in evidence as the objects of men's obsession. Several of her male characters are seeking some idealized version of the stereotypic happy family. Robert Forester, in *The Cry of the Owl,* enjoys surreptitiously watching Jenny working in her house because of the vision of domesticity she represents. Coming off a bitter divorce, he finds that Jenny is helping him recover a sense of purpose. What, he wonders, lies beneath the sense of routine that Jenny has come to symbolize? "Chaos? Nothingness? Evil? Pessimism and depression that just might be warrantable? Just plain death, a stopping, a void so frightening nobody cared to talk about it?"[55] But Forester discovers that his quest for an idyllic family life is unobtainable. Jenny is not the stable, domestic woman he has imagined her to be, and what begins as Forester's seemingly innocent attempt to imagine a happy family life ends in murderous chaos.

Similarly, David Kelsey, in *This Sweet Sickness,* has created an elaborate fantasy existence of a comfortable family life built around his former girlfriend, Annabelle. A young, handsome, and successful engineer, Kelsey lives a secret double life, having bought a house in a neighboring town where he stays on weekends and imagines living with Annabelle. But Annabelle is married to someone else and has no interest in Kelsey. In fact, the cultured and sophisticated Annabelle of Kelsey's imagination bears little resemblance to the real woman, who is rather plain and unimaginative. Meanwhile Kelsey has no interest in real women, spurning the advances of his neighbor Effie, whom he dismisses as the coarse product of a debasing, sex-obsessed popular culture.[56] Annabelle tells him, "You're quite heartless—in a way, Dave. You seem to live entirely in your own head and you don't know anything at all about other people, the people around you."[57] Finally, Kelsey's sickness makes impossible his attempt to create a happy family life. Just before his suicide at the novel's end, Kelsey realizes that "nothing was true but the fatigue of life and the eternal disappointment."[58]

A Fear and Anticipation of Failure

As one of the few female artists working in the underground culture, Highsmith exhibited a strong fascination with the social construction of gender roles, the official repression of sexual deviance, and the potentially pathological effects of the return of the repressed. Throughout her oeuvre runs a strong subtheme of homosexuality among her male characters (interestingly, this theme is most explicit in *The Price of Salt,* her only novel during this period to feature female main characters). A strong homoerotic attraction marks many of Highsmith's male relationships. Bruno, in *Strangers on a Train,* dislikes all women except his mother, seeing them as stupid and promiscuous.[59] He is fully devoted to Guy and grows jealous because Guy would rather spend time with Anne.[60] After both he and Guy have committed their murders, Bruno has the passing thought that if he were to kill Anne, he and Guy could really be together.[61] But this relationship does not run only one way. Though Guy professes to hate Bruno, he secretly admits to himself that somehow he enjoys seeing him—"some torture that perversely eased."[62] At another time, Guy pictures himself as Bruno's lover, an image that infuriates him, but which he cannot deny.[63]

Like Bruno, Tom Ripley is uninterested in women and develops a strong attraction to Dickie Greenleaf. Haunted by a humiliating childhood memory in which his aunt had derided him as a "sissy," Tom rankles at any insinuation that he is a homosexual.[64] At the same time, his attitude toward Dickie is marked by homoerotic feelings both strengthened and twisted by his refusal to consciously admit them. He grows jealous of the time Dickie spends with Marge, and the first time he dresses in Dickie's clothes, he imagines himself, as Dickie, telling Marge that he does not love her because of his feelings for Tom.[65]

Intimations of homoeroticism also run through *The Glass Cell*—in Carter's relationship with Max[66]—and, more overtly, in *The Tremor of Forgery*—in Howard's relationship with the admittedly gay Anders.[67] But for Highsmith, the theme of homosexuality is not meant to be taken literally. Rather, as a symbolic device, it undermines the certainties of postwar American culture.

Homosexuality, in the Cold War period, served as a common bogeyman in much the same way communism did. In fact, a strong connection existed between the two. From June through December 1950, for instance, the Senate engaged in a formal inquiry investigating the presence of "homosexuals and other moral perverts" in government. In the same type of language used to describe communists, the Senate report concluded, "One homosexual can pollute a Government office," and gays were barred by executive order from employment in all federal jobs.[68] The link between homosexuality and communism became common in American culture. Arthur Schlesinger Jr., for instance, once described communism as "something secret, sweaty and furtive like nothing so much, in the phrase of one wise observer of modern Russia, as homosexuals in a boys' school."[69] This equation of communism and homosexuality can also be seen in the popular right-wing image of an effete and ineffectual eastern establishment that had "lost" China, as well as in the term "pink," used to describe communist sympathizers, but also closely associated with effeminacy.[70]

Homosexuality also threatened the sanctity of the suburban ideal. The nuclear family, nestled snugly in its home, epitomized the American dream. But homosexuality challenged that concept, signaling a pernicious deviance that threatened the very fabric of the American way of life. "According to the common wisdom of the time," social historian Elaine Tyler May has written, "'normal' heterosexual behavior culminating in marriage represented 'maturity' and 'responsibility'; therefore, those who were 'deviant' were, by definition, irresponsible, immature and weak."[71] Philip Wylie argued in his bestseller *Generation of Vipers* (1942) that such men were the victims of overbearing mothers who had effectively emasculated their husbands and smothered their sons with attention. This "Momism" had created in the son a strong sense of dependence on the mother and thus made nearly impossible any healthy relationship between himself and other women.[72]

By portraying homosexuality as a running undercurrent in postwar culture, Highsmith tapped into these popular images to challenge the validity of Americans' self-conception. The virile men of action who populated Cold War culture, keeping Americans safe from communism and effeminacy—from John Wayne to Mike Hammer—were a far cry from Highsmith's gallery of weak, insufferable, craven, murderous male characters. Like Bruno in *Strangers on a Train,* some are victims of Momism.[73] But even the most seemingly well-adjusted, like Guy, are obsessed with the weakness they are forced to keep hidden deep inside themselves, convinced that if unleashed it could rapidly undo everything they have so painstakingly built. As Guy thinks at one point, "There was inside him, like a flaw in a jewel, not visible on the surface, a fear and anticipation of failure that he had never been able to mend. At times, failure was a possibility that fascinated him."[74] For Guy, this weakness is crystallized and brought to the surface in his perverse attraction to Bruno, which, as he knows it will, proves his undoing. For Highsmith, homosexuality symbolized the inherent counterforces built into the dominant cultural values, threatening at all times to subvert them.

Highsmith extended her critical investigation of the era's dominant gender assumptions by working several variations on the Oedipal conflict, with attendant implications regarding American men. Like the era's dominant social and political culture, Highsmith's universe was male-centered. But unlike the dominant cultural icons, her men possess deep psychological flaws, making them unfit for the moral leadership American policy makers claimed as their inheritance.

Bruno, in *Strangers on a Train,* represents the classic Oedipal pattern. He tells Guy on their first meeting that he hates his father but gets along well with his mother. "'We even go to parties together.' He laughed, half ashamed, half proud, and suddenly uncertain and young. 'You think that's funny.'" He is beset by castration fears, saying of his father's refusal to give Bruno his inheritance, "I mean it's a hell of a thing, isn't it, when your own father robs you. Now he says he won't give [the inheritance] to me because I won't work, but that's a lie. He thinks my mother and I have too good a time as it is. He's always scheming up ways to cut in."[75] A bit later he says that his father's hobby is collecting cookie cutters. "My mother's always telling him to go back to his cookie cutters."[76] In getting Guy to murder his father, Bruno completes the Oedipal cycle.

Bruno's mother represents the type Wylie railed against. She has emasculated her husband, forcing him into the decidedly unmasculine habit of collecting kitchen utensils. She has created, in Bruno, an unhealthy attachment to herself, making it impossible for him to have a healthy relationship with another woman. Bruno announces his distaste for all women, and when Guy reminds him that his mother is a woman, Bruno responds, "I never seen another woman like my mother."[77] When he conceives the plan to exchange murders with Guy, Bruno is proud of himself but disappointed that he will not be able to tell his mother.[78] After murdering Miriam, he imagines giving an interview in which he would brag about his plan. As he answers imaginary questions, he thinks, "What significance did it have that your victim was female?"—then wonders, "Where had that question come from?"[79] In context of the era's popular-cultural imagery, it is obvious where the question came from. Suffocated by an overbearing mother, rendered incapable of building normal romantic relationships, Bruno is little more than, in Guy's words, a "neurotic child."[80]

Not all of Highsmith's male protagonists follow a classic Oedipal trajectory. For instance, David Kelsey in *This Sweet Sickness* remains at a pre-Oedipal stage, a pattern outlined by Tania Modleski in her discussion of Edgar Ulmer's classic noir film *Detour.* When Annabelle leaves Kelsey, like Al Roberts in *Detour,* he responds less like a jilted lover and more like a child who has been abandoned by his mother. As Modleski described the process, "the heroine's early abandonment of the hero may be seen to correspond to the child's unwelcome discovery that his mother has a life independent of his own."[81]

Kelsey creates an elaborate fantasy life in which he and Annabelle share a happy (and seemingly chaste) life in a remote house he has bought. But to explain his absence every weekend to his neighbors, Kelsey fabricates a sick mother to whom he is hopelessly devoted and must regularly return home to help.[82] But women only exist for Kelsey on this idealized plane, in which mother and wife are conflated into one comforting image of home. In reality, Kelsey finds women tedious and small-minded.[83]

Modleski argued that the fundamental psychological fear expressed in *Detour* is that of "women's independence, self-sufficiency and wholeness, and of the anger and greed stimulated in the male by the specter of female autonomy."[84] In the same way, Kelsey is furious to discover Annabelle has a life apart from him. Her independence inspires a series of increasingly hysterical fantasies in Kelsey that set in motion a chain of events culminating in murder and suicide.

Highsmith spun yet another variation of the Oedipal conflict in *The Two Faces of January.* Rydal Keener, a young American, has moved to Greece to escape the influence of his father, a brilliant Harvard professor, from whom he has long been estranged. When he receives word of his father's death, Rydal decides against returning home for the funeral. Chester McFarland, a small-time American con man who has escaped to Athens just ahead of the law, is a dead ringer for Rydal's late father, and his young wife Colette vaguely reminds Rydal of his cousin Agnes—whose teenage love affair with Rydal had been the cause of his falling out with his father.[85] Rydal enters into a relationship with Chester and Colette, self-consciously seeking to work out his ambivalent feelings toward his father.

Rydal first meets Chester just after the older man has accidentally murdered a Greek policeman who came to question him, and, without hesitation, Rydal helps Chester dispose of the body.[86] Rydal thinks his decision to help Chester implies a "lurking respect for his father," a thought that makes him uncomfortable.[87] As he writes to his brother, "[Chester] is helping me to see Papa a little better, maybe to see Papa with less resentment, more humor; I don't know, but God knows I would like to get rid of resentments. I am older now. That's what matters, of course. By an odd coincidence, his wife, much younger and quite attractive and vivacious, reminds me of—that unhappy mistake of my youth. A psychological purge by some sort of re-enactment that I don't even understand yet is going on in me—and I am sure it is all for the good."[88]

Chester distrusts Rydal, certain the young man plans to blackmail him. He also grows increasingly jealous of Rydal's friendship with Colette. Thus, Chester and Rydal have a fierce argument, which reminds Rydal of his fight with his father over Agnes.[89] Chester tries to kill Rydal but accidentally kills Colette instead.[90] The two then engage in an extended chase across Europe in which both are pursued by the police.

As Rydal alternately pursues and flees from Chester, he still seeks to understand his feelings toward his father. He maintains a strange respect for Chester, even helping him escape from the police on one occasion. In the end, Chester is captured and mortally wounded. In a disappointing, too-neat conclusion, Chester makes a deathbed confession, proclaiming his guilt and absolving Rydal of all blame. When Rydal learns of Chester's confession, he thinks, "It was like hearing of his own father breaking down, hearing of something unbelievable."[91] Finally, Rydal admits to himself that he respects and cares for Chester and, by implication, his father. He knows the police will never be able to understand this attitude, for it is "impossible to explain, to the bureaucratic mind, the intricacies of his emotions in regard to Chester, in regard to Colette."[92]

Highsmith's unsettling themes undermined the certainties of the postwar American consensus. Her subterranean explorations into the national character challenged the moral and psychological fitness of Americans when they were proclaiming themselves moral leaders of the world. Highsmith destabilized the era's dominant assumptions by positing a world in which even the most fundamental beliefs may be overturned. The British novelist and critic Brigid Brophy has argued that Highsmith began this deconstruction of the orthodox paradigm by her very approach to the literary genre in which she worked. Mystery and crime novels, according to Brophy, normally seek to reassure the "Ego." The chaotic, violent, irrational events that take place normally occur around the hero, whose job it is to unravel the seemingly irrational events and fit them into a logical paradigm. Highsmith, however, dissolved "the hero's integrity as an Ego. The suspense is no longer whether the violent events will catch up with him; it's whether he will do them. And even if he doesn't do them in fact, he does in fantasy; he's admitted ownership of the violent material in the book."[93] Similarly, Highsmith admitted ownership of the violent material lying just beneath the surface of American culture.

Part Four

Little Shop of Horrors

Independent Filmmakers

"Lots of Socko"

The Independent Cinematic Vision of Samuel Fuller

The 1964 movie *The Naked Kiss* opens with a close-up of a beautiful woman (Constance Towers) staring angrily into the camera, her arm drawn back. She then throws a punch directly into the camera. The point of view immediately switches to the woman's, and the viewer sees an obviously drunk man reeling backward from the punch. Switching back to the man's view, the camera shows the woman take a step forward and throw another punch. This rapid shifting of point of view continues for a few seconds as the man pleads, "I'm drunk, Kelly, please." He reaches toward her, and a close-up shows him grab at her hair, which comes off in his hand, revealing that she is completely bald. The camera then shifts to a low-angle, long shot showing the now bald Kelly continue to beat the man until he falls helplessly to the floor. She proceeds to take out his wallet and remove some money, announcing, "I'm taking only what's coming to me," and then throw the wallet and the rest of the money in his face. Picking up her wig, she turns to a mirror. The camera point of view shifts to that of the mirror's as the viewer looks close-up at Kelly putting on her wig, straightening it, and applying her makeup. As she finishes, the film's opening credits flash on the screen. Welcome to the world of Samuel Fuller.

In a series of low-budget movies made between 1949 and the mid-sixties,

Fuller staked out his vision of America, a world populated with pickpockets, prostitutes, safecrackers, infantry soldiers, assassins, and lunatics. In Fuller's view such figures represent the hope of America's redemption, constantly finding themselves pitted against hypocritical pillars of respectability, communist agents, and the internal contradictions of postwar American ideology. Throughout Fuller's oeuvre, the Cold War ethic of pluralism runs amok as a wide range of characters debate what it means to be an American and a member of a viable community. Such discussions are filled with fascinating contradictions and jarring juxtapositions, as when, for instance, an accurate and damning indictment of American racism is made by a North Korean prisoner of war in *The Steel Helmet* (1951). But the most fundamental juxtaposition in Fuller's work is the often crude interpolation of these serious themes into plots that emphasize action and violence as well as sensational and cartoonish story lines whose ludicrous touches often defy description (for example, a reporter in an insane asylum accidentally wanders into the nymphomaniac ward, wherein he is set upon by a bevy of horny broads).

In the context of postwar B-moviemaking, Fuller's work generally met the criteria of success—it was inexpensively and quickly made and turned respectable profits. Like virtually all B-movies, Fuller's were largely formulaic, genre films.[1] While these standards severely constrained some filmmaking impulses, the B-movie format also offered opportunities unavailable in larger-scale productions. Especially for directors whose worldviews fell outside the parameters of mainstream American culture, the B-movie market provided the chance to create a body of work that might be too weird and idiosyncratic for other venues. Within this format, Fuller worked comfortably while simultaneously managing to subvert many of the conventions and deconstruct the formulaic and generic expectations of B-movie audiences.

During the period of his greatest productivity, Fuller was virtually ignored by serious film critics in the United States. Though individual movies of his occasionally received favorable reviews, typically he was reviled by such arbiters of taste as Judith Crist, who wrote that Fuller's *Shock Corridor* (1963) "hasn't got the decency to qualify as a lower B-level film. It's coated with sexual jargon, psychiatric and political palaver and pathetic photographic effects . . . but nothing can hide the film's infantile pretensions and drooling preoccupation with sensation."[2] But while Fuller was without honor in his own country, his work was being discovered and championed by a group of French film critics around the journal *Cahiers du Cinema,* who articulated the doctrine of *la politique des auteurs,* which viewed a film's director as the "author" whose personality the work expressed.[3] Fuller, who wrote, directed, and sometimes produced his own work—and whose interests, temperament, and style were indelibly stamped on all his films—served as a natural exemplar of the auteur at work, and he developed a devoted following first in France and then throughout Europe, particularly among younger filmmakers.[4]

Beginning in the mid-sixties, sparked by Andrew Sarris's influential adaptation of the "auteur theory" of French film critics,[5] Fuller began to attract a growing cult following in the United States, especially among younger critics and directors impressed with his ability to defy Hollywood conventions. In *The American Cinema* (1968), Sarris labeled Fuller "an authentic American primitive,"[6] while Peter Bogdanovich called him "probably the most explosive talent ever to blast its way through Poverty Row,"[7] and Dennis Hopper gave Fuller a bit role in his 1971 film *The Last Movie.* Ironically, Fuller's career came to a virtual standstill just when his critical reputation was on the rise. From 1965 to 1980 he directed only one American movie, *Shark* (1969), which he disowned because of his dissatisfaction with studio interference in the editing of the film.

Fuller's admirers have not always felt comfortable with the object of their affections. Especially among leftist cultural critics, his virulent anticommunism and penchant for ambiguity and contradiction have not rested easily. Calvin Green, writing in the leftist film journal *Cineaste,* said, "Put quite bluntly, Sam Fuller is a chauvinist whose jingoistic fervor goes beyond the irrational, amounting to a morbid hysteria."[8] While some on the left have dismissed Fuller as a hopeless political reactionary, others have sought to excuse his anticommunism as not really being what it seems. The French critic Luc Moullet stated that Fuller's vision of communism was so abstract and conventional and so closely paralleled his images of Nazis and gangsters that his anticommunist preachments should not be taken seriously.[9] George Lipsitz argued that "Fuller views the American struggle against communism . . . as pre-eminently a confrontation with itself."[10] Similarly, many on the left have mistaken Fuller's war films—fraught with the chaos and moral ambiguity of the common soldier's view of war—as unambiguously patriotic and prowar.[11] The left's irony-poor understanding of Fuller was epitomized by Robert Hatch's review in the *Nation* of Fuller's comeback movie, *The Big Red One* (1980)—based on Fuller's own experiences as an infantryman in World War II—which Hatch dismissed by saying, "Over all, it suggests that there is something pretty fine about the great game of kill or be killed, and that, as for World War II, we Americans won it. Given thirty-five years of hindsight, a man might be expected to contribute something more profound to the subject than another variation of 'Once more unto the breach dear friends.'"[12] Interestingly, this rejection of Fuller's politics by those on the left has not led to his being embraced by the right, which has been equally baffled by Fuller's taste for contradiction and confusion. Writing in the *National Review,* John Simon stated, "Fuller's films . . . do not so much display 'a primitive artist at work' (Sarris) as they do a poster artist at his glaring worst. The dialogue is as simplistic as the ideology."[13]

Though Fuller's dialogue *is* often simplistic (sometimes embarrassingly so), his ideology seldom is. As much as any artist in the postwar period, Fuller captured the cacophony of voices that comprised American cultural discourse, including many of those that had been driven out of the mainstream. Furthermore, Fuller used the process of filmmaking itself to articulate this multivocal dialogue, drawing on a wide range of images from sources in both popular and high culture, from tabloid journalism, stripteases, and comic books to Beethoven and Euripedes. Finally, Fuller's work resists the trappings of midcult and transcends the genres in which he worked. His films refuse to obey established formulas or offer easily digestible morals. They consistently flaunt expectations and resist closure. Within the heart of mass culture, Fuller launched an all-out assault on the easy assurances and palliatives of the dominant cultural sensibilities.

How Hard You Shout It

One of the first major influences on Fuller's intellectual development was his experience in the news business. Born in 1911 in Worcester, Massachusetts, Fuller worked as a boy hawking papers in his hometown. Following the death of his father in 1922, he and his mother moved to New York City, where he also sold papers on street corners. "I learned early," he later recalled, "that it is not the headline that counts, but how hard you shout it."[14] At the age of fourteen he began working as a copy boy for the Hearst tabloid, the *New York Journal,* and, at fifteen, he was covering the police beat for the *Evening Graphic* and collecting suicide notes. After a few years in New York, Fuller worked his way across the country as a journalist, ending up as a police reporter for the *San Diego Sun.* During the Depression he supplemented his income by writing pulp novels and movie screenplays, beginning with *Hat's Off* in 1936.[15]

Fuller's most successful novel, the psychological thriller *The Dark Page,* was published in 1944,[16] but Fuller was not around to enjoy the book's publication, having enlisted in the army in 1942. As a member of the First Infantry Division ("the Big Red One"), Fuller saw action from North Africa through the invasions of Sicily and Normandy to the liberation of the concentration camps in Czechoslovakia, earning a Bronze Star and Silver Star. When he learned that *The Dark Page* had been published, he was digging a foxhole in France. He wrote in a letter at the time: "We hit an area that was hot and dug in. Foxholes have to be deep, not too deep, for too deep means you can die from concussion in case a shell lands near your hole. Well, we were digging and your V-mail came and I rested in my hole and really felt good because I hadn't lost contact with civilization."[17] This combination of a dogface's view of the necessities of survival and the desire to maintain "contact with civilization" represents a tension prominent in much of Fuller's later work. His war experiences thus constituted the second major influence on Fuller's intellectual development. For Fuller, the absurdity, chaos, violence, moral ambiguity, and ubiquity of death that defined war would also symbolize society in general. Like James Jones and Norman Mailer, Fuller learned to hate authority figures and distrust abstract ideologies as a result of his service in World War II.[18]

After returning from the war, Fuller wrote screenplays until 1949, when Robert Lippert, head of the independent Lippert Productions, offered him the chance to direct one of his own scripts. With a salary of $5,000 and a budget of $118,000, he filmed *I Shot Jesse James* in ten days. From the beginning, Fuller staked out a reputation as a different type of filmmaker, both thematically and stylistically. The movie, which he once described as "a Western with no chases,"[19] is a sympathetic, fictionalized biography of James assassin Robert Ford. Even more than for its revisionist storyline, *I Shot Jesse James* was notable in how it reflected Fuller's heightened sensitivity to visual forms. As Sarris has said, the movie "was constructed almost entirely in close-ups of an oppressive intensity the cinema had not experienced since Dreyer's *The Passion of Joan of Arc.*"[20]

Catching a Look That's New

In *The Dark Page,* Carl Chapman, city editor of the tabloid *New York Daily Graphic,* hourly repeats to his staff his favorite slogan, "Lots of socko,"[21] a slogan that also summarizes Fuller's approach to filmmaking. The action, chaos, and consistent sense of the unexpected that are fundamental parts of every Fuller film were built into the very methods he used to make them. Some of these filmmaking techniques were foisted on him by the constrained budgets of his B-movies, but mostly they grew out of his eccentric personality and desire to keep both actors and viewers from settling into a comfortable complacency.

Carrying a .45 on the set, Fuller would fire the pistol into the air rather than call "action" because, he said, "I don't like to shout and I want them ready to go. When they hear a shot I get a reaction. I like reactions."[22] Occasionally, after intensive rehearsal of a scene, until each actor knew exactly what he would be doing at each moment, Fuller would rearrange the set just before filming to get a sense of "realism in [the actor's] face, because he's really looking. And he looks around and I catch a look that's new. And that's what I do through the scene."[23] For example, in filming *Fixed Bayonets* (1951)—a Korean war film set in winter—after rehearsing a scene Fuller sent the cast out for air and, while they were gone, turned on a large ice machine and iced down the set. "Then I called the actors back in," he remembered in a 1968 interview. "Were they surprised! Those falls, there's no acting in them. Didn't you get a feeling of panic? It was real. They were slipping all over the place. They knew there were explosions going on, and they had to get out of there."[24]

Fuller also conveyed action through his creative and mobile camera work. For the opening scene of *The Naked Kiss* he strapped cameras to the actors themselves and literally had Constance Towers punch the camera.[25] At other times, he used extremely long takes—as long as ten minutes—that move from set to set.[26] And Fuller's extensive use of close-ups—put to brilliant effect, for instance, in the scene in *Pickup on South Street* (1953) in which Candy realizes that Joey and his cronies are communists—heightens the sense of isolation that permeates all of his films.

The Gift of Ambiguity

Critic Raymond Durgnat has dubbed film "the mongrel muse," writing that "the great difficulty in talking about cinema style is that cinema is a *potpourri* of art forms, sharing elements in common with each, but weaving them into a pattern of its own."[27] The multiple and contradictory voices emerging out of a Fuller film reflect the diversity of sources and references on which he drew. Borrowing from a wide range of materials in both high and popular culture, Fuller created a pastiche that shattered standard generic formulas and offered consistently startling juxtapositions.

Perhaps most obviously, Fuller drew inspiration from the tabloid newspaper, the style of journalism in which he had been brought up. Several of his protagonists are journalists, such as Johnny Barrett in *Shock Corridor,* while *Park Row* (1952) is a paean to nineteenth-century journalism. His movies often have the quality of "scoops." *The Steel Helmet* was the first movie made about the Korean War and *China Gate* (1957) one of the first made about Vietnam. They also have the feel of lurid exposes. *Shock Corridor* concerns abusive conditions in a mental hospital, and *The Naked Kiss* focuses on the corruption beneath the surface of an idyllic small town. Large, screaming headlines often play a crucial role in establishing mise-en-scène ("Connors Defies Uncle Sam," "Grant Killed By Prostitute"). Film critic J. Hoberman classifies such popular artists as Fuller, comic-strip artist Chester Gould, and the photographer Weegee as "abstract sensationalists" who, coming out of the urban working class, perfected the tabloid vernacular of the industrial proletariat. "The tabloid . . . developed an esthetic of shock, raw sensation and immediate impact, a prole expressionism of violent contrasts and blunt, 'vulgar' stylization. At once cynical and sentimental this mode fed on incongruity, mordant humor and the iconography of the street. The work of the tabloid school is brutal in both form and content, as assaulting as the cities which gave it sustenance and the subways where it was digested."[28]

In plot and imagery, Fuller's films also often resemble comic books.[29] For example, the vision of war permeating *The Steel Helmet*—one of weary existentialism that, Hoberman wrote, "suggests *Waiting for Godot* rewritten by Mickey Spillane"[30]—is virtually nonexistent in early-fifties popular culture except in the period's comic books.[31] Michael Gould has argued that Fuller utilized comic-book imagery to express a surrealist sensibility. His cinema of exaggerated sparsity is surreal, Gould wrote, in that it "makes the viewer immediately encounter the image (a shock effect) rather than permit him to gradually absorb it through the clutter of elaborate frills."[32] Fuller conveyed character types with a minimum of props, exaggerated makeup, closeups, or often, in comic-book style, with names like Candy, Cuddles, Lucky Legs, Short Round, and Runt.

As several commentators have noted, the pared-down sets and archetypal characters that give Fuller's movies a comic-book quality also bear strong resemblance to the theater of Bertolt Brecht. Nicholas Garnham has argued that both Fuller and Brecht use society's outsiders—especially prostitutes and gangsters—to criticize the hypocritical morality of mainstream society.[33] Like Brecht, Fuller eschewed realism in favor of a more stylized acting and set construction. His creative use of B-movie budgets produced some strange effects, heightening the surreal quality of his films. Most of the action in *Shock Corridor,* for instance, takes place in the hallway of a mental institution. For this set, Fuller built a short corridor, painted the continuation of the hallway, and used midgets in the background to give a sense of perspective.[34]

At a time when the Stanislavskian method was invading Hollywood, Fuller maintained a Brechtian sense of character and acting. "He uses dialogue," according to Garnham, "as a means of delivering slogans rather than as an aspect of behavior."[35] His characters tend to be painted with broad strokes, and he favored a similarly broad acting style. This combination of subject and style created characters who are more cartoonish than the era's Stanley Kowalskis and Jim Starks, but who also more effectively conveyed Fuller's sympathy for common people.

The difficulty of categorizing Fuller's films has plagued many critics because the filmmaker's eclectic borrowing from other cultural and cinematic forms complicates traditional generic formulas. Thus, Phil Hardy has stated that all Fuller films are war movies, while for Garnham they are all westerns, and for Lipsitz they are all urban dramas.[36] According to Paul Schrader, *Pickup on South Street* is a transitional movie between film noir and the more bourgeois crime dramas of the late fifties, while Jon Tuska has said that despite the film's conventional happy ending—a violation of one of the basic tenets of film noir—*Pickup*'s theme and style place it firmly within the noir tradition.[37] In his suggestive discussion of *Pickup,* Frank McConnell argued that Fuller merged two genres—the propaganda spy thriller, perfected in World War II and updated for the Cold War; and film noir. "In *Pickup,*" McConnell said, "these two traditions of filmmaking cohabit and interfere with each other."[38] Thus the Manichean worldview of the thriller is undercut by the moral and psychological complexities of the noir vision. In fact, McConnell's general point applies to Fuller's entire oeuvre in that the various cinematic sensibilities mingle and frequently subvert standard formulaic assumptions, conveying what Moullet called Fuller's "gift of ambiguity."[39] A feeling of moral uncertainty more appropriate to film noir, for example, overlays *The Steel Helmet*—the American patrol is riven by racial and class divisions, and the main spokesman for anticommunism is the detestable Sergeant Zack—disassembling its patriotic war film trappings. The corny love story that dominates the middle section of *The Naked Kiss* plays off well-known cinematic structures before the film's noir sensibilities deconstruct the entire genre. In Fuller's world, nothing is exactly what it seems to be, and the intertextual nature of his references made way for his assault on audiences' expectations.

Fuller stood firmly within Manny Farber's description of the tradition of "underground films," which were "slicing journeys into the lower depths of American life,"[40] and his work reveled in its defiance of midcult sensibilities. The defining traits of midcult, according to Dwight Macdonald, include the following: it is formulaic; its sole standard of success is popularity; it offers the "built-in reaction," wherein "it is impossible not to identify the emotion [the artist] wants to arouse. . . . One is never puzzled by the unexpected"; it features an incessant editorializing—"the Midcult audience always wants to be Told"; it employs elements of High Culture and even the avant-garde while simultaneously smoothing away any critical, disquieting, or potentially subversive elements in favor of a vaguely uplifting and affirmative message.[41] Fuller, however, consistently undermined these principles, thwarting popular expectations and denying the audience the luxury of settling into a comfortable complacency. When Zack shoots and kills an unarmed prisoner of war in *The Steel Helmet,* one may react in a variety of ways, by cheering or being horrified or some combination of the two, but Fuller seeks to elicit no identifiable built-in reaction. The shooting is made even more disconcerting by Fuller's matter-of-fact presentation and refusal to take sides.

"Imagine a Western," Macdonald wrote, "in which the hero loses the climactic gun fight or an office romance in which the mousy stenographer loses out to the predatory blonde."[42] But such events were commonplace in Fuller's universe. Throughout his films Fuller employed formulaic imagery for the express purpose of overturning clichéd plot lines and denying his audience the uplifting and sentimental catharsis of midcult. At the end of his western *Forty Guns* (1957), during the final gun battle, the villain grabs the hero's lover and uses her as a shield. The hero opens fire anyway, wounding the woman and killing the villain. In fact, this ending was imposed on Fuller by the studio; originally he had the hero kill them both.[43] Similarly, in *The Naked Kiss,* he brutally interrupts a stock love story plot when Kelly, on the day before her wedding to the debonair philanthropist Grant, discovers him molesting a young girl and bludgeons him to death with a telephone. Fuller said, "The original impression I wanted was of a wonderful, almost dull, very, very ordinary love story: the poor girl from the wrong side of the tracks, the rich man who falls in love with her. Well, I hate those kind of stories."[44] With a vengeance, Fuller sought to shock audiences out of their complacency and reassert life's disconcerting arbitrariness. As he said in a 1977 interview, "Why do we always have to have a nice boy, and the heavy has to be a bad boy? I don't understand that, I never will. It's not exciting to me if the man says to the girl, "Look, I'll meet you in the corner drugstore at five o'clock." I wouldn't write that . . . not unless I knew . . . when the girl walks into the corner drugstore, she's going to have her head blown off."[45]

In the same way, Fuller defied audience expectations in his use of high culture.

Where midcult employed high culture to give a veneer of respectability without challenging the fundamental message of affirmation, Fuller used elite cultural references to reinforce his films' sense of dislocation and alienation. Classical allusions pop up in unusual contexts, standing in uncomfortable juxtaposition to the often tawdry story lines. *Shock Corridor,* for instance, begins and ends with a quote of Euripedes: "Whom God wishes to destroy he first makes mad." In *The Naked Kiss,* Kelly and Grant share a passion for European culture, listening to Beethoven and quoting Goethe, Byron, and Baudelaire. Fuller's sense of irony is reflected here in the radically opposite meanings of Kelly's and Grant's cultural sensibilities. For Kelly, the prostitute, an interest in serious art reinforces her sense of independence and worldly wisdom and accentuates her status as an outsider—Griff, the policeman, tells her he cannot appreciate Beethoven because he is tone deaf. For Grant, the world-traveling millionaire/child-molesting pervert, this taste for European culture heightens the aura of decadence surrounding the revelation of his sickness.

Fuller most fully stood in contrast to the dominant midcult sensibilities of Cold War America in his insistence on portraying the ugliness of life. "In Fuller," Moullet commented, "we see everything that other directors deliberately excise from their films: disorder, filth, the unexplainable, the stubbly chin, and a kind of fascinating ugliness in a man's face."[46] At a time when the cinema was coming to be dominated by the flawless, plastic visages of stars like Rock Hudson, Paul Newman, Natalie Wood, and Janet Leigh, Fuller consistently chose unattractive actors like John Ireland, Gene Evans, Thelma Ritter, Rod Steiger, and Claude Akins. His images were frequently grotesque, such as the closeup of the bald Constance Towers, her face twisted with rage, which literally assaults the viewer at the beginning of *The Naked Kiss.* And when, after beating up her pimp, she turns to the mirror and puts on her wig and makeup, transforming herself from grotesque to beautiful, Fuller laid bare the ugliness underlying the flawless exteriors of American consumer culture.

Only Ninety-nine Percent Nuts

Near the end of *Merrill's Marauders* (1962), the story of the five-hundred-mile march by American troops through the dense, Japanese-controlled Burmese jungle, one soldier says, "When this is all over you know what I'm going to do? I'm going to get married, going to have about six kids. I'll line them up against a wall and tell them what it was like here in Burma. If they don't cry, I'll beat the hell out of them." This overwhelming desire to make people understand the true nature of war marked many of Fuller's movies and grew directly out of his own war experience. But such a view was out of keeping with the dominant, midcult sensibilities of the Cold War period. Paul Fussell has argued that the one-dimensional, affirmative culture that had been formulated during World War II carried over into the postwar era at the expense of "complexity, irony, skepticism and criticism." This high-minded culture emphasized unity, patriotism, and sincerity. When James Jones accepted the 1952 National Book Award, in a comment as accurate for filmmakers as for writers, he said, "The only thing wrong with literature in our time is that it lacks . . . malice, envy and hate. . . . The fear of rascality in our writers is unwittingly turning them into moralists."[47]

Fuller never feared rascality, and his work refuted the banal highmindedness of the dominant middlebrow culture. His war films focus on all the elements that most of the period's war films and literature denied: death, exhaustion, monotony, divisiveness, chaos, ambiguity, absurdity, the lack of glory, and the mere quest for survival. He said, "War is monstrous. You pee, and you eat, and you look at your weapon, and you march, and you kill, and you eat, and you look at your weapon, and you march and you kill. You pull back and while you pull back you kill. You move forward, you kill, and it's dark. . . .You sleep, and you get up, and it goes on day, after day, after day. It's not really a nightmare, it's not even a group of robots. It's just a wheel. It keeps going around and around."[48] The Sisyphean monotony of the dogface's life permeates Fuller's war films, and he even sought to integrate that monotony into the filmmaking process. "We rehearse for a week," he said. "[The actors] carry packs, they gripe, they grouch, they bitch, they get dirty. I have them take their uniforms home so they can sleep in them. They look wrinkled and dirty; there's no smellovision, but the flavor is of urine."[49]

The Steel Helmet, Fuller's first war movie, bears resemblance in its view of death to the works of two other World War II veterans, Joseph Heller's *Catch-22* and Kurt Vonnegut's *Slaughterhouse Five.*[50] As Morris Dickstein has observed, because of these novels' peculiar, nonchronological structure, they "do not slowly gravitate toward death like straightforward novels with unhappy endings. . . . They are drenched in death on all sides."[51] Though Fuller adopted a chronological narrative form, the film is similarly immersed in death. The first three characters introduced have all, in a sense, returned from the dead. Behind the opening credits, the camera focuses on a helmet with a bullet hole. After the credits finish, the helmet rises to reveal it is worn by Sergeant Zack (Gene Evans), whose entire unit has just been massacred, shot through their heads at point-blank range with their hands tied behind their backs. Zack survived by the merest fluke; the bullet entered his helmet, spun around inside, and exited without hitting his head. Zack is discovered by Short Round, a South Korean boy whose entire family was killed by North Korean artillery. After cutting Zack free, Short Round tags along, very much against Zack's wishes. The two then run into Corporal Thompson (James Edwards), an African American medic whose entire unit was captured and massacred. Thompson alone survived because the North Koreans had needed him to treat their wounded.

The three wander in the fog until they meet an American patrol, similarly lost, under the leadership of the hapless Lieutenant Driscoll (Steve Brodie). Zack agrees to lead the patrol to a nearby Buddhist temple to establish an observation post in exchange for a box of cigars, but he resents Driscoll's leadership. Driscoll pays no attention to his own highly competent sergeant, the Nisei Tanaka (Richard Loo), because of the lieutenant's racism, but despite Zack's racism (he constantly refers to Tanaka as "Buddhahead"), the two sergeants share a mutual respect. The patrol is largely composed of misfits, racially and culturally diverse, and everyone is judged on the basis of what he did during the last war. Zack, Thompson, and Tanaka are "retreads" (World War II veterans), while Driscoll spent the war stateside. "I heard you were killed in France," Driscoll says on first seeing Zack. "You had plenty of chances to leave the States and find out," Zack replies.

Having established the observation post, the patrol captures a North Korean major hiding in the temple. Well-educated and fluent in English, the North Korean taunts Thompson, saying, "I just don't understand you. You can't eat with them unless there's a war on." He goes on to point out that Thompson cannot even sit where he wants on a bus. When Thompson replies that as an outsider the North Korean is in no position to pass judgment, the prisoner spits in Thompson's face. Later he says to Tanaka, "You've got the same kind of eyes I have" and reminds him of the placement of Japanese Americans in relocation camps during World War II. Tanaka responds that he and many other Japanese Americans fought in the last war, earning over three thousand Purple Hearts. But Thompson and Tanaka can only dismiss the North Korean's criticism after admitting the validity of his charges. At a time when the United States was promoting itself to the Third World as the champion of democracy, Fuller's sense of paradox and irony allowed him to have a communist character articulate a trenchant criticism of American racism.

Fuller's taste for ambiguity and complexity can also be seen in the character of Zack, who, more than anyone else, expresses the dogface's view of war. He shows his mordant sense of humor in advising a private how to tell the difference between a North and South Korean: "He's a South Korean if he's running with you; he's a North Korean if he's running after you." He dislikes officers, telling Driscoll disdainfully, "If I was right all the time I'd be an officer." He is unsentimental about death, saying, "A dead man's nothing but a corpse. Nobody cares who he is now." And he is virulently anticommunist, warning of "rice paddies crawling with commies just waiting to slap you between two slices of rye bread and wash you down with vodka." At a time when popular-cultural heroes included Douglas MacArthur, John Wayne, and Mike Hammer, Zack fills a similar role, that of a tough, ruthless, and efficient anticommunist. But apart from his skill as a soldier, there is little admirable about Zack. He mercilessly bullies his men and shoots an unarmed prisoner. And during the climactic battle sequence, while all the men Zack had derided fight bravely, he cracks and wanders aimlessly through the battle scene. Once again, Fuller established clichéd characters and situations only to subvert them.

Images of exhaustion and chaos dominate *Merrill's Marauders*. Though the story is of a great military triumph—the Allied victory at Myitkyina, North Burma—there is nothing glorious about Fuller's view of war. The soldiers battle exhaustion, hunger, typhus, and malaria as well as the Japanese while traveling through jungles and swamps and over mountains. The toll on them is enormous. The doctor who examines the men says, "I have never seen human beings in such condition. They're just drained. Physically and psychologically drained." But Brigadier General Frank Merrill (Jeff Chandler) drives them onward, insisting, "When you're at the end of your rope, all you have to do is put one foot in front of the other. Just take one more step." The tedium of the march and palpable physical deterioration of the soldiers[52] are periodically interrupted by the terrifying and confusing violence of battle. In the greatest battle scene of Fuller's films, American and Japanese soldiers fight at a rail yard in Shaduzup. As they run among a group of giant concrete blocks and climb over them, the soldiers never know what lies just around the corner, and so they fire blindly. Fuller said that the scene was actually toned down. "The film's producers took out a couple of things I wanted in that scene. I wanted to get an effect of people shooting blindly, of Americans shooting other Americans. Because it's panic! . . . But I had to draw the line. After all, I was told, . . . you're going to be showing it to mothers and fathers, and they're going to say, 'What is this? It's enough that if our boy is shot, he's killed by an enemy. Does it have to be his own friend who shot him?' Yes! It does. That's what happens."[53] The movie ends before the Americans reach Myitkyina, thereby avoiding any clichéd final battle victory scene. Instead, a voice-over narrator says that of the three thousand members of Merrill's Marauders who began the march, only one hundred remained in action at the end. But the ultimate absurdity occurs when this narration and the image of a handful of bedraggled soldiers trudging toward the final battle is followed by a studio-imposed conclusion, a commercial for the U.S. Special Forces. As the character based on Fuller in *The Big Red One* comments, "Surviving is the only glory in war," a statement expressing the theme of all Fuller's war films, but one that does not make an effective recruiting slogan.

Fuller's cinema emphasized the confusion of wartime, both physical and moral. In the ambiguous universe of battle, where hesitation means death, normal rules and definitions do not apply. "We don't murder," the Sergeant (Lee Marvin) explains to his troops in *The Big Red One,* "we kill." Thus, Fuller did not understand the controversy surrounding Zack's shooting of an unarmed prisoner in *The Steel Helmet.* "You see, I think it's a little stupid, when you're in a war, to hold your fire just because a man holds his hands up. Five minutes before that, he's shooting at you. He runs out of ammunition; he can put his hands up. I mean, certainly there's no law. If there's a law in war, then we're really completely nuts. Now, we're only ninety-nine percent nuts."[54]

Fuller recognized the difficulty of conveying the confusion and terror of war through the medium of film. "If we could have weapons behind the screen," he once said, "and if, when the picture starts, once in a while, someone in the audience was hit, that would give the audience a feeling for the tension of war. Naturally, you're not going to get anybody to come to the second performance."[55]

I'm Just Interested in Character

In the western *Run of the Arrow* (1957), O'Meara (Rod Steiger), a Confederate veteran, refuses to become an American citizen after the Civil War and moves to the West to live among the Indians. On the way he meets Walking Coyote (Jay C. Flippen), a Sioux who had scouted for the Union Army. Walking Coyote tells O'Meara that he could have been a Sioux chief. When O'Meara asks why he had not, Walking Coyote says disdainfully, "Ah, I can't stomach politics." This sentiment might well have been voiced by Fuller, too. Throughout his films, he expressed a distaste for all overarching political systems and ideologies, concentrating instead on the dehumanizing effect of these systems at the individual level. In doing so, he articulated a political sensibility that would become increasingly common in the sixties and seventies, which held that the personal is political.

For years Fuller's reputation as an ardent anticommunist obscured the larger message of his films. In fact, Fuller distrusted all abstract ideologies. He hated the depersonalizing aspects of systems and theories, and he demanded that humans confront each other as individuals. In a typically Fullerian bit of irony, O'Meara shows his humanity toward his hated enemy Driscoll (Ralph Meeker) in *Run of the Arrow* by shooting him through the head rather than allowing him to be skinned alive by the Sioux tribe O'Meara had joined.

"I'm just interested in character," Fuller has said,[56] and his characters are motivated by the most personal of reasons. Zack agrees to lead the patrol to the temple in *The Steel Helmet* in exchange for a box of cigars. Lucky Legs (Angie Dickinson), the half-Chinese saloon owner in *China Gate,* guides the French patrol to the Chinese arms cache only after a guarantee that her son will be sent to the United States. And Tolly Devlin (Cliff Robertson) helps the district attorney crack the organized crime ring in *Underworld U.S.A.* (1960) only to gain revenge on the mobsters who murdered his father. "I never like a man to do something heroic," Fuller stated in 1968, "for any chauvinistic or false premise other than emotional, personal necessity."[57]

When the police in *Pickup on South Street* try to enlist Skip McCoy's (Richard Widmark's) help in tracking down the communists by appealing to his patriotism, he snarls disdainfully, "Are you waving the flag at me?" For Fuller, as for Skip, such blind patriotism is almost as distasteful as communism because it glosses over the tensions, divisions, and hypocrisy of Americanism. In *Shock Corridor,* reporter Johnny Barrett (Peter Breck) goes into an insane asylum to solve a murder there. By the early and mid-sixties, mental hospitals had come to serve a variety of symbolic uses in American culture. In Ken Kesey's *One Flew over the Cuckoo's Nest* (1962), the institution represents an authoritarian state, dominated by women, that emasculates men,[58] while in Philippe de Broca's 1967 French film *King of Hearts,* which attracted a large cult following in the United States, the kinder, gentler insanity of the inmates is portrayed as preferable to the destructive insanity of the war raging outside. For Fuller, the insanity of his patients is merely an intensification of broader cultural tensions. In their rare lucid moments, the inmates tell Barrett their stories. Stuart (James Best) recalls his father's instruction, which offered nothing positive and taught him only to hate. With no moral safety net to fall back on when he was captured by the North

Koreans during the war, he had been an easy target for brainwashing. Vilified as a traitor and hounded by reporters on his return, he went crazy and became convinced that he was Confederate General Jeb Stuart. Trent (Hari Rhodes) had been the first black student to integrate a southern university. The constant hatred and harassment of whites and the nagging fear that he would let down his race drove him insane, until he now thinks he is a member of the Ku Klux Klan and marches down the corridor carrying a sign reading, "Democracy and Integration Don't Mix; Go Home Nigger" and trying to organize the inmates into a lynch mob. Boden (Gene Evans) had been a brilliant physicist who played a role in the development of the atomic bomb. Thinking about the possible consequences of his creation had driven him insane, and now he has the mind of a six year old. Coming in 1963, *Shock Corridor* spoke directly to the contradictions of American Cold War culture, where hatred, racism, and calculating the destruction of the world were commonplace for millions of people not in asylums.

The Precipitous Slide of Existentialism

In style and content, Fuller's films feature strong existential overtones. Various of his movies express the existential motifs that Robert Porfirio has identified as characteristic of American film noir. Like noir, Fuller's world is populated by nonheroic heroes. From Sergeant Zack and Skip McCoy to Tolly Devlin and Johnny Barrett, Fuller's protagonists tend to be selfish, immature bullies. His characters represent the existential concept of alienation and loneliness. They live on the margins of society as pickpockets, prostitutes, or the insane. The world of Fuller's films is, like the noir world, marked by chaos, violence, and paranoia. It also, as Porfirio has said of film noir, features a strong sense of the absurd. As Farber remarked, Fuller's iconoclasm frequently turned his movies into "black comedies"[59] filled with absurdities, such as dialogue which often consisting of strings of bad clichés, the attack of the nymphomaniacs in *Shock Corridor,* and a Japanese fan dance performed by a white stripper in *The Crimson Kimono* (1959) as a symbol of interracial understanding.

As in film noir, Fuller's vision is of humans under a sentence of death, especially in his war films. But, Porfirio wrote, "The precipitous slide of existentialism towards nihilism is only halted by its heavy emphasis on man's freedom," and Fuller's films all feature a moment of choice. According to Garnham, "In all Fuller movies there is a crucial moment when the violence inherent in any battle, any conflict, bursts into the open. This is the moment when the protagonists are finally committed to physical involvement, a commitment that Fuller is constantly forcing upon his audience."[60] Thus, Lucky Legs sacrifices her own life and ignites the fuse to blow up the Chinese weapons dump in *China Gate*. Finally, as Porfirio has noted of film noir, Fuller's characters are constantly trying to impose meaning on their absurd universe by creating a sense of sanctuary and order.[61] Many of his characters seek to establish some kind of viable community or family life. Robert Ford kills Jesse James so that he will no longer be a wanted man and can settle down and marry his sweetheart. O'Meara seeks to join the Sioux tribe in his effort to deny his Americanness in *Run of the Arrow*. The multiracial and multiethnic platoons in Fuller's war movies serve as communities for the disparate soldiers. And Kelly, in *The Naked Kiss,* hopes to shed her outsider status and integrate herself into a respectable community until she discovers the sickness at the heart of that community.

Authentic American Primitive

Andrew Sarris's characterization of Fuller as an "authentic American primitive" has drawn sharp reaction from many Fuller defenders, who seem to equate "primitive" with "neanderthal."[62] Apart from the fact that in the modernist lexicon, "primitive" is not a pejorative (it could also be applied to Picasso, Stravinsky, and jazz), such a criticism misses Sarris's primary emphasis on Fuller's authenticity. In his films, Fuller expressed a vision of authenticity that would not become commonplace until the New Left of the sixties. As Marshall Berman pointed out, from the mid-nineteenth century to the end of the 1950s, the political left and right had largely agreed in equating capitalism and the liberal state with individualism, and radicalism with "a 'collectivism' that negated individuality. Political thought was frozen into this dualism until the cultural explosion of the 1960s redefined the terms. The New Left's complaint against democratic capitalism was not that it was too individualistic, but rather that it wasn't individualistic enough: it forced every individual into competitive and aggressive impasses (zero-sum games) which prevented any individual feelings from being expressed."[63] In the same way, Fuller viewed the modern American system as depersonalizing and corrupt. The policemen in *Pickup on South Street* are as cold and ruthless as the communists when they convince Candy to risk her life by passing the microfilm to her contact. In *Underworld, U.S.A.,* both the organized crime syndicate and the district attorney's office are run as large, faceless businesses, feeding off people and casting them aside when they are used up. It is no accident that in Fuller's world the only people who can stand up to this large, dehumanizing system are those who are already outside it.

"The moral complexity of Fuller's movies," Garnham commented, "is part of their modernity."[64] For Fuller, this complexity is symbolized by the United States. Despite his hatred for the large bureaucratic structures and depersonalizing ideologies, Fuller saw the United States as the greatest hope for the world. But it is not a vision that fit in well with the dualistic worldview of most Americans in the Cold War period. Fuller's America is filled with ambiguity and paradox. Phil Hardy has indicated that the appropriate symbol for Fuller's vision of America is to be found in *Run of the Arrow,* in which O'Meara constantly wears a hat marked with the insignia of the Virginia Sixth Volunteers, rides a Union cavalry horse branded U.S., speaks with an Irish brogue (which is never explained), and lives among the Sioux, where he serves as a scout for the U.S. Cavalry.[65] Similarly, at the end of the big battle scene in *The Steel Helmet,* Fuller conveyed an unorthodox vision of America in the three exhausted survivors: a black medic, a Nisei sergeant, and a bald youth who had been the constant butt of everyone's jokes.

To Fuller, America is not a static entity but is in a constant state of flux, of becoming. Many of his films have open endings to symbolize this uncompleted process. *The Steel Helmet,* made at the height of the Korean War, coming so soon after Fuller's experiences in World War II, concludes by proclaiming, "There is no end to this story." *Run of the Arrow,* a film about regional division and racial hatred, made in 1957 in the wake of southern resistance to the Brown decision and the emergence of the Civil Rights movement, ends with the printed words, "The end of this story can only be written by you." Appropriately, the statement that best captured Fuller's paradoxical vision of America is expressed by a lunatic. In *Shock Corridor,* Trent, the black man who believes he is a Klansman, says during a brief lucid moment, "I always had pride in my country, called it *'esprit de corps':* it's inside me, I love it. It's even a blessing to love my country, even when it gives me ulcers."

8

Roger Corman's Low-Budget Modernism

Surveying the set of his 1962 movie *The Raven,* director Roger Corman decided it would be a shame to tear it down after only a single use. As he would later remember, he thought, "If I could write a script in one week and get some actors, I could walk right into that set and shoot another picture for very little money."[1] Boris Karloff, one of *The Raven*'s featured stars, agreed to stay for two days of filming, and Corman cast a young, unknown supporting actor from *The Raven* (and a member of Corman's regular ensemble), Jack Nicholson, in the lead role. He then hired Leo Gordon, another occasional member of Corman's ensemble, as both actor and screenwriter, to write sixty pages of dialogue. Corman told Gordon not to worry that no one seemed to know exactly what the plot was, because he would write a script around the scenes they filmed at a later date. When *The Raven* finished filming on a Friday, and before the sets were torn down on Monday, Corman spent the weekend shooting *The Terror.*

Corman's agreement with Karloff provided a small sum and a $15,000 deferred payment out of any money over $150,000 the film earned. During the two days of filming, Corman worked the eighty-year-old actor—already in poor health—extremely hard, using him, as Karloff would later complain, in every scene he shot. The story, such as it was at that point, concerned Andre Duvalier

(Nicholson), a French officer during the Napoleonic wars, who becomes lost from his regiment, pursuing a mysterious woman to the castle of Baron von Leppe (Karloff). Also present in the two days of shooting were Corman regulars Jonathan Haze as the mute Gustav and Dick Miller as the Baron's servant, Stefan.

After Karloff's departure, Corman attempted to complete the picture around other projects, hiring Jack Hill to finish the script. In order to make a story of the footage shot with Karloff, Hill changed some of the characters (who had never been too well defined anyway). The previously mute Gustav, for instance, suddenly becomes quite talkative, and the woman Duvalier has been following inexplicably keeps appearing and disappearing, and, on occasion, turning into a hawk. To complete filming, Corman farmed out much of the second-unit directing to his young assistants, including Francis Ford Coppola, Monte Hellman, and, finally, Nicholson. Dealing with the work of six different directors (including himself) and two screenwriters, Corman realized the story made little sense and decided to add a scene in which Duvalier grabs Stefan and exclaims, "I've been lied to ever since I got to this castle . . . now tell me what's going on!" At this point, Stefan narrates a story that is supposed to connect the disparate threads of the plot, a laughably implausible yarn about how the Baron is not really the Baron but an impostor who years ago murdered von Leppe and took his place, and now, in his madness, is convinced he truly is the Baron. Finally completed after nine months, *The Terror* was released in 1963. It was, as Nicholson would recall years later, "the only movie I ever made that didn't have a plot," to which Corman would rejoin, "He's right. It had no plot, but I'm not certain that it's the only movie he's ever made that hasn't had one."[2]

The story does not end there. By 1966, Karloff still had not received his $15,000 because, as Corman claimed, *The Terror* had not earned the $150,000 necessary for Karloff's deferment to kick in. Corman proposed a deal: he would pay Karloff the $15,000, thereby erasing the debt from *The Terror,* if Karloff would agree to two days of filming on a project to be shot in early 1967. Corman then offered his young assistant, Peter Bogdanovich, the opportunity to direct his first feature film if he could come up with a good role for Karloff. The result, the brilliant and chilling *Targets*—which Corman produced—featured Karloff as an aging horror actor, Byron Orlock, who is retiring because, as he says, horror movies cannot keep pace with the horrors of everyday life. "My kind of horror isn't horror anymore. . . . No one's afraid of a painted monster," Orlok comments as he looks at a newspaper headline: "Youth Kills Six in Supermarket." Orlok's story is intercut with that of a young Vietnam veteran who murders his family, climbs a tower, shoots numerous passersby, and then hides out in a drive-in, where Orlok is making an appearance to promote his new movie. In a gripping climax, the film cuts back and forth between the paltry horror on the drive-in screen and the real horror as the sniper shoots several of the theater's patrons before being disarmed by Orlok. And the movie showing on the drive-in screen is—naturally—*The Terror.*[3]

The tangled story of the making of *The Terror* illustrates several important aspects of Corman's career. First it demonstrates his independent filmmaking sensibilities, his pioneering work in a style a later generation would dub "guerilla filmmaking." For Corman, such things as standing sets and intact film crews were irresistible inducements to try to squeeze out another picture on a minuscule budget. Such practices established Corman as the dominant figure in B-filmmaking in the fifties and sixties, directing over fifty movies—nearly all low-budget, independent films—between 1955 and 1971 and producing scores of others. The making of *The Terror* is also significant in how many young and unknown talents who figure into the story went on to play prominent roles in American cinema in later years. Nicholson, Coppola, Hellman, and Bogdanovich are only a few of the many talents discovered and nurtured under Corman's tutelage. Finally, the story is representative of one of the predominant visions of Corman's oeuvre. Not so much in *The Terror*—a rather silly, generic horror film—but in the Corman-produced *Targets,* modern life is portrayed as arbitrary, meaningless, and terrifying. Here the realities of the Cold War and vacuousness of American culture create horrors that far outstrip the imaginations of our most pessimistic artists.

A Certain Moral Viewpoint

"The films of a nation," the great German film critic Siegfried Kracauer commented, "reflect its mentality in a more direct way than any other media."[4] Though perhaps problematic when viewed as a universal principle, this statement is especially appropriate to the work of Corman for several reasons. Corman's métier was the exploitation film, a B-movie type that became increasingly common in the fifties and early sixties. These films focused on timely and sensational topics presented in as graphic a manner as possible, with a lurid advertising campaign that usually promised far more than the picture delivered, all geared for a teenage audience.[5] Many of Corman's subjects were drawn from contemporary topical concerns, such as juvenile delinquency (*Teenage Doll,* 1957), rock-and-roll (*Rock All Night,* 1956; *Carnival Rock,* 1957), reincarnation (*The*

Undead, 1956), the beatnik scene (*A Bucket of Blood,* 1959), integration (*The Intruder,* 1961), motorcycle gangs (*The Wild Angels,* 1966), and psychedelic drugs (*The Trip,* 1967). The classic example of Corman's drawing his subject material from the headlines came with *War of the Satellites* (1957). As he said later, "The first Russian Sputnik had just been launched when a friend called me with a story idea about satellites. I called Allied Artists and said I would have a script in two weeks and the film could be shot in ten days and cut in three weeks. The film was actually shot in eight days, and within two months of the headline event we had the first movie about the new space age."[6] In other cases, Corman sought to imitate the popularity of current successful movies. For instance, when he agreed to produce Coppola's first directorial feature, *Dementia 13* (1963), he told Coppola to replicate the plot of *Psycho* (1960).[7] Similarly, Corman followed the successful *Invasion of the Body Snatchers* (1956) with two similar stories, *It Conquered the World* (1956) and *Not of This Earth* (1956). He made *The Wasp Woman* (1959) to cash in on the success of *The Fly* (1958), and *Atlas* (1960) sought to mimic a string of successful Hercules movies. Because his filmmaking ethic called for him to draw most of his subjects by ripping them out of current headlines or plagiarizing other successful movies, Corman, more than most filmmakers, was highly attuned to public sensibilities. While all producers and directors are concerned with making profits, few have been as consistently successful at it as Corman, who always seemed to know what the public would buy.

Kracauer further explained his thesis by arguing that film is a collective, collaborative enterprise rather than the work of an individual. "Since any film production unit embodies a mixture of heterogeneous interests and inclinations, teamwork in this field tends to exclude arbitrary handling of screen material, suppressing individual peculiarities in favor of traits common to many people."[8] This statement is especially true of Corman, but with an interesting twist. Corman's obsession with keeping his budgets low led him to hire a wide range of young people just entering the business. If a person were willing to work long hours for low pay, Corman provided an unprecedented learning experience, giving untested talent opportunities they would never be able to gain in larger studios. This practice also allowed Corman to tap into the emergent sensibility of those coming of age in the postwar era, a crop of actors, screenwriters, and directors who would play a crucial role in shaping American cinema from the mid-sixties on. Such actors as Nicholson, Charles Bronson, William Shatner, Peter Fonda, Robert DeNiro, and David Carradine were all given their first major roles in Corman films. Similarly, the list of screenwriters and directors who apprenticed under Corman includes many of the major names in cinema in the past thirty-five years: Coppola, Hellman, Bogdanovich, Robert Towne, Nicholas Roeg, Dennis Hopper, Martin Scorsese, Paul Bartel, Jonathan Demme, Ron Howard, Joe Dante, and John Sayles.

Corman's role in the development of the underground culture differed in important respects from that of other artists in the emergent paradigm. His major significance was not limited to the critical vision of American culture conveyed in the content of his art. While many filmmakers with critical or eccentric philosophies—like Samuel Fuller, Edgar Ulmer, and Edward D. Wood Jr.—did use the B-movie format as a vehicle to articulate their worldviews, Corman rarely used his art to openly propagandize any particular point of view. Rather, he influenced postwar American culture as much by the manner in which he created his art as by what his films were about. Ethan Mordden commented regarding *The Terror,* "With his abundant tracking shots, his inflamed color sense, his sly *homages* to the masters (and to himself), and his laissez-faire use of his players' wildly unaligned acting habits and their English, transatlantic, and downright urban-American accents, Corman has devised something new in horror, movies we enjoy not to see what happens but to see *how it is done.*"[9]

Mordden's point extends beyond Corman's sixties horror movies, for in his creative use of low budgets and his maverick independence, Corman pioneered a new cinematic sensibility. In the limited sets of his early movies (especially *A Bucket of Blood* and *Little Shop of Horrors,* 1960), he made no attempt to hide his low budgets, but flaunted them. The cheapness of the sets, costumes, and special effects and the absurdity of the plots and dialogue self-reflexively called attention to the medium and its limitations. At other times, his location shooting, use of nonprofessional actors in supporting roles (such as the townspeople in *The Intruder* and members of the Venice, California, chapter of the Hell's Angels in *The Wild Angels*) created a strange variant of postwar European neorealism. Was it an homage or a parody? Similarly, the stylized overacting of such veterans as Vincent Price, Ray Milland, Boris Karloff, and Basil Rathbone in Corman's early-sixties horror films can be seen as either the product of a director who does not know how to control his actors or the result of an emergent "camp" ethic of deliberate artificiality. (In Bogdanovich's *Targets,* Karloff/Orlok bemoans the film critics who characterize his acting as "camp.") Finally, Corman's homages to such great directors as Ingmar Bergman and Federico Fellini—especially in *The Masque of the Red Death* (1964) and the psychedelic imagery of *The Trip*—

may be viewed as crude attempts to give his exploitation pictures a patina of respectability or as self-conscious efforts to obliterate traditional distinctions between high and popular culture. In short, while Corman's films usually worked at
the level of pure exploitation, they also provided ample opportunity for a media-
savvy audience to recognize them as an elaborate in-joke.

At the same time, one cannot completely dismiss the message of Corman's
art. Few of the films are explicitly political, and yet throughout Corman's oeuvre
there runs a common theme, or set of themes. As David Carradine remarked,
"If you've ever looked at Roger's pictures, you probably noticed that even the
most depraved ones have a certain moral viewpoint—a political viewpoint, if
you will, or a social attitude."[10] In face of the official optimism of the dominant
Cold War culture, Corman consistently presented a dark vision of American
life, a world populated by homicidal nebbishes, scientists with God complexes,
decadent and emotionally twisted aristocrats, and cowardly gangsters. It is a
dreary world always on the verge of destruction, in which the most commonplace assumptions, from the supremacy of patriarchy to the belief that knowledge equals power, are dramatically overturned. It is, in short, an unremittingly
modernist worldview.

The literature regarding Corman falls into two categories. Most biographies are
gossipy, anecdotal accounts, focusing on Corman's often outrageous filmmaking
exploits.[11] The other group consists of authors who insist on taking Corman seriously as a director, occasionally to the point that their analysis becomes a virtual parody of academic writing on popular culture.[12] The best work is Gary
Morris's auterist study, which draws on structuralist and Freudian theory to il-
luminate many of Corman's major recurring images.[13] None of these works,
however, adequately reconstruct the cultural context in which Corman worked.
And both types ultimately oversimplify his role in postwar American film either
by treating him solely as an exploitation director or as a genuine artist. Even
Morris's study is fatally flawed. To support his contention that Corman is a serious auteur, Morris concentrated exclusively on Corman as a director. But such
an emphasis distorts Corman's career because it ignores his other crucial roles
as producer, distributor, discoverer, and nurturer of talent and inspiration. Even
on its own terms, Morris's work misrepresents Corman, for in stressing the seriousness of Corman's work, Morris focused on the director's ten most important films. This approach misses one of the distinctive elements of Corman's
career—nowhere does it convey the sense of fun, of pure silliness, of such low-
budget pictures as *Swamp Women* (1955), *The Viking Women and the Sea Serpent*

(1957), or *The Creature from the Haunted Sea* (1960). For every one of Corman's "serious" films, there were at least two along the lines of *Teenage Caveman* (1958), starring Robert Vaughn as the angst-ridden title character in what could best be described as a combination of *Rebel without a Cause* and *One Million B.C.* with an ending that prefigured *Planet of the Apes* by a decade.

Low-Budget Aesthetic

Born in Detroit in 1926, Corman was the son of a successful engineer who moved the family to Beverly Hills when Roger was a teenager. After high school, he attended Stanford University, earning a degree in engineering, and spent two stateside years in the navy during World War II. Corman's education convinced him that he did not want to be an engineer, and, after college, he spent a year at Oxford on the G.I. Bill studying English literature, and then worked a variety of low-level jobs, such as messenger and story analyst, for some of the major Hollywood studios.[14]

In 1953, Corman sold his first script, *House by the Sea,* to Allied Artists for $3,500. The title was ultimately changed to *Highway Dragnet* to cash in on the popularity of the television series *Dragnet.* In addition to screenwriting, Corman demanded, and received, an associate producer's credit on the movie. As he would write in his autobiography, "*Highway Dragnet* actually did all right. What I learned from this first hands-on experience in filmmaking was that there are very few great successes or total failures."[15] Using his money from *Highway Dragnet* and his associate producer's status, Corman raised $12,000, with which he produced *The Monster from the Ocean Floor* (1954). Originally, he said, the film "was to be called *It Stalked the Ocean Floor.* The title was later changed because the distributors felt it was too cerebral."[16] Corman was able to raise $50,000 for his next project, *The Fast and the Furious* (1954), directed by and starring John Ireland. Because of the financial success of his first two movies, Corman received offers from Republic, Columbia, and Allied Artists to distribute the film. Instead, he wanted to use that success as leverage to establish a longer-term deal. He turned to James Nicholson and Samuel Arkoff, who had just established a new company, the American Releasing Corporation (ARC), which would soon change its name to American International Pictures (AIP) and establish itself as the leading independent film company in postwar America. AIP eventually would produce and/or distribute over thirty of Corman's films. Corman made his agreement with Nicholson and Arkoff because it allowed him the greatest degree of independence available in the business. He remembered later, "I told them I'd finance my own films but wanted to get back my negative costs—what it costs to make the movies—as soon as I finished each one. Essentially, I was asking for an advance upon turning over the negative so I could keep going."[17] Nicholson and Arkoff agreed and then took *The Fast and the Furious* on tour around the country to show distributors, allowing AIP to obtain financial backing.[18]

When Nicholson, Arkoff, and Corman created ARC/AIP, the film industry was in serious financial straits. The primary threats came from suburbanization, the rise of television, and the dismantling of the major studios' vertical integration of the market. As families moved to the suburbs, they tended to look for entertainment in their living rooms on television, and urban theaters were increasingly left empty. The Supreme Court's ruling in the Paramount Decision in 1948 dealt the industry a further blow. In its opinion, the Court ruled that the major studios' ownership of theater chains—a common practice since the days of the silent films—constituted a violation of the Sherman Anti-Trust Act. By the early fifties, then, studios were no longer able to guarantee widespread bookings for their films.[19]

The industry dealt with these crises by attempting to portray what television could not, through a wide variety of means, from 3-D films to giant spectaculars. The result was that fewer movies were produced as more money was pumped into the blockbusters. But this process had deleterious effects on neighborhood theaters and the newly emerging drive-ins, which needed double bills and faster turnover of films than the studios were offering. The independents stepped into this void, providing enough films to satisfy theater owners and often establishing direct economic connections with theaters. ARC, for example, raised 20 percent of its early financing directly from theater owners.[20] Corman also made some of his early movies directly for theater owners. *Swamp Women* and *Teenage Doll* were shot in New Orleans and the nearby bayou country and financed by a pair of New Orleans brothers who owned a drive-in chain and wanted to establish their own distribution company.[21]

Equally important, independent film companies in the fifties understood that their movies needed to be geared to teenagers, a different audience than Hollywood had traditionally targeted. Arkoff and Nicholson realized that postwar teens had an unprecedented amount of disposable income and were desperate to get out of the house and so were a natural audience for neighborhood theaters and drive-ins.[22] AIP became the first film company to specialize in exploitation pictures aimed at teenage audiences, but other independents quickly followed suit. The result was a spate of teen-oriented genres, especially science fiction, horror, juvenile delinquency, and rock-and-roll, or, frequently, some combination of them (such as AIP's *I Was a Teenage Werewolf*).

Corman worked comfortably within this context but always jealously guarded his independence. His agreement with AIP, which usually was made on a film-by-film basis, financed his filmmaking. AIP was primarily a distributing company (through the fifties it did not even have its own studio), and so Corman shot his movies independently. He also made films for Allied Artists, AIP's major independent competitor, and several other independents. On occasion, Corman shot movies for one of the major studios: *I, Mobster* (1958) and *The St. Valentine's Day Massacre* (1967) for 20th-Century Fox, and *The Secret Invasion* (1962) and *The Tower of London* (1962) for United Artists. But every time, Corman quickly backed away from any long-term commitment to the large studios. For a few years in the late fifties and early sixties, he even established his own distributing company, Filmgroup, which distributed some of his own pictures and several lurid exploitation movies, such as *Date Bait*.[23] Corman also used Filmgroup to help create several more worthy low-budget gems, including the directorial debuts of Hellman, *The Beast from the Haunted Cave* (1959), and Coppola, *Dementia 13* (Corman produced both films). Also, he served as executive producer of Filmgroup's *Night Tide* (1960), a haunting, atmospheric thriller directed by Curtis Harrington.[24]

Thus, Corman made a deliberate choice to work with low budgets both for the economic and artistic freedom they allowed. Gary Morris has pointed out that this artistic freedom influenced both Corman's style and content. The low budgets freed him in the sense that he felt no need to elicit flawless (or even very good) performances from his actors or make sure that his shots matched or his sets looked perfect or even realistic. Moreover, according to Morris, "A certain amount of deprivation also frees the director from the meddlesome presence of front-office bureaucrats, and takes him out of the conscious service of the culture at large, which uses film and other forms to endorse its existence and values."[25] Corman reveled in his films' low budgets, perfecting a style of filming the pictures as cheaply as possible. He normally shot scenes in a single take. If a mistake occurred, he usually left it in. During the shooting of *The Viking Women and the Sea Serpent,* for instance, Corman set a personal record of seventy-three separate camera set-ups in one day, filming so fast that in one scene, one of the Viking women is wearing sunglasses.[26] The work was physically and emotionally draining on his actors and crew, and because he was unable to afford stuntmen and -women, the actors performed their own stunts. During the filming of *Gunslinger* (1956)—which in his memoirs Corman bemoaned as the only time he had gone over schedule (it was planned for six days of shooting and took seven because it rained constantly)—actress Allison Hayes expressed a sentiment commonly held by actors in a Corman movie: "Tell me Roger, who do I have to fuck to get off this picture?"[27]

Unlike most B-movie directors, Corman did not attempt to hide his low budgets. Rather, he used his cheap, tawdry sets to emphasize the marginal, alienated, and emotionally twisted people who populate his universe. Like a handful of other B-film directors—notably Edgar Ulmer—Corman developed what Morris termed a "low-budget aesthetic," using the limitations imposed on him by financial considerations to make a social comment. The limited number of actors, the few, sparsely furnished sets, the unbelievable special effects and ridiculous-looking monsters of Corman's fifties movies created a universe that was simultaneously claustrophobic, barren, paranoid, vacuous, and absurd. "The very dreariness of these black-and-white dramas," according to Morris, "is an early indication of Corman's view of the world as a closed, empty, pointless place."[28]

Establishing himself as an independent director who defied Hollywood conventions, Corman also consistently undermined standard cinematic formulas. With its downbeat ending and dour sensibility throughout, *Carnival Rock* eschewed the standard teen rock-and-roll melodrama formula, in which the music provided at least temporary relief. In other early films, he deconstructed several traditional film genres—such as westerns and gangster movies—by the crudely obvious tactic of placing women in the lead roles. Especially fascinating is *Gunslinger,* a western in which both the hero and villain are females. Rose Hood (Beverly Garland) is the wife of the sheriff. When he is gunned down, she assumes his office, vowing to clean up the town. The major criminal is Erica Page (Allison Hayes), a saloon owner who, through a series of leveraged buyouts, is acquiring land rights to the section of town where the railroad is scheduled to be built. Erica has a stable of hired guns she uses to eliminate competition, primarily Jake Hays (Jonathan Haze), whom she delights in sexually taunting and humiliating.

Corman's vision, however, cannot be considered unambiguously feminist. In several films he drew on contemporary cultural images and blatant Freudian imagery of castrating females with voracious sexual appetites to warn of women who are too powerful. Particularly in a series of performances by the fine actress Susan Cabot, Corman portrayed female characters who threaten to emasculate and manipulate men, preventing them from developing into mature and responsible adults. In *Sorority Girl* (1957), Cabot played a rich girl whose distant, emotionally abusive mother and absent father have made her into a psychopath. She constantly browbeats her sorority sisters and relentlessly paddles the pledge assigned to her for the smallest infractions. When she is spurned by the resident BMOC (Dick Miller), she plots to destroy him, blackmailing him by getting one of her pregnant sorority sisters to accuse him of being the father. In the end her plan backfires, and the whole sorority turns against her. In *The Wasp Woman*, Cabot portrayed Janice Starland, a former model and president of Starland Cosmetics. Janice is charming, friendly, and savvy, but her company profits are falling because she is nearing forty and losing her youthful looks, so she can no longer be the company cover girl. When the eccentric Dr. Zinthrop comes to her with a formula made from the venom of queen wasps, which he claims reverses the aging process, Janice puts him on the payroll and demands to be his first guinea pig. She ignores a friend's warning that socially, queen wasps are on the same level as black widow spiders—both are carnivorous, paralyzing their mates and eating them alive slowly. Soon, Janice looks twenty years younger, but, as a side effect, at night she turns into a giant wasp who kills and devours several male victims. In *Machine Gun Kelly* (1958), Cabot was cast as Kelly's (Charles Bronson) moll Flo, a castrating harpy who belittles Kelly, pushing him deeper into a life of crime with her constant taunting. "I gave you the machine gun, the name, the reputation," she tells him. "I gave you a backbone." By himself, Kelly is a sniveling coward, terrified of death. He cannot fire his gun until Flo derides his toughness. In the final gun battle with the FBI, Kelly wants to give up, but Flo will not let him. When he does surrender, an FBI agent asks, "Why didn't you shoot it out?" and Kelly replies, "Because I knew you'd kill me." By ironically portraying Flo as "the balls" behind Kelly's crime spree, Corman tapped into common antifeminist imagery of the postwar era, but he complicated that simple formulation by consistently casting women in the most interesting and complex roles.

Throughout Corman's movies run many images common to Cold War films, but he often subverted standard assumptions about these images by placing them in uncommon contexts. *It Conquered the World,* for instance, was one of the wave of invasion movies of the fifties that reflected the official fear of communism. It belonged to the subgenre of anticommunist invasion films (including *Invasion of the Body Snatchers* and *I Married a Monster from Outer Space*) in which the invaders take over the bodies of people, rendering them cold, dispassionate automatons. The film further reflected what Peter Biskind identified as the conservative distrust of intellectuals, especially scientists.[29] Tom Anderson (Lee Van Cleef) is a brilliant scientist who has established contact with Venus, a civilization far more advanced than Earth's. When he learns that the Venusians want to colonize Earth, he actively assists them, proclaiming it "the greatest day in the history of mankind." Anderson's friend, Paul Nelson (Peter Graves), is not so sure, especially when the Venusians begin taking over the bodies of humans, making them emotionless and unquestioningly obedient. Anderson tells Nelson that in the modern world, genius and progress are the constant victims of stupidity, fear, and greed. "I'm in on the beginning of ultimate freedom."

But Nelson demurs, telling Anderson, "I'd have to take a long, hard look at anything that was going to change the world and me so completely." When Nelson's wife is taken over by the invaders, he cold-bloodedly shoots her. In the end, Nelson, a small contingent of soldiers, and a belatedly repentant Anderson track the invader down to a cave, where they attack the absurd-looking monster (which resembles a giant vegetable) and kill it with a blowtorch. At the end of the movie, Nelson makes a speech that reflects the consensus liberal vision of freedom according to such intellectuals as Erich Fromm and Arthur Schlesinger Jr. "Men have to find their own way and make their own mistakes. There can't be any gift of perfection from outside ourselves. And when men seek such perfection they find only death, fire, loss, disillusionment and the end of everything that's gone forward. Men have always sought an end of toil and misery. But it can't be given, it has to be achieved. There is hope; but it has to come from inside—from man himself."

Images of impending apocalypse also recurred in Corman's fifties science fiction films (as well as in the ritual fire that destroys the claustrophobic sets at the end of most of his sixties Poe films). Several of Corman's movies were set after the Earth has been destroyed by nuclear war. At the end of *Teenage Caveman,* the viewer learns that the characters are not inhabiting a prehistoric world, but a posthistoric one. When Robert Vaughn meets the creature who has terrified his tribe, he discovers that the creature is really a survivor of the apocalypse who gives Vaughn a history book whose last chapter is titled "The Atomic Era." The movie ends with a straightforward antinuclear message. Elsewhere, Corman used the threat of nuclear war to portray the arbitrariness of a godless universe. One of the few survivors of the apocalypse that opens *The Day the World Ended* (1956) remarks, "My brother is dead out there. He was only thirty feet

from me. He's dead and I'm not. . . . You know the irony of it? He was studying for the ministry. He was going to be a man of God." Thus, while Corman
occasionally reflected the staunch anticommunism of the era's dominant culture, he also demanded that we consider the potential ultimate consequences
of Cold War policies.

It's Hideous and It's Eloquent

In style and content, Corman's early films displayed a strongly modernist sensibility. The minimalism of the sets and the bleakness of the world portrayed
reflected the pessimism of a Kafkaesque universe. But in a series of dark comedies made in 1959 and 1960, Corman extended this vision into what J. Hoberman
would label "vulgar modernism." With this term, Hoberman referred to "a
particular sensibility that is the vulgar equivalent of modernism itself. By this
I mean a popular, ironic, somewhat dehumanized mode, reflexively concerned
with the specific properties of its medium or the conditions of its making." As
examples of this sensibility, Hoberman cited cartoonist Tex Avery, the creators
of *Mad* magazine, and television comedian Ernie Kovacs. Such artists derived
much of their humor by self-consciously calling attention to the artificiality and
limitations of their specific medium (for example, Kovacs's producer called to
him from off camera, "This isn't the way we rehearsed it," while Avery had one
of his cartoon characters shoot a member of the audience, whose silhouette
drops dead) and by drawing on the audience's familiarity with other media texts
to create a pastiche of intertextual references (such as *Mad*'s parodies of advertising, television, films, and comic books).[30]

Throughout his early career, Corman deliberately accentuated his films' cheapness with his ridiculous monsters (as in *It Conquered the World* and *The Day
the World Ended*) and terrible special effects (which in *The Viking Women and
the Sea Serpent* look like they were filmed in someone's bathtub). For those
unsure if he was joking, though, Corman tipped his hand with a trio of black
comedies: *A Bucket of Blood, Little Shop of Horrors,* and *Creature from the
Haunted Sea.* With these films, Corman paired his tawdry, alienating universe
with a modernist comic vision (found in a variety of other cultural sources from
Mad to the works of such literary black humorists as Richard Condon and
Thomas Pynchon) in which Western civilization, in Hoberman's words, is "a
clutter of cultural detritus."[31]

A Bucket of Blood, which takes place in a beatnik coffeehouse, opens with a
closeup of beat poet Maxwell Brock reciting ridiculous poetry:

I will talk to you of art, for there is nothing else to talk about. . . .
Life is an obscure hobo bumming a ride on the omnibus of art. . . .
Creation is—all else is not.
What is not creation is graham crackers.
Let it all crumble to feed the creator.

The story concerns Walter Paisley (Dick Miller), a bus-boy at the coffeehouse, who listens attentively to Brock's poems and seeks to live by them. Walter is scorned by the beats and abused by Leonard, the coffeehouse owner. Certain that art is an avenue to being accepted by the coffeehouse crowd, Walter goes to his small flat and ineptly attempts to sculpt a bust. When the landlady's cat gets stuck in his wall, Walter takes a knife, tries to cut a hole to allow the cat to escape, and accidentally kills it. Horrified, he hides his deed by covering the cat with clay and calling it "Dead Cat."

At the coffee house, "Dead Cat" is an instant cause célèbre, and Walter is praised and feted. Brock gives a speech in his honor, and groupies gather around him, one of whom passes him a packet of heroin. An undercover officer witnesses this transaction and follows Walter home to arrest him. To escape, Walter kills the policeman and covers him with clay, creating a new work, "Murdered Man." Carla, an attractive beatnik artist and the object of Walter's affection, calls it a "masterpiece. . . . It's hideous and it's eloquent. It expresses modern man in all his self-pity." Leonard, meanwhile, learns Walter's secret but is loathe to turn him in because of the attention Walter's reputation is bringing to the coffeehouse. Walter continues to murder to create his sculptures, while his fame grows. Brock composes a poem in Walter's honor ("The bird that flies now pays later through the nose of ambidextrous apathy/necrophiles may dance together on the placemats in an orgy of togetherness"), while Leonard organizes an exhibition of Walter's work. At the show, the clay begins to chip off the sculptures, revealing what lies beneath. Walter flees, pursued by the crowd at the exhibit, and hangs himself in his apartment, causing Brock to exclaim, "I suppose he would have called it 'Hanging Man'—his greatest work."

A Bucket of Blood derived much of its humor from its mixture and juxtaposition of various popular-cultural referents—the beat scene, horror movies, low-budget movies, and Jewish folk humor (especially the figure of the schlemiel). But in *Little Shop of Horrors,* the references are both more varied and more fundamentally integrated into the story's humor. Like several of Corman's films, this one was inspired by a standing set. Corman asked screenwriter Chuck

Griffith to rewrite his *Bucket of Blood* script for the existing set, and Griffith transformed the coffeehouse into a flower shop and the schlemiel-protagonist into an employee who cultivates a venus flytrap that develops a taste for human blood. After three days of rehearsals, Corman shot the interiors in two days, and Griffith directed the second-unit exteriors.[32]

The story concerns Seymour Krelboin (Jonathan Haze), who works in a flower shop owned by Gravis Mushnik, a miserly eastern European immigrant. Mushnik's heavily-accented English is filled with malapropisms: "What am I," he asks a customer looking for a bargain, "a philatelist?" The shop serves a variety of eccentric regular customers, including Mrs. Shiva, who is constantly buying flowers for recently deceased relatives, and Fouch (Dick Miller), who enjoys eating carnations: "I'm crazy about kosher flowers." Seymour breeds the plant, which he names Audrey Jr., after Mushnik's daughter. When Seymour discovers that Audrey Jr. lives on human blood, he must continually hunt up more victims, while the petulant plant demands still more, crying out, "Feed me!" "I'm starved!" or "I need some chow!"

Film critic Danny Peary has pointed out that *Little Shop of Horrors* contains many references that only an audience well versed in popular culture could decipher. First, Audrey Jr. is a parody of the ridiculous monsters populating low-budget science fiction and horror films of the fifties, like those Corman had made. The movie's staging has the actors facing forward, as if playing before a live audience, in the style of fifties television situation comedies. The police investigating the murders marvelously satirize the heroes of television's *Dragnet* when Sergeant Fink and his partner, Smith, engage in deadpan dialogue:

> Smith: How are your kids?
> Fink: I lost one yesterday.
> Smith: How did it happen?
> Fink: Playing with matches.
> Smith: Those are the breaks.

The whole troupe works together, Peary has pointed out, like a Yiddish repertory company, and the script is filled with recognizable ethnic types and humor. Most fundamentally, the movie is a satire of and paean to low-budget filmmaking, delighting in its own limitations.[33] In one of the most famous scenes, Seymour visits a dentist and kills him. Before he can drag the body back to Audrey Jr., a young masochist, Wilbur Force (Jack Nicholson) arrives, anxious for his checkup. Seymour poses as the dentist and begins drilling Wilbur's teeth, while Wilbur screams in ecstasy. Nicholson recalled shooting the scene: "Jonathan Haze was up on my chest pulling my teeth out. And in the take, he leaned back and hit the rented dental machinery with the back of his leg and it started to tip over. Roger didn't even call cut. He leapt onto the set, grabbed the tilting machine, and said, 'Next set, that's a wrap!'"[34]

The third movie in Corman's trilogy of black comedies, *The Creature from the Haunted Sea,* similarly mixed a variety of popular-cultural references, including spy stories, gangster pictures, horror films, and cartoons. The story is set in Cuba immediately after the revolution. In a cartoon prologue, a narrator comments that the country's complexion was changing, while drawings of peasants instantly sprout Fidel Castro beards. While the voice-over narration proclaims that the country has been "liberated," the drawings depict an execution and show the revolution's opponents fleeing the country after looting the national treasury.

The plot concerns some Cuban military officers who make arrangements with an American gangster to take them and their chest of gold out of the country in his boat. "As an American gambler and gangster," they tell him, "you are above suspicion." They want to reach a safe haven and plot a counterrevolution. "Don't worry, we'll be back," they say, "and if you think you're seeing executions now—oh boy!" The gangster (Anthony Carbone) plans to murder the Cubans one by one, telling them a legendary sea monster has been doing the killing. Things get complicated when a monster really does show up and begins killing. The movie ends with almost the entire crew dead and the monster sitting atop the chest of gold at the ocean's bottom. The creature, easily the most absurd of all Corman's monsters, was made for $150 out of a wetsuit, Brillo pads, tennis balls (for the eyes), and pipe cleaners (for the claws).[35]

In many ways, these three films are the cinematic equivalent of the contemporary genre of literary black humor. The grim and fatalistic vision, in which death is the only final reality, mirrors that of such authors as Kurt Vonnegut and Joseph Heller. The ridiculous names (Walter Paisley, Seymour Krelboin, Gravis Mushnik, Wilbur Force, Mrs. Shiva) and one-dimensional characters are used to heighten the sense of alienation, a tactic also used by authors like Heller and Pynchon. Morris Dickstein has pointed out that black humorists, even non-Jewish authors like Pynchon and Thomas Berger, have commonly used the figure of the schlemiel to emphasize the insignificance of the individual in modern life.[36] But Corman took the character of the alienated, insignificant nebbish even further, portraying him as driven by his anonymity and powerlessness into fits of mass murder in a desperate attempt to establish his significance. Later, in *Targets,* Corman and Bogdanovich would work a terrifying variation on the theme that the anonymous schlemiel is not harmless but gains fame and notoriety as he becomes increasingly bloodthirsty.

The Color of Gunpowder

The Corman legend focuses as much on how he made films as on the films themselves, but with *The Intruder* the movie-making process and the picture's content combined for a classic example of guerilla filmmaking. Based on the novel by Charles Beaumont (see chapter 4), *The Intruder* is a brilliant examination of American racism, far more nuanced in its depiction of the situation and radical in its critique than mainstream late-fifties/early-sixties movies about race (almost all of which starred Sidney Poitier). The film's ultimate commercial failure—Corman claimed it was the first movie he ever lost money on—in no way diminishes its artistic success.

The story concerns Adam Cramer (William Shatner), a racist demagogue who tours the South in the wake of the Supreme Court's Brown decision, whipping up local resistance to court-ordered desegregation. Arriving in the town of Caxton, Cramer finds most whites uneasy with the idea of integration, but resigned to it. Cramer rallies the local white population, from the leading citizen to the poor whites, to forcibly oppose the arrival of black students in the high school. But once he has aroused the people's passions, he realizes he is losing control of the situation. A black church is bombed and the minister killed, a passing car carrying a black family is attacked, and the leader of the black students, Joey Green, whom Cramer has framed on a rape charge, is nearly lynched by a white mob. "You started something you can't control," someone tells Cramer. "You think you're the boss? Wake up. That mob's the boss now." In the end, Cramer is discredited just before the student can be lynched.

Lending power to the story are the realistic touches Corman built into the filming of the movie. Anxious to find a southern-looking location that was not in the Deep South, Corman filmed *The Intruder* in the Missouri boot-heel town of Sikeston, casting local townspeople in all but the lead roles. While Sikeston is not in the Deep South, Jim Crow remained the way of life in southern Missouri in 1960. Beaumont, who wrote the screenplay and acted in the film, observed, "No dressing up was done for *The Intruder.* The film was shot in and about a community corresponding exactly to that described in the novel. It was drab and unlovely and gray, the color of gunpowder. It was real. If anything it was too real. . . . The most controversial scenes in the novel (also in the screenplay) were enacted publicly, often with the confused assistance of the very elements under attack. Young Negroes were recruited and photographed in the schools to which they cannot go. Angry bigots were persuaded to act the roles of angry bigots."[37]

Corman kept the film's plot as much a secret as he could, and only he and Shatner were allowed to have copies of the full script. Corman said that when they shot scenes in which Cramer addresses large crowds, local extras were swept up in the rhetoric: "One scene was a meeting with Cramer in an old cafe. I got some truly great faces on camera—old, toothless, lined, weary rural American faces, with their worn-out overalls and the whirring overhead fans in the stifling heat. It looked authentic—Bill [Shatner] rattling off racist idiocies about 'niggers ruining the human race' and these old men mumbling and nodding sleepily in agreement. 'Yeah, yeah, right, get those niggers.' They knew it was a movie, they were paid extras, but they *believed* in Bill Shatner. They loved him as Cramer the racist." Corman and his crew were eventually run out of town by the sheriff, with Corman sneaking back into town to get the final, establishing shot of the school.[38]

The Intruder depicted the depths and complexities of American racism far more accurately than such consensus films as *The Defiant Ones*. Shatner's Adam Cramer is not a stock villain but a subtle and nuanced character, alternately charming and ruthless. Neither he nor the white townspeople succumb to any of the liberal palliatives of mainstream films on race relations (as does the Tony Curtis character in *The Defiant Ones* or the Spencer Tracy character in *Guess Who's Coming to Dinner?*) about learning to accept and live with, if not love, integration. The only white voices of reform, the newspaper editor and school principal, are portrayed as increasingly impotent, powerless to protect the black community as tensions escalate. Corman also captured the divisions within the black community. As the students walk to school together for the first time, led by the minister, one elderly man comments, "You Negroes gonna cause some of us niggers to get killed." Though the movie's commercial failure convinced Corman to steer clear of blatantly political messages, *The Intruder* stands as a testament to the artistic viability and radical courage possible in guerilla filmmaking, much as Herbert Biberman's *Salt of the Earth* (1954) had done at the height of the blacklist era.

No Escape

In the early sixties Corman began working more often with larger budgets and longer (fifteen-day) shooting schedules, primarily in a series of stylish AIP films loosely based on the stories of Edgar Allan Poe.[39] Having forsworn further explicit moralizing, Corman actually deepened his social critique by presenting a pessimistic vision of humans futilely seeking to establish some meaning in a godless universe. The world of the Poe films, according to Gary Morris, is "dense and overripe to the point of rottenness. Corman fills his frames with images of rot and decay that signify his obsession (through death-obsessed lead characters) with death."[40] All of these films portrayed an aristocratic elite that is decadent, psychopathic, overly refined, and brutal.

The worldview Corman conveyed in his Poe films was one of unrelenting pessimism. *The Masque of the Red Death* (1964) opens with an old woman walking through a burnt-out field and encountering a Bergmanesque, red-hooded figure who gives her a white rose, which he turns red, and says, "Take this to your village. Tell them the day of deliverance is at hand." The village is then struck by the Red Death, and the old woman is the first victim. The Satan-worshiping Prince Prospero (Vincent Price) remarks at one point, "Can you look around this world and believe God rules it? Famine, pestilence, war, disease, death—they rule it." One of the villagers, under sentence of death, says to Prospero, "You're a madman," to which the prince replies, "And yet I will live and you will die." While the plague rages outside the castle, Prospero holds a wild, decadent, Felliniesque party for the principality's aristocrats in his castle (much like the siege party in Thomas Pynchon's *V.*). But Death eventually invades the party, killing Prospero and his guests, and the movie ends with a quote from Poe: "And darkness and decay and the red death held illimitable dominion over all."

In several of his other sixties films, Corman extended his modernist vision. *X—The Man with the X-Ray Eyes* (1963) opened with the surrealistic image of a disembodied eyeball, a scene reminiscent of Luis Buñuel's surrealist classic *Un Chien Andalou* (1928). The story concerns Dr. James Xavier (Ray Milland), a scientist who performs experiments that will allow him to see far more of the "actual wave spectrum" than humans can normally see. The absurd hubris of humans trying to understand the chaos of the universe is captured when Xavier's friend, Dr. Brandt, says, "My dear friend, only the gods see everything," and Xavier replies, "My dear doctor, I'm closing in on the gods." For Corman, though, enlightenment does not bring peace of mind, only increasing alienation.

Xavier is ostracized by the scientific community, which considers him insane. After he inadvertently causes Brandt's death, he flees, eventually working as a faith healer, telling people what is physically wrong with them. When an elderly woman asks if she has cancer, Xavier replies in terms that convey Corman's view of life, "It's nothing. Just tiredness and age and nothing."

Meanwhile, Xavier's eyesight has become so acute he cannot escape its effects. In a scene replete with ironic Christian imagery, Xavier (that is, Savior) comes to understand that knowledge is not power but impotence, that the truth will not make him free. Pursued by the police, Xavier drives into the desert. Unable to drive well because he sees too much, he is pursued by a helicopter from which issues a disembodied voice through a loudspeaker, like the voice of God: "You cannot escape. There is no escape." Wrecking his car, Xavier wanders through the desert until he comes upon a tent revival meeting. "Come forward," the preacher intones, "and save your soul." Xavier says, "I've come to tell you what I see. There are great darknesses—farther than time itself and beyond the darkness, a light that glows and changes. And in the center of the universe, the eye that sees us all." "You see sin and the devil," the preacher informs him, and quotes the Gospel: "If thine eye offends thee, pluck it out." As the congregation takes up the chant, "Pluck it out," Xavier does exactly that, and the movie ends with a closeup of his two bloody, empty sockets.

The grim, existential pessimism of *X—The Man with the X-Ray Eyes* reappeared in several of Corman's other sixties movies. In two brilliant westerns directed by Monte Hellman, *Ride in the Whirlwind* (1967) and *The Shooting* (1967)—for which Corman served as uncredited producer—characters are caught up in life-and-death struggles they had no part in creating, though they quickly realize their innocence is wholly irrelevant. Similarly, in several excruciating scenes in Bogdanovich's *Targets,* the point of view is from the tower through the rifle scope, focusing on the sniper's next victim. The viewer gets the sense of looking through the eyes of a ruthless and vengeful god and comes to understand the utter arbitrariness of life. One is left in the position of motorcycle gang leader Heavenly Blues (Peter Fonda) at the conclusion of *The Wild Angels.* Asked to say something at the funeral of a fellow biker, he can only reply, "There's nothing to say." When the funeral erupts in a fight between the Angels and the townspeople, police sirens sound in the distance as the Angels flee, and someone encourages Blues to run. "There's nowhere to go," he responds as he begins shoveling dirt into the grave, awaiting his inexorable fate.

Defiantly Pluralistic

Corman retired from directing after *Von Richtofen and Brown* (1970), and did not direct another film until *Frankenstein Unbound* (1990). In 1970 he founded New World Pictures, an independent film company that specialized in producing such exploitation movies as *Private Duty Nurses, Women in Cages,* and *The Student Teachers* as well as importing such distinguished foreign films as Bergman's *Cries and Whispers* (1976), Fellini's *Amarcord* (1974), and François Truffaut's *The Story of Adele H.* (1975). In typical Corman fashion, he avoided playing his highbrow imports in art house theaters, booking them instead in the drive-in circuit.[41] The cultural blending that marked New World Pictures represented the logical culmination of Corman's career and represented one of the major characteristics of the underground culture, the breaking down of traditional distinctions between high and popular cultures.

In her 1965 essay, "One Culture and the New Sensibility," Susan Sontag identified an emergent cultural sensibility among younger artists that was based on an equal familiarity with elite, avant-garde, and popular cultures. "The new sensibility," she wrote, "is defiantly pluralistic; it is dedicated both to an excruciating seriousness and to fun and wit and nostalgia. . . . The voracity of its enthusiasms (and of the supercession of these enthusiasms) is very high-speed and hectic."[42] For a generation of filmmakers following in Corman's wake, his formulaic exploitation pictures were part of the cultural dialectic out of which their own artistic vision grew. As Martin Scorcese commented about his years studying film at New York University, "There's no such thing as studying film at NYU. At NYU they made you study [Bergman's] *Wild Strawberries.* I studied *Wild Angels* in movie theaters. Every morning at NYU you had to light a candle to Ingmar Bergman. They had little shrines to Bergman all over the place. I love Bergman pictures but it was Corman's movies we studied in those strange dives all over New York."[43] In his own work, however, Corman went beyond simply evincing a familiarity with both elite and popular cultures and actively sought to merge the two. Thus his career, which under the old paradigm would have been considered a series of irreconcilable contradictions, symbolizes the ironic mixture of seriousness and playfulness that marked the underground culture's new sensibility. Corman created a world that simultaneously reflected the bleak pessimism of postwar modernist philosophy and the silliness of low-budget, genre movies, one that interpolated the influence of avant-garde European cinema into the crudest form of American consumer culture.

Part Five

Cracks in the Consensus

Liberal Artists

Richard Condon
and the Paranoid
Surreal Style in
American Politics

In the process of researching his second novel, *The Manchurian Candidate* (1959), Richard Condon spoke with a wide range of intelligence experts about brainwashing and various other mind-control techniques. During the course of his interviews, according to investigative journalist John Marks, "inside sources may well have filled him in on the gist of a discussion that took place at a 1953 meeting at the CIA on behavior control. Said one participant, ' . . . individuals who had come out of North Korea across the Soviet Union to freedom recently apparently had a blank period of disorientation while passing through a special zone in Manchuria.'"[1] Out of this material Condon fashioned a bizarre, absurd, and chilling tale of a joint Chinese-Soviet plot to brainwash an entire American patrol in the Korean war and turn one member into an all-American hero, who, upon returning to the United States, would be celebrated and feted by those in power and rise to a position of influence. Once there he would be manipulated by agents of the international communist conspiracy, using advanced mind-control techniques, into carrying out a series of assassinations designed to bring Soviet agents into positions of tremendous influence within the United States. Condon's book became a runaway bestseller and, in 1962, was made into a brilliant film directed by John Frankenheimer and starring Frank Sinatra, Laurence Harvey, Janet Leigh, and Angela Lansbury.

On November 22, 1963, Americans mourned the assassination of their young president. The arrest and subsequent murder of Lee Oswald, a pathetic little ex-Marine and Marxist hanger-on, raised an abundance of questions that continue to haunt the national memory. One of the most puzzling enigmas concerned the brief period in which Oswald defected to the Soviet Union before returning to the United States. What happened to Oswald during the time he lived in the Soviet Union? Might he have been the victim of brainwashing and turned into a remote-control assassin? Could he have been a real-life "Manchurian candidate"? The similarities between Condon's fictive tale and reality were uncomfortably palpable, and in the aftermath of the assassination, the film version of *The Manchurian Candidate* was withdrawn from public release, not to be reissued for twenty-five years.

The voluminous Warren Commission Report, designed to pin responsibility for the assassination on the alienated and psychopathic Oswald, did little to allay suspicions that a broader conspiracy existed that, either through incompetence or design, was being covered up by those in top levels of government. Conspiracy theories flourished, especially on the left and among younger people increasingly disaffected with their government's policies in Vietnam. Despite the warnings against this conspiratorial worldview by such elder left statesmen as Dwight Macdonald and I. F. Stone, who dismissed criticism of the Warren Report as "paranoid nonsense,"[2] such leftist journals as the *National Guardian* and *Ramparts* introduced the writings of Mark Lane, Jim Garrison, and a host of other conspiracy theorists into a broader popular discourse. As the more recent success of such works as Don Delillo's *Libra* (1988), Oliver Stone's *JFK* (1991), and Norman Mailer's *Oswald's Tale* (1995) demonstrates, the abundance of theories and intensity of debate show no signs of abating.

The old master, Condon, weighed into this fray on several occasions. A month after the assassination, he wrote in *The Nation* that the president's murder, like his own novel, was both cause and consequence of the broader milieu. "With all Americans," he said, "I . . . contributed to form the attitudes of the assassin; and . . . the assassin, and Americans like him . . . contributed to attitudes which . . . caused me to write the novel."[3] Assuming Oswald's guilt, as did almost everyone in the assassination's immediate aftermath, Condon expressed what, according to Christopher Lasch, would become the staple of establishment liberals' interpretation of Kennedy's death—that the president's obvious social superiority fueled the resentment of society's losers until one such outcast took it upon himself to strike back. Condon wrote: "Lee Oswald's indicated murder of Mr. Kennedy seems motivated only by his resentment against the most successful man in the world; resentment against a . . . man who was so rich in spirit that he made no effort to conceal his superiority. . . . From the view of this resentment, as long as this fellow stayed out of . . . Oswald's path he would be all right, but when he came laughing into Dallas, and the newspapers printed a map that showed he would drive right past where . . . Oswald worked for a lousy fifty bucks a week, it was more than this classical resentment could bear."[4]

But in his later works Condon rejected the view that Oswald acted alone and entered into the growing cultural discourse of assassination-conspiracy theories, albeit in allegorical fashion.[5] In *Winter Kills* (1974), Nicholas Thirkield, half brother of the Kennedyesque Tim Kegan, undertakes an investigation of his brother's assassination, which took place fourteen years earlier. Enlisting the aid of his father, the Joseph Kennedyesque billionaire Tom Kegan, Thirkield uncovers a series of seemingly contradictory conspiracies, only to discover in the end that he has been sent on a wild goose chase by the true mastermind of the assassination, his own father. Believing his money had purchased the presidency for his son, Tom Kegan had become embittered when Tim, realizing the extent and illegality of his father's influence, disassociated himself from Tom and charted his own course as a reform president.[6] In his later novel, *Death of a Politician* (1978), Condon traced the career of Walter Slurrie, a Nixonesque character whose close connection with the Secret Police, a CIA-type organization, had implicated him in Kennedy's assassination. Reflecting one of the most popular conspiracy theories, propounded by Carl Ogelsby, Oliver Stone, and others, Condon here posited that Kennedy was assassinated by the CIA because he intended to withdraw American troops from Vietnam.[7]

This bizarre dialectic of fact and fiction—wherein yesterday's fantasy becomes today's (possible) reality and thus creates ever wilder fantasies—highlights a glaring blind spot in the consensus liberal paradigm. In his classic work *The Paranoid Style in American Politics,* Richard Hofstadter defined this "paranoid style" as the exclusive property of "the radical right," the provincial and alienated denizens of small-town America, raised in an atmosphere of xenophobia and religious fundamentalism and fueled by a populist resentment of their social betters.[8] Lasch said that this view represented the underlying belief of the establishment liberal interpretation of the assassination, allowing Kennedy's defenders to celebrate his "style" and unfulfilled promise while minimizing his

sparse record of actual achievements. But as Lasch recognized, by the late sixties and early seventies, another vision had become prevalent in liberal popular
culture. "Side by side with the official mythology," he wrote in 1983, "of a be-
leaguered government threatened by riots, demonstrations, and unmotivated, irrational assassinations of public figures, a popular mythology has taken shape
in the last thirty years that sees government as a conspiracy against the people
themselves."[9] Such films as *The President's Analyst* (1967), *The Parallax View*
(1974), *The Conversation* (1974), *Three Days of the Condor* (1975), and *All
the President's Men* (1976) reflected the mainstreaming of paranoia in liberal
culture. Michael Rogin has argued that, contrary to the beliefs of Cold War liberal intellectuals, this process shows that "the countersubversive tradition occupies not the political margins of America but its mainstream."[10]

Condon, a premature paranoiac, recognized early on the political demonology
at the core of consensus liberal ideology. In his various novels he portrayed paranoia as one of the defining characteristics of modern American life. His world
is rife with real and imagined conspiracies, his characters at the mercy of vast
and intricate plots manipulating them without their knowledge, or delusions that
they are the victims of such a plot. A similar theme permeated the works of
such contemporary authors as Thomas Pynchon and Kurt Vonnegut, but Condon avoided the suprahistorical or extraterrestrial machinations of, for instance,
the "Tristero" conspiracy of Pynchon's *The Crying of Lot 49* (an alternative
postal system dating back over several centuries) or the interplanetary meddling
of Vonnegut's *The Sirens of Titan.*[11] Instead Condon firmly situated his paranoid
framework within recognizable institutions. The absurdity of Condon's world is
a bare exaggeration of the absurdity he finds in the real world, "horror tales," as
Julian Smith has said, "of the natural, not the supernatural."[12]

Similarly, Condon excelled at portraying the vacuity and viciousness at the
heart of the American dream. Several of his protagonists live out rags-to-riches
success stories, but, in Condon's world, the only way to rise to a position of
wealth and power in the American rat race is through a brutal disregard for
those who stand in the way. Such a process has its psychic costs, both personal
and social, and Condon sought to lay bare the dehumanizing and destabilizing
effects of the American culture of success.

To Be Accepted by the Reader

As an author, Condon specialized in giving fits to literary critics seeking to cat-
egorize him. Writing in the *New Yorker,* Whitney Balliett described Condon's

first two novels as "brilliantly, highly individualistic, and hopelessly unfashionable demonstrations of how to write stylishly, tell fascinating stories, assemble plots that suggest the peerless mazes of Wilkie Collins, be very funny, make acute social observations, and ram home digestible morals. They demonstrate, in short, a good many of the things that were expected of the novel before the creative-writing courses got its practitioners brooding in their mirrors."[13] On the other hand, in 1959 *Time* designated *The Manchurian Candidate* one of the "ten best bad novels" of the year, marked by "a superstructure of plot that would capsize Hawaii, and badly insufficient philosophical ballast."[14] Four years later, though, *Time* included Condon in a list of ten young American authors—among them Walker Percy, Joseph Heller, John Updike, Philip Roth, and Ralph Ellison—who were spearheading a revival of the American literary scene.[15] When, in the midst of writing *Catch-22,* Heller read a review of *The Manchurian Candidate,* he said, "I had a feeling, well, here's a guy who's writing the same book I am; I'd better read this quickly because he might have already written it."[16] For Vonnegut, Condon was a "very middle-European" sort of writer who "echoes . . . Fredrich Durrenmatt, Max Frisch, *und so weiter.*"[17] In Herbert Mitgang's view, Condon wrote "Chinese-meal novels" in which "you feel hungry an hour later, but all those sweet and pungent sauces tantalize you right up to the fortune cookie."[18] To Roger Sale, "Condon is James M. Cain minus the rawness that makes Cain occasionally powerful. He is Thomas Pynchon without style or imagination," while to Herbert Gold he was "Nabokov without tears."[19]

All of this says much more about the difficulty literary critics have dealing with square pegs and round holes than it does about Condon, who always, as Julian Smith commented, "prefer[red] five ninety-five from an esthetically crippled reader to the kindest words from Edmund Wilson and his friends."[20] Openly disdainful of the literary establishment, Condon argued the novelist's chief ambition should be entertainment and not art. "For no work of fiction has ever changed anything," he wrote in 1977, "any more than flashlights have. . . . It was economics that altered the condition of slavery, not *Uncle Tom's Cabin.*"[21] Continuing, he wrote, "Novels which are toasted as works of art at the time of publication almost always drown in the wine. . . . Therefore, to be accepted by the *reader,* who is intently committed to the novel he has acquired as being entertaining, as a writer who heals and diverts hundreds or dozens of readers who wish to be turned away from a few of the unbearable moments of their lives— that is not a bad model of work for anyone with art on his or her mind."[22] Taking seriously his calling as a professional writer, Condon once told an interviewer he worked seven hours a day, seven days a week and looked down on those who worked more slowly. "When I hear about writers who took seven years to write a book, I know they drank martinis for breakfast."[23] An enormously prolific author, between 1958 and his death in 1996 Condon wrote twenty-six novels and an autobiography, and coauthored a cookbook and an Academy Award–winning screenplay adaptation of his own novel *Prizzi's Honor* (1985).[24]

This mercenary view of his work derived largely from the fact that writing was Condon's second career, the result of a midlife crisis. Born in New York City in 1915, Condon began working as a publicist for a variety of Hollywood studios, starting with Disney in 1937. At Disney, one of his first assignments had been to coordinate publicity for the cartoon short "The Practical Pig," a sequel to "The Three Little Pigs." Condon's bright idea was to strike a deal to tie the cartoon in with National Pork Week, which would bring extensive newspaper advertising and get the nearly eight thousand pork outlets in the country to hang posters featuring Disney's porcine protagonists. When he shared his public relations brainstorm with Walt Disney, however, Disney was aghast. "Those pigs are our actors!" Uncle Walt cried in horror. "How do you think L. B. Mayer would feel if you made a deal with the National Morticians Association for Clark Gable and Greer Garson to advertise National Embalming Week?"[25]

Condon survived Disney's outrage and established a successful career in Hollywood. But by the mid fifties, several ulcers and a desire for a less public life caused him to change careers, and he wrote his first novel, *The Oldest Confession,* in 1958. Writing also allowed Condon and his family to engage in several of his passions, especially traveling and living abroad (in Spain, Mexico, Switzerland, and Ireland) and cooking. A connoisseur of the good life, Condon's books are filled with loving descriptions of food and cooking as well as learned disquisitions on such subjects as wine, travel, art, architecture, and bullfighting. Condon's taste for high culture was an interesting companion to his overarchingly pessimistic view of life and his frankly populist conception of the writer's trade.

We Have Become the Monster

An atmosphere of barely suppressed violence and insanity pervades Condon's universe from the first page of his first novel, *The Oldest Confession.* The Madrid hotel, owned by the book's protagonist, James Bourne, had been headquarters for the Soviet General Staff during the Spanish Civil War, while the cooks in the German restaurant attached to the hotel had been flown to Madrid by the

Luftwaffe. "To those of a romantic turn, like James Bourne, these conditions should have made the hotel seem endemically sinister, but the warm press of spring helped to shoo away the sachet of old death. It was still there, however, but like a touch of insanity in a well-to-do family, it was never mentioned."[26] A few pages later, Condon placed his novel and the issues it raised specifically within the context of the post–World War II period: "When one moves from airport to airport one can observe the restlessness which has come to the world since Hiroshima."[27]

The problems arising from World War II and its aftermath, especially the difficult moral questions, were among Condon's major recurring themes. In *The Oldest Confession,* he told the story of Bourne, scion of a wealthy American family and a successful businessman in his own right, who renounces the immorality of business to become a high-class thief. "Bourne had chosen crime as his career because, in a manner entirely clear to him, he had known that the only way he could achieve a sense of honesty while doing what he had obviously been born to do, had been expensively trained to do, as had most all other men of his class—that is, to amass money—was to steal it. By the stated dishonesty of stealing money illegally, as opposed to the evaded dishonesty of acquiring it as he had among his father's friends, Bourne felt clean, honest and integrated."[28]

At a time when the dominant images of business in popular culture were overwhelmingly positive, Condon denounced the ethics, not just of specific businessmen, but of the entire business class. Unlike Sloan Wilson's *The Man in the Gray Flannel Suit* or even Rod Serling's *Patterns,* Condon did not confine his criticism to pondering the difficulties of maintaining one's values in the cutthroat business environment. Instead, he saw the entire enterprise as corrupt. As Bourne says to his wife Eve, contrasting their profession with standard business procedure, "There is hardly a business in existence today which does not practice cheating and dishonesty. If we are to accept these degrees of dishonesty, then we must make allowances for honest criminality like yours and mine. There is absolutely no doubt about our dishonesty, no shadings or degrees, so there may be no possible doubt about our complete honesty, either."[29] Condon specifically contrasted Bourne's criminal profession with the dominant icons of the era's business culture. "Criminality implies a lack of herd discipline, yet in its more demanding strata it calls for infantile discipline of the kind utilized by a small boy or salesman who will work to remember baseball batting averages back to Nap Lajoie. . . . The non-organization man, the abjurer of gray flannel clothing, the comforting agony at rest behind the masochistic mask, all are compounded when practiced by the higher criminal orders."[30] While Bourne rationalizes his actions on the basis of the immorality of modern business, he owes his success to integrating business principles into his crime. He keeps his account books meticulously and uses an insider's knowledge of business operations to craft his intricate heists.[31] And following his last caper, in which he had swindled a Parisian insurance company out of nearly 100 million francs, he reinvested two-fifths of his profit in annuities with the same company, certain it would have beefed up its security against any such future fraud.[32]

Despite Bourne's rationalizing, his plot to steal several Spanish art master-pieces and replace them with duplicates goes terribly awry, ending with Bourne's two closest friends dead and Bourne serving a lengthy prison term. The first murder occurs when another criminal tries to horn in on the art theft. But as Bourne tells Eve, they bear no responsibility because "the murder of one man has no connection with the life or death of another."[33] Eve knows better, though, telling him, "That's what sin is, Jim. If we go any further doors will close all around us and we'll never get out."[34] Finally Eve pierces the hypocrisy of Bourne's rationalizing, telling him that though his father's business ethics were hopelessly corrupt, Bourne's are equally so. "You're your father's son," she says, "grubbing for money and keeping a double set of books, and you'd even bargain with a murderer for an edge."[35]

The unraveling of a carefully planned crime, with resulting deadly conse-quences, was a common theme in Condon's work. In an age that increasingly relied on experts and fail-safe plans, artists working in the emergent under-ground culture, like Condon and filmmaker Stanley Kubrick—in such movies as *The Killing* (1956), *Dr. Strangelove* (1964), and *2001: A Space Odyssey* (1968)—frequently portrayed a world in which the most carefully crafted plans of experts backfire with fatal repercussions. In his later work, *Arigato* (1972), Condon specifically related this theme to the Cold War dependence on experts when he described an impossible heist, the theft of several thousand cases of expensive wine, planned by a public policy think tank.[36]

Condon similarly faced the problem of modern morality arising out of World War II and its aftermath in his novel of Nazi Germany and occupied Paris, *An Infinity of Mirrors* (1964). The story of Paule Bernheim, a beautiful French Jewess, who, in 1932, marries Wilhelm (Veelee) von Rhodes, a young German officer stationed in Paris, the novel traces the contours of modern evil from the cowardice of the German army to the silence of the German people to the collaboration of the French church, press, and intelligentsia in the face of the Nazis and their "final solution."

Condon's use of humor and his focus on the darker, sexual side of Nazism convey what Hannah Arendt called the "banality of evil." This emphasis left some critics frothing that Condon had written an "immoral" novel.[37] But, in fact, his depiction of the ridiculousness of Nazi bureaucratization placed in startling juxtaposition the horrors committed by these bureaucrats and their strict observance of the most mundane administrative regulations in carrying out their holocaust. In the book's most vivid scene, Paule and Veelee's seven-year-old son is picked up by the French police in a sweep of Parisian Jews, who are to be deported. Along with nearly thirteen thousand others, the boy is taken to the Velodrome d'Hiver, a stadium built for bicycle races. In leasing the Velodrome to the Germans, the owners had insisted that no one wearing street shoes be allowed to walk on the banked wooden track. Thus, the stadium is filled with terrified people, over four thousand of them children, most of whom are refugees and speak no French, without food, water, or adequate toilet facilities, while the public address system repeatedly blares the warning in French, "Attention! Attention! Walking on the board track while wearing shoes is strictly forbidden. Attention! Those who walk upon the board track with shoes on will be immediately and severely punished!"[38]

In Condon's view, the evil unleashed by Nazism infects all who come in contact with it. When Paule and Veelee undertake to punish those responsible for their son's death, they succeed in kidnapping the Nazi official responsible, beating him to the point that he is unrecognizable, and loading him on a train bound for Auschwitz. As the train pulls away, Paule realizes that in the modern world, no one can plead innocence. "We have killed a monster," Veelee tells her. "We have become the monster," Paule replies.[39]

The Overcommunications Industry

Condon worked throughout his career to break down the barriers between high and popular culture. Like the films of Samuel Fuller and Roger Corman, his novels often deal with sensational topics picked off newspaper front pages. *An Infinity of Mirrors* came at a time when William Shirer's *The Rise and Fall of the Third Reich* was a best-seller and Arendt's *Eichmann in Jerusalem* provoked a heated debate among Jewish and non-Jewish intellectuals. *The Manchurian Candidate* dealt with brainwashing and right-wing conspiracy theories,

The Ecstasy Business (1967) with the Hollywood celebrity industry, *Mile High* (1969) with organized crime, and *Winter Kills* with Kennedy assassination theories. Elsewhere, Condon worked within well-established popular genres: the western in *A Talent for Loving* (1961), the political thriller in *Whisper of the Axe* (1976), among others, and the criminal caper in *The Oldest Confession* and *Arigato*. As Leo Braudy has written, "Condon . . . [has] completely moved away from the modernist obsession with literary language and [is] experimenting instead with the ability of the rhythms of daily speech and popular culture to embody the plain-speaking clarity of [his] satire. By destroying the gap between 'serious' and 'popular' culture, [he] make[s] us realize that the myths and images we may consciously disdain affect us more deeply for our ignorance of them."[40]

Though Condon seemed to rip his plot lines off the front pages of the tabloids, his views in many ways reflected the dominant liberal consensus. Like most liberal intellectuals, he tended to see the public as one undifferentiated mass audience, and implicit in most of his works is the idea that this mass public can be easily manipulated by a secret and powerful cabal. Similarly, like a wide range of intellectuals from Daniel Boorstin to Dwight Macdonald, Condon deplored the effect of the modern mass media on the public. In *Some Angry Angel* (1960), his novel of a newspaper gossip columnist, he wrote, "In order to sell all its uncountable editions, the newspaper industry had to foster moral anarchy and then to enforce its acceptance by the unending publication of frightening details in ceaseless and salaciously informative stories concerning obscure crime, adultery, betrayal, rape, degradation, indignity, race hatred, lust, graft, violence, prejudice, greed, fear, corruption, and suspicion until all America's children had learned that no adult authority was to be respected, until those children could become adults and prove that tenet."[41] Or, as he said later in the same novel, "The newspaper industry worked hard to manufacture the attitudes and rationales of indecency and violence, which they then claimed to report objectively, as news."[42]

In his attack on Joseph McCarthy and his followers in *The Manchurian Candidate,* Condon reflected the dominant view of most liberal intellectuals. Richard Rovere, in his influential book on McCarthy, portrayed the senator as both a ridiculous bumbler and a dangerous demagogue, who, with no real intellectual attachment to the issue of anticommunism, used it as a tool to nihilistically bludgeon everyone who challenged him, but who also wanted to be accepted as "one of the boys" by other senators and those in the press.[43] Condon similarly portrayed his McCarthyesque character Johnny Iselin as an incompetent boob who is brilliantly manipulated by his wife. She encourages him to lie about his war record in his campaign speeches, to go without shaving each weekend (because it "made him like some slob, like a farm hand or some Hunky factory worker"), and to keep changing numbers when saying exactly how many communists were in the State Department (so that people would discuss how many there were, not whether there were any at all).[44] When Iselin complains that the other senators tease him in the cloakroom about his constantly changing numbers, she finally lets him stick with fifty-seven, "as it could be linked so easily with the fifty-seven varieties of canned food that had been advertised so well and so steadily for so many years."[45] Like Rovere's McCarthy, Condon's Iselin cares nothing about the issue of communism itself, but sees it as a way to gain publicity.[46]

Iselin's followers are largely from the Midwest and Texas, the type of narrow-minded provincials Hofstadter had insisted were especially prone to the "paranoid style in politics." In describing the guests at a party thrown by the Iselins, Condon placed Iselin's supporters in a tradition of paranoid, populist-style demagogues: "The older guests who shook hands with the Iselins that night had been followers of Father Coughlin; the group just younger than them had rallied around Gerald L. K. Smith; and the rest, still younger, were fringe lice who saw Johnny's significance in a clear, white light. The clan had turned out from ten thousand yesterdays in the Middle West and neolithic Texas, and patriotism was far from being their last refuge."[47] Unable to articulate their own views, these people "exchanged opinions they rented that week from Mr. Sokolsky, Mr. Lawrence, Mr. Pegler, and that fascinating younger fellow who had written about men and God at Yale."[48]

While Condon seemed to accept many of the principles of the liberal consensus view, he also satirized the basic assumptions of liberal intellectuals. In important ways, the plot of *The Manchurian Candidate* is the reductio ad absurdum of the liberal consensus. Liberals did not minimize the threat posed by communism but believed that the tactics of McCarthy and the right wing of the Republican Party were not the most effective means of fighting communism. As Arthur Schlesinger Jr. worried, "This time we might be delivered through the incompetence of the right into the hands of the totalitarians of the left."[49] But, Condon wondered, what if it were not incompetence? Suppose, instead, that it was part of some brilliantly designed master plan for the communists to gain power through the far right wing of American politics. In the novel, by brainwashing Korean war soldier Raymond Shaw, Senator Iselin's stepson, and turning him into a remote-control assassin, the communists plan to have him undertake a series of assassinations that will carry Iselin to the presidency, where he will be, as he always has been, manipulated by the top communist agent in the United States, Raymond's mother and Iselin's wife. Interestingly, this plot, in significant ways, mirrored that of Mickey Spillane's *One Lonely Night* (1951), in which a virulently anticommunist politician is secretly a member of the Communist Party and sees his election as an important step in the communist takeover.[50] By using the same plot elements as Spillane—the bane of liberal intellectuals for his neanderthal politics and formulaic masscult thrillers—and working them from a liberal perspective, Condon showed that paranoia is not the exclusive property of the right wing, but the basis of all American politics.

According to Leo Braudy, Condon stands with such novelists as Pynchon, Heller, Norman Mailer, Thomas Berger, William Burroughs, and Ken Kesey as creators of "the most original novelistic style of the 1960s . . . [that is,] paranoid surrealism . . . [which] drew equally on the facts of national life and the clichés of popular fiction to create a world where technology, politics, and history had run wild and the only possible humanism was gallows humor."[51] Paranoia dominated Condon's literary landscape, and plots bordering on the ludicrous were given a disconcerting reality. In his political thrillers, there is no such thing as an accident. If the incompetence of the McCarthyites seems to do the international communist conspiracy more good than harm, then that is by design. Similarly, in *Mile High* Condon worked from the premise that it was no accident that Prohibition solidified the position of organized crime in the American economy because it was planned and executed that way. In *The Vertical Smile* (1971), he claimed that student and black rioting in the late sixties were orchestrated by the Republican National Committee so that the party could win elections with a "law and order" campaign.[52] Just as Hofstadter defined the paranoid style, so Condon's plots frequently suggest that conspiracies exist not just here and there, but are *"the motive force* in historical events. History *is* a conspiracy, set in motion by demonic forces of almost transcendent power."[53] But Condon saw these conspiracies as metaphors rather than realities. In several other books, notably *Some Angry Angel* and *Any God Will Do* (1966), he emphasized the arbitrariness and capriciousness of life, while in *The Oldest Confession* and *Arigato* he examined the unintended consequences of failed conspiratorial plans. In later works, specific settings make a paranoid worldview seem more appropriate, such as Mafia society in *Prizzi's Honor* (1982), and the overlapping world of church, business, and politics in fifteenth-century Italy in *A Trembling upon Rome* (1983).[54]

Condon utilized another strategy of surrealism with his close attention to detail. His books reflect painstaking research, and he often included a bibliography of sources to give the novel a sense of reality. Several critics have complained about this tendency. Mordechai Richler, commenting on the forty-seven books cited as sources in *An Infinity of Mirrors,* said it was "a novel not so much to be reviewed as counter-researched," while David Dempsey claimed the book "might have been a better novel if it weren't such good history."[55] On the contrary, Condon's emphasis on research and verisimilitude heightened the fantastic nature of the stories he tells, a technique similar to that used by surrealist painters. According to art critic Clement Greenberg, "The Surrealist represents his more or less fantastic images in sharp and literal detail, as if they had been posed for him. . . . The more vividly, literally, painstakingly the absurd and the fantastic are represented, the greater their shock. For the sake of hallucinatory vividness, the Surrealists have copied the effects of the calendar reproduction, postal card, chromeotype, and magazine illustration."[56]

This emphasis on facts also reflected a pattern of American politics in which what Condon labeled the "overcommunications industry"[57] constantly inundates the public with so many facts that it only leads to further confusion.[58] With his learned asides on the history of the Medal of Honor, political conventions, and the theories of brainwashing techniques in *The Manchurian Candidate;* or the modernization of cattle-ranching techniques in the nineteenth century in *A Talent for Loving;* or the history of anti-Semitism in *An Infinity of Mirrors;* or any number of other topics, Condon asserted that Americans do not suffer from a want of facts, but from an overload of information. The end result is to reinforce the sense of powerlessness of ordinary people and increase their reliance on experts, because only they have the ability and resources to understand and interpret the constant barrage of facts. This process explains why, for instance, I. F. Stone's dissection of the Pentagon's 1965 white paper on Vietnam, "Invasion from the North," was so empowering for the antiwar movement because, for the first time, it gave lie to the official claim that only the government, with its legion of highly trained experts, could make sense of the vast amount of information on the war.[59]

Condon frequently heightened this paranoid surrealism through his use of what Joe Sanders has termed "borderline fiction," which occupies the literary territory between fantasy and reality, borrowing heavily from science fiction literature.[60] The fantastic nature of his plots also blurred the distinction between the realm of science fiction and reality. His use of such contemporary scientific techniques as brainwashing reflected the science fiction writer's interest in the possibilities of modern technology and its effects on humans, while also demonstrating, according to Sanders, that "one obvious trait of borderline fiction is that it does not use very esoteric or scientific or supernatural inspiration; rather it is based on trends and fears already existing in the public mind."[61] Condon's prodigious use of research to give his work a greater sense of reality also contributed to its fantastic and unsettling nature. If, at times, Condon's fictional characters were obviously thinly disguised variations on easily recognizable public figures, his occasional obvious rearranging of historical fact was all the more disconcerting. Some of these anachronisms may be explained as mistakes: a Mexican bandit in the 1870s named after the American single-tax advocate Henry George, when George would not become internationally famous until the late 1870s and certainly would not have been well known enough when the child had been named several decades earlier;[62] or a boy who gets a 1904 autograph of President William McKinley, who had died three years earlier.[63] But many of the changes are plainly deliberate, such as changing the date of Johnny Iselin's (that is, Joe McCarthy's) first charges of communist infiltration in the State Department from 1950 to 1957;[64] or, in his later work, *Death of a Politician,* placing the Castro revolution in the early fifties, so that the Nixon character (Walter Slurrie) could have been vice president during the 1953 Bay of Pigs invasion (sic).[65] As in the work of science fiction writer Philip Dick, in several of Condon's novels we are obviously inhabiting an alternative universe. "The rearranging of historical perspective is hideous," Sanders has commented, "but Condon's vision of American as nightmare is hard to dismiss."[66]

A Talent for Loving

Beneath the surface of the complacency and conformity of Cold War society, Condon saw American culture as marked by a psychopathic, internecine warfare both within the family and in public life. Far from providing comfort and a sense of belonging, in Condon's universe families are a psychological prison from which each person seeks desperately to escape. As Sanders has said, "At the root of each central character's problems—and thus of the problems experienced by the world each dominates—is a crime by one generation against the next."[67] On the humorous end of this spectrum is the curse of the Catalonia family in *A Talent for Loving,* handed down from Don Jaime Arias de Catalonia, a captain who traveled with the Spanish explorer Hernando Cortés, who had insulted the Aztecs by trying to pass off his obscene journals as the writings of the Aztec god Quetzalcoatl. According to this curse, upon a family member's first romantic kiss, he or she becomes overwhelmed by an ardent passion that never abates.[68] On the darker end of the spectrum is Edward Courance West in *Mile High,* who is embittered by having been deserted as a child by his dark-skinned Sicilian mother and, as an adult, feels the need to sexually possess and then murder all the dark-skinned women who remind him of her.

The classic example of this character is Raymond Shaw's mother. Michael Rogin, in discussing the film version of *The Manchurian Candidate,* pointed out that Condon drew his terrifying vision of the manipulative, disempowering mother from well-known images of American popular culture in the forties and fifties, especially from the concept of "momism" as introduced by Philip Wylie. A well-known writer for women's magazines, Wylie authored the best-seller *Generation of Vipers* in 1942, in which he argued that women in twentieth-century America had lost the household functions of the preindustrial period. Thus a woman's primary means of acquiring status and power were to encourage the men in her life to depend on her and pay obeisance to her. Wylie portrayed mothers as tyrants who turn their husbands into weak and sniveling Walter Mittys and their sons into men who were incapable of romantic love because of their obsession with their mothers. In the period following the Great Depression, when so many men had been out of work, and World War II, when women had left the home to work in the factories, Wylie's vision raised serious concerns.[69]

Mrs. Iselin emerges as a viper out of America's darkest imagination. A woman driven by power but constrained by the definition of a woman's proper role, she exerts her influence by discarding one husband, who is not sufficiently ambitious, and marrying Iselin, who is stupid enough to be easily manipulable. Precisely how she became a communist is never explained, but it was a truism of Cold War thought that no one could become a communist for honest sociopolitical reasons. Thus, there must be some hidden personality flaw, probably the result of sexual deviance.[70] Mrs. Iselin's insanity is explained by her incestuous relationship with her father, a pattern she continues with Raymond.[71] She renders the otherwise virile Johnny impotent, and their marriage is never consummated.[72] She is a brilliant political tactician whose flawlessly logical plan will make her the most powerful person in America. But she is also completely insane, and her fury at the communists for choosing her son to become the assassin who will pave her way to power makes her determined that, once in power, she will engage in an all-out nuclear war with the Soviets and Chinese.[73] Though Raymond detests her, he is unable to escape her control until, in the book's final scene, he shifts his aim at the last second from his intended target, the Republican presidential nominee, and instead shoots his mother, Johnny, and himself.[74]

Living Had Become a Palindrome

Just as Condon ripped the mask off the comforting image of the suburban American family that dominated Cold War culture, so did he peel away the mystique of the self-made man. In such novels as *Some Angry Angel* and *Any God Will Do,* Condon used the traditional form of the rags-to-riches success story, but instead of being inspiring, these narratives are garish nightmares that reveal the emptiness and superficiality of twentieth-century American life. Daniel Tiamat, the protagonist of *Some Angry Angel,* is driven by an overwhelming ambition not to be like his father, an alcoholic and chronically unemployed Irish immigrant. Tiamat rapidly rises through the ranks as a journalist at the *New York Daily Press,* marries the boss's daughter, and lands the coveted position as the paper's gossip columnist, though he is warned, "A gossip column is a deadly weapon in the hands of a primitive conceit like yours."[75]

Quickly Tiamat becomes the most celebrated gossip columnist in the country, building an extensive network of paid and amateur informers. The similarities between this system and the network of anticommunist informers who played such a prominent role in Cold War politics were not lost on Condon, who pointed out that among Tiamat's informers were "some forty-two thousands from the Federal payroll under such droll classifications as information chiefs, press aides, P.R.O. section heads, advisory spokesmen, public education chairmen, and senators. All these federal informers competed for attention with one another and with the White House rumor mill. . . . On every staff there was one man who could get through to Dan in exchange for a few top secrets in the areas of defense, finance, atomic energy, and witch hunts. This was not to be considered treasonable because the items they gave Dan were rarely, if ever, true anyway."[76]

As Tiamat becomes more celebrated, his personal life rapidly disintegrates into a miasma of alcohol and drugs. Beset by constant doubts that he deserves his power, prestige, and wealth, he lets it all slip from his grasp. In rapid succession, he is fired from his prestigious gossip column and made the *Press*'s lonely hearts columnist, Miss Friendship; his wife dies in a freak accident; and he is stricken with polio.[77] As Miss Friendship, Tiamat, like Nathanael West's Miss Lonelyhearts, confronts the lives of quiet desperation that have become the norm in modern America. Embittered by his rapid fall, Tiamat lashes out at his correspondents, daring his first letter writer to commit suicide because of the meaninglessness of her life. When she does so, Tiamat is stunned. After this, he settles into a pattern of offering what solace he can, guided by the writings of Bishop Sheen and Norman Vincent Peale, but the bleakness at the core of modern life, which he is forced to confront daily, wears him down. By the time of his tenth anniversary as Miss Friendship, at a dinner held in his honor, Tiamat can only stand painfully on crutches and say, "All of us, in one voice and with one mind and wish, if the brutality of our living and the shock of it have not snatched our voices and our sanity—all of us, with that one voice—let us curse God together."[78]

Like all of Condon's novels, *Some Angry Angel* has enough plot for five novels by most other writers. In the story of Daniel Tiamat, Condon not only offered a savage satire of the American dream but also an unflinching examination of the narcissism, desperation, and vacuity of American culture. Tiamat encounters this first among the social and cultural elite while working as a gossip columnist. In that position he inhabits a world filled with "some of the highest-seeded bores of [his] generation. . . . They fostered unchanging conversation about one unchanging topic: self."[79] After being transformed into a grotesque—a raging, bitter, wheelchair-bound drunk—Tiamat inhabits a world of other grotesques, offering ersatz solace to his fellow victims "of a stern God whom he imagined looking rather like Bernard Baruch with a beard."[80] America's frenetic celebrity culture cannot mask the desolation and grotesquery at its core. Modern American life has twisted and mutilated what it means to be human, what it means to live in a community. Condon wrote, "The buildings and pavements of New York reflected sheets of heat that wet everything with their heaviness. Thirteen million people were embedded in the heat. Their mass stretched for fifty-five miles in the horizontal directions. They existed in eighty-nine million rectangular rooms where, every evening of every year, an average of sixty-four people hanged themselves because of loneliness. . . . New York had become a city mutated beyond the original meaning of any city into the most ominous meaning of all cities. Within it, living had become a palindrome."[81]

Condon similarly skewered the great American success story in *Any God Will Do*. In the character of Francis Vollmer, he created his vision of the quintessential American—fact-obsessed, technically adept at a wide range of activities but lacking a true affinity for any of them, scheming, paranoid, and totally insane. Having grown up in an orphanage, Vollmer is obsessed with tracing his lineage, convinced he is the illegitimate son of some European royalty. Preparing for his entrance into continental aristocratic society, he memorizes encyclopedias, studies French cooking, and practices his sexual technique until he is extremely accomplished in each field. In none of these areas, however, is his technical prowess matched by an emotional commitment. As one character says, "Everything he has sought to learn has the quality of 'personality.' He can chat about building a bridge, for instance, with statistics and anecdotes about bridges, engineers, steel, rivers and the bridge in literature, dentistry, billiards, and symbolism, but one is at the same time certain that he would not know a bridge if he were crossing one."[82]

Worried about Vollmer's obsession with his parentage, his wife consults the orphanage and discovers that his father had been a dwarf who worked as a circus clown and died in a circus fire. Refusing to believe it, Vollmer sails for Europe to find his true parents, but he becomes increasingly obsessed with a fear that he is being stalked by dwarfs who want to cut him down to a height of eighteen inches. With his wealth of knowledge and skills as cook and lover, Vollmer makes a favorable impression on the upper-class Europeans with whom he comes in contact, though one complains, "He's crashingly unilateral. Everything flows toward self. . . . He suffers from snobbism carried to its ultimate degree, far beyond the we-are-better-than-anyone-on-earth-so-let-us-help-you-or-we-will-kill-you sort of thing which other rich Americans try so hard to project."[83]

Vollmer's paranoid delusions continue to haunt him, and he is driven hopelessly insane, convinced the dwarfs have won. His fear of dwarfs reflects his unconscious realization that he does not deserve the wealth and acclaim that have come to him. He reflects Hofstadter's characterization of the American paranoid: "This enemy seems to be on many counts a projection of the self: both the ideal and the unacceptable aspects of the self are attributed to him."[84] But as one of his aristocratic lovers comments, Vollmer is "among the blessed" because he has a purpose in life, he has something to believe in, which sets him apart from most people. "Everything is getting blander and the world is a wreck and Francis is mad," she says, "but at least he believes in something which should exist: *noblesse,* the obligation to self, to one's own, and his belief has made him a princely man. If he had believed in God with the same fervor, he would be the Archbishop of Canterbury."[85] By the end, Vollmer is reduced to an empty shell, possessing only the empty "personality" skills he has perfected, unable even to recognize those closest to him. "There was no meaning to life," the novel concludes. "One only did the best one could."[86]

A Fairy Princess with Syphilis

Condon is sometimes classified, along with as Pynchon, Vonnegut, Heller, and John Barth, as a black humorist. If Condon's skill as a writer is not quite on a level with theirs, then one should heed Russell Jacoby's warning: "In plotting cultural life often the less original thinkers register most faithfully the zeitgeist."[87] Condon's bleak vision of humans at the mercy of vast, impersonal forces, combined with his penchant for absurdist comedy, reflected Morris Dickstein's description: "Black humor is pitched at the breaking point where moral anguish explodes into a mixture of comedy and terror, where things are so bad you might as well laugh."[88] Condon's surreal conspiracies portrayed a world gone mad, in which sinister forces, from communist brainwashing experts to German SS officers to the mass media, can manipulate individuals at will, and experts work out elaborate scenarios without in the least considering the devastating human costs of these plans. And yet there remains a strongly humanistic core in Condon's vision, an empathy for the grotesque characters who populate his world, from the pathetic outcasts who write Miss Friendship seeking sympathy to Francis Vollmer, whose insane belief in his aristocratic lineage represents modern humanity's desperate attempt to imbue life with some meaning. Like such writers as Vonnegut and Harlan Ellison, and such political movements as the early New Left, Condon fused a belief in the overwhelmingly powerful and potentially destructive modern technological state and a sympathy for that society's outcasts, especially those who resist the dehumanizing tendencies of modern life. But Condon's view is bleaker than Vonnegut's, Ellison's, or the New Left's, for the resistance of his characters is not political (as in Vonnegut's *Player Piano* or Ellison's "'Repent Harlequin!' Said the Ticktockman"),[89] but, like Vollmer's, a further retreat into a solipsistic insanity. In a world that is, to use Condon's description of Manhattan, "rich in facades not unlike the possibilities of a fairy princess with syphilis,"[90] such an alternative is the only one left for people who want to maintain their humanity.

10

Another Dimension

Rod Serling,
Consensus Liberalism,
and *The Twilight Zone*

In 1956 television's hottest playwright, Rod Serling, wrote a teleplay for CBS's *United States Steel Hour* entitled "Noon on Doomsday," based on the notorious lynching of Emmett Till. A fourteen-year-old black Chicagoan, Till had been murdered the previous year while visiting relatives in Mississippi for whistling at a white woman, and his killers were acquitted by an all-white jury. When, while working on his screenplay, Serling told a reporter that his script was based on the Till case, U.S. Steel received hundreds of letters from southerners protesting the planned show. According to Serling, "Since many of the protesting letters and telegrams were from White Citizens Councils, I thought the Steel Company would merely consider the source and leave the production alone. This was not the case. Down went the flag and the biggest corporation in the world put on its own private Appomattox."[1] As he would remember in an interview a few years later, "I wrote the script using black- and white-skinned characters initially, then the black was changed to suggest 'an unnamed foreigner,' the locale was moved from the South to New England—I'm convinced they would have gone to Alaska or the North Pole and used Eskimos except that the costume problem was of sufficient severity not to attempt it. But it became a lukewarm, emasculated, vitiated kind of show."[2] Eventually, even a bottle of

Coca-Cola was excised because it was feared that the soft drink, brewed and bottled in Atlanta, threatened to raise the specter of regionalism.[3]

Two years later, Serling once again sought to portray the Till case in dramatic form with his teleplay "A Town Has Turned to Dust" on CBS's *Playhouse 90*. Serling's script again ran afoul of the show's sponsors. But whereas there had been only a single sponsor for "Noon on Doomsday," with the *Playhouse 90* show at least seven different sponsors were allowed to raise objections and influence the script's final form. To appease the show's advertisers, a network executive issued the following script guidelines:

> 1) In Act 1, completely eliminate fact that earlier killing was colored man. He will have name like "Diego" without specifically labelling him Mexican.
> 2) Modify reason why attack occurred to eliminate whistling at girl connotation. Use simple explanatory line indicating boy had gotten out of line and didn't know his place rather than making a pass at a woman of a different class.
> 3) Entire script to be carefully examined to soften implication Anna and Mexican kid enjoy jumping in the hay together.

Also, in order not to offend any Mexican American groups, all anti-Mexican epithets were eliminated. In Serling's original script, the sheriff commits suicide, but that too was changed because one of the sponsors, Allstate Insurance, objected that suicide led to serious complications in resolving policy claims. Finally, one of the characters needed a name change, because his original name, Clemson, was also that of an all-white southern college.[4]

Serling often complained publicly about such censorship of his work, claiming that craven network executives and advertisers denatured his message, squelching anything that hinted of topicality or controversy. While this plaint was valid, it also oversimplified his experiences as a television playwright. By the time he wrote "Noon on Doomsday," he had four years' experience writing over sixty screenplays for network television and well understood the possibilities and limitations of the medium. Furthermore, as Joel Engel has stated, television actually gave Serling more freedom to deal with controversial topics than he would have been allowed in any other medium with the same potential audience. "Only television," Engel noted, "was willing, albeit reluctantly, to tackle such themes."[5] Finally, in his effort to escape the constant scrutiny of sponsors and network censors, Serling created his fantasy series *The Twilight Zone* (1959–1964), which not only allowed him to broach a host of controversial

issues—such as nuclear war, prejudice, blacklisting, and lynching—in allegorical fashion, but also offered a much more fundamental critique of the
dominant paradigm than had characterized Serling's previous realistic, topical
dramas.

More than any other artist working in the emergent postwar underground culture, Serling consistently confronted power in its most naked form. Whereas
most of the artists under consideration worked in marginal genres, such as pulp
fiction and B-movies, Serling's talents were best suited for what rapidly became
the dominant American mass medium in the postwar era. As a television playwright, he was constantly forced to run the gauntlet of corporate sponsors, who
directly financed the shows and, concerned that no segment of the buying public be alienated, took a close interest in the content of the programs.

The result was a fluid and complex working environment. As a new, rapidly
expanding mass medium focusing in its early years on live drama, television
needed to develop a large pool of talented writers. Throughout the early fifties
it succeeded in this aim, attracting such brilliant young authors as Gore Vidal
("Visit to a Small Planet"), Paddy Chayefsky ("Marty"), Horton Foote ("The
Trip to Bountiful"), Reginald Rose ("Twelve Angry Men"), J. P. Miller ("Days
of Wine and Roses"), William Gibson ("The Miracle Worker"), Serling, and others. But the excitement of so many unknown talents working in a new medium
whose boundaries were still being tested was tempered by the economics of the
process. To finance these programs, the networks needed corporate sponsors,
but to obtain this sponsorship, they had to produce shows the advertisers believed
would not offend potential customers. More than anything else, corporations
demanded an absence of controversy.

Writers were torn between the desire to present compelling and timely plays
and the fear of incurring the wrath of sponsors and network executives. Playwrights reacted in a variety of ways. They usually tended to precensor themselves, avoiding subjects they knew would be unacceptable. Often they concentrated on small-scale stories—personal, realistic dramas that, if they raised
larger sociopolitical concerns, did so only by implication. Such teleplays as
Chayefsky's "Marty," Foote's "The Trip to Bountiful," and Serling's "Requiem
for a Heavyweight" represented this tendency. Some persisted in writing controversial material and fighting the networks and sponsors to maintain the
integrity of their material. What finally appeared in such instances usually were
watered-down versions of the author's original concept, revised to eliminate the
most potentially divisive elements. In Rose's "Thunder on Sycamore Street"

(1954), based on a true incident in which a black family moved into a white neighborhood only to be met by a mob of racist white neighbors, the new family was transformed from black to one in which the father is an ex-convict.[6] In Serling's "The Arena," a story of backdoor maneuvering and infighting in the U.S. Senate, the author was forbidden to mention any current political issues. As he would write in 1957, "So, on the floor of the United States Senate (at least on *Studio One*), I was not permitted to have my senators discuss any current or pressing problem. To talk of tariff was to align oneself with Republicans; to talk of labor was to suggest control by the Democrats. To say a single thing germane to the current political scene was absolutely prohibited. So . . . [the audience was] treated to an incredible display of Senators shouting, gesticulating and talking in hieroglyphics about make-believe issues . . . in a kind of prolonged, unbelievable double-talk."[7]

In addition to corporate censorship, television was subject to the broader fear of political nonconformity that marked Cold War culture as a whole. Late in 1947 *Counterattack: The Newsletter of Facts on Communism* began publishing the names of people in the entertainment industry engaged in communist or what it deemed "communist front" organizations. Three years later, the editors of *Counterattack* published *Red Channels: The Report of Communist Influence in Radio and Television,* a 215-page book listing 151 entertainers—primarily performers, directors, and writers, most of them prominent—whom they accused of being pro-communist. Many careers were ruined by such charges, and everyone in the industry learned the danger of even the appearance of leftist sympathies.[8] For those who forgot, even in unguarded moments, there were forces at work to remind them.[9]

Despite the pressure to avoid controversy, most of the censorship Serling and other television writers faced was not directly political, but typically reflected the logic of consumer capitalism at its most absurd. For instance, in preparing "The Haven" (1953), a story of marital infidelity and incest, author Tad Mosel was informed that the network had some objections to the script. Certain that he would be forced to tone down the "immoral" aspects of his play, Mosel was told, "In the first act there was a reference to an 'old Chevy,' and since this constituted a rather gratuitous plug for Chevrolet, would [you] mind changing it to 'old crate'"?[10] Serling too was frequently forced to rewrite his scripts for the most ridiculous reasons. In his teleplay "The Fateful Pilgrimage," he was told to change the words "American" and "lucky" in dialogue, because the show was sponsored by a cigarette company and these were the names of rival brands.[11]

This practice was widespread throughout the industry. Many of these changes were amusing. In 1953, for instance, *Studio One* changed the title of its adaptation of Rudyard Kipling's "The Light that Failed" to "The Gathering Night" because the sponsor was Westinghouse, which manufactured light bulbs. Others were frightening, such as the American Gas Company forcing the deletion of any mention of Nazi gas chambers in the *Playhouse 90* production of Abby Mann's "Judgment at Nuremberg."[12]

For most of the crop of great early television playwrights, the pressures of the hectic schedule of live television combined with the often absurd interference of corporate sponsors and network executives proved too much, and, by the late fifties, many had left the medium.[13] But Serling's talents were suited almost solely for television. Whereas Foote moved into film, Vidal returned to fiction, and Chayefsky wrote drama and film scripts, Serling eventually tried all these options and failed. Forced to remain in television, he needed to find a way to escape the constantly watchful eyes of the network and sponsors.

Serling's stroke of genius came with his conception of *The Twilight Zone.* By creating a fantasy series, he freed himself from the tyranny of others constantly meddling with his scripts. As his wife Carol remembered, "The TV censors left him alone either because they didn't understand what he was doing or believed that he was truly in outer space."[14] Serling, in other words, was forced to go underground, to raise the issues that interested him through indirection, irony, and paradox. He found he could write the morality plays he wanted if, for instance, he used aliens rather than racial minorities. But in the process of going underground, Serling's critical vision deepened well beyond the liberal pietism of his realistic dramas. In *The Twilight Zone,* he destabilized, deconstructed, and subverted the certainties and eternal verities of the dominant Cold War worldview.

Walking Distance

Serling was born on Christmas Day, 1924, in Syracuse, New York, into a lower-middle-class Jewish family. In 1926, the family moved to Binghamton, New York, where his father ran a meat market. A gregarious and charming child, Serling was always popular and, as an adult, looked back nostalgically on his childhood in Binghamton. This halcyon vision of childhood symbolized a desire to escape the pressures of adulthood in several *Twilight Zone* scripts. In reality, though, Binghamton may not have been as idyllic as Serling remembered. Although the Serlings maintained little of their Jewish cultural heritage and sought to assimilate into the mainstream culture (the family celebrated Christmas, for instance), Serling occasionally fell victim to anti-Semitism. In high school he was both banned from a non-Jewish fraternity and expelled from the Jewish fraternity for dating Gentile girls.

Immediately after graduation, Serling enlisted in the military, volunteering to be a paratrooper. At five feet four inches, he was initially rejected as too short, but through sheer perseverance Serling was assigned to the 511th Parachute Infantry Regiment of the Eleventh Airborne Division. In 1944 Serling's regiment was shipped to the Pacific, landing on the Philippine island of Leyte, where the men spent thirty brutal days marching through jungles and over mountains. During his tour of duty, Serling was wounded in the leg and saw many die as a result of enemy fire. But the death that affected him most deeply was that of his best friend, who was crushed by a crate of supplies air-dropped to the regiment by American planes. Serling's biographer Joel Engel has written, "His strong sense of irony, so essential to his best writing, may have been born at that moment."[15] After Leyte, Serling's regiment made its first jump on February 3, 1945, thirty miles south of Manila, where they engaged in bitter combat. Along with the rest of the 511th, Serling was preparing for an invasion of Japan when the atomic bomb brought the war to an end.

Following his stint in the army, Serling attended Antioch, a small, liberal arts college in Ohio, where he gained invaluable experience as a manager of the campus radio station, eventually creating a weekly dramatic anthology show for which he wrote and directed either an original script or an adaptation. After graduating, he began working for a radio station in Cincinnati, writing a variety of scripts, from documentaries about small towns in the listening area ("In most cases," he remembered, "the towns I was assigned to honor had little to distinguish them save antiquity. Any dramatization beyond the fact that they existed physically, usually had one major industry, a population and a founding date was more fabrication than documentation.")[16] to testimonials for patent medicine commercials and "gimmicks" for the afternoon ladies' program. In the meantime, he was also freelancing television scripts with some success. In 1951 he quit radio and devoted himself full-time to writing for television.[17]

As Engel has pointed out, Serling picked the right medium at the right time. Unlike film or drama, television was desperate for scripts and short of experienced writers. For established movie screenwriters and playwrights, writing for television would have been a major step down (and one that, in the early fifties, was not even financially remunerative), while radio writers had no experience with a visual medium.[18] Television producers were willing to accept scripts from anywhere, even Cincinnati (where Serling remained for several years, even after establishing himself).

Soon the television industry developed a crop of talented, young writers and directors, among them Arthur Penn, John Frankenheimer, George Roy Hill, Sidney Lumet, and Franklin Schaffner. The resultant "Golden Age of Television" placed a heavy emphasis on live anthology shows: in the 1953–1954 season, there were twenty-five such anthology dramas.[19] Because television was in its infancy, many producers encouraged their staffs to experiment and test the boundaries of the medium. Worthington Miner, for instance, of CBS's *Studio One,* created a modern-dress version of "Julius Caesar" (1949) to emphasize the totalitarianism of Mark Anthony.[20] Other shows dealt with controversial topics. Reginald Rose's "The Gathering," made for *Studio One,* showed the effects of an air raid on a family only to reveal in an ironic twist that the characters were Russian and the raid was in Moscow.

But live television worked best in small-scale, realistic dramas with lots of closeups to cover the space limitations in the studios and increase the intimacy of the viewing experience, since people watched these shows alone or in small groups. The most successful example of this type of drama was Chayefsky's "Marty" (1953), a touching story of a thirty-something butcher's love affair with an unattractive woman he meets at a dance. Rod Steiger's brilliant performance, Chayefsky's naturalistic dialogue, and the play's authentic working-class milieu worked together to create a landmark in dramatic television. As Erik Barnouw has pointed out, though, subtle and realistic dramas like "Marty" ran counter to the growing commercial dominance of television. "Most advertisers were selling magic. Their commercials posed the same problems that Chayefsky drama dealt with: people who feared failure in love and in business. But in the commercials there was always a solution as clean-cut as the snap of a finger: the problem could be solved by a new pill, deodorant, toothpaste, shampoo, shaving lotion, hair tonic, car, girdle, coffee, muffin recipe, or floor wax. The solution always had finality. Chayefsky and the other anthology writers took these same problems and made them complicated. . . . All this was often convincing—that was the trouble. It made the commercial seem fraudulent."[21] As the power hierarchy in television quickly solidified, corporate sponsors came to exert more direct pressure on the contents of shows, and the nuanced and complex worldview created by such writers as Chayefsky was gradually squeezed out.

Patterns

Throughout the Golden Age of Television, Serling consistently portrayed a world mirroring the consensus liberal vision. He fully accepted the Cold War view that communism posed the major threat to the world. In his 1952 teleplay "I Lift My Lamp," he told the story of Anna, a refugee from the Communist government of Czechoslovakia who emigrates to the United States. Pursued by her former lover, now a government agent, Anna refuses to return with him. Standing beneath the Statue of Liberty, he defends his decision to join the party, asking, "What could be worse than chaos?" "Communism," she replies.[22] Similarly, in his 1955 teleplay "The Rack," Serling examined the effects of brainwashing on American prisoners of war in Korea. During the court-martial of a soldier accused of collaborating with the enemy, the defense counsel denounces the special cruelty of the Chinese Communists: "We pass laws as just as possible. Because no country can condone treason and exist. But we base these laws on certain truths that we think are permanent. One of the truths is that there's a certain level of morality that all men must recognize. Then we find a group of men who'll threaten and browbeat and mentally torture to get what they want and who don't recognize that morality. And now we find ourselves having to judge a man who committed a crime only because under unusual circumstances he had no benefit of that morality."[23]

This staunch anticommunism continued throughout Serling's *Twilight Zone* scripts of the early sixties. In "The Whole Truth,"[24] a used-car salesman buys an old Model A and discovers, to his astonishment, that whoever owns the car cannot help telling the truth about everything. Beset by this handicap, his successful business rapidly crumbles until, with a flash of brilliance, he sells the car to the world's greatest liar, Nikita Khrushchev. In "The Mirror,"[25] Serling showed the rapidity with which idealistic hope can turn to paranoid terror in his characterization of a Castro-style revolutionary leader of a Central American country.

While Serling reflected the virulent anticommunism of the consensus, he was also outspokenly critical of right-wing Cold Warriors. In one of his first public political acts, Serling wrote a letter to the pro-McCarthy *Cincinnati Enquirer* in March 1954: "For the benefit of all [who support McCarthy], let it be submitted that not all of us who flinch at McCarthy's methods are Communists, or even Communist excusers. Our basic tenet of American justice that recognizes a man's innocence until guilt is proven will be with us long after the fog-horn echoes of the *Enquirer*'s and Joe McCarthy's campaign to delineate people in the Either-Or classification."[26] This view was also expressed in Serling's work. In his *Twilight Zone* script for "The Monsters Are Due on Maple Street,"[27] he criticized the mob mentality and the search for scapegoats that characterized the Cold War era, while in his adaptation of Price Day's short story "Four O'Clock,"[28] he alluded to the blacklist in portraying a fanatic who, intent on using his miraculous power to identify evil people, discovers that he is the evil one. And in his most successful film screenplay, an adaptation of Fletcher Knebel and Charles Bailey's best-seller *Seven Days in May* (1964), Serling portrayed a MacArthur-style general who plots a military coup to overthrow the president because of his opposition to the president's nuclear disarmament treaty with the Soviets.

Within this liberal worldview, Serling sought to uncover the troubling paradoxes of American culture. At the same time, in his pre–*Twilight Zone* scripts he typically sought some acceptable form of closure. For instance, his two powerful war teleplays, "The Strike" and "The Rack," managed to be simultaneously antiwar and proauthority. "The Strike,"[29] a Korean war drama, concerned the inexperienced Major Gaylord, who, because of the exigencies of war, has been put in command of a division of five hundred soldiers retreating from a Chinese offensive. Having sent out a patrol of twenty men on a reconnaissance mission, Gaylord is now forced to call for air support to napalm the area where he believes the patrol to be. Others assure him it is necessary to sacrifice the patrol to save the division, but Gaylord cannot accept this rationalization. As one character explains, command has paralyzed Gaylord by humanizing the war for him. "His job has always been logistics. So many men form this line. So many men go in this column. So many men eat so much and fire this much and can go this far with this number of vehicles. All of a sudden he gets put into a situation where men aren't just numbers. They're flesh and blood. They've got identity. And when you cross 'em off—it isn't just arithmetic anymore." When someone else comments, "The boy is not what you'd call officer material," the first speaker responds, "This boy could be chief of staff—except for a flaw. In times of sanity—it's an attribute. Concern for fellow man. Now it's a flaw."[30] The play ends with Gaylord ordering the air strike and the clear implication that, though regrettable, such sacrifices are necessary in wartime.

"The Rack" was even more staunchly promilitary. As in "The Strike," Serling excelled at dramatizing the moral complexity of the issue. Captain Ed Hall, a decorated veteran, is accused of collaborating with the enemy in a Chinese prisoner camp. Hall's father is a regular army colonel who cannot understand how his son could have committed treason. But as Hall says, "The pat, black-and-white, all-in-order Army. They could never understand what's cowardice in one man is just simple collapse in another. How could they understand? A machine with three million parts. A machine can't understand. How could it?"[31] Hall's lawyer argues that a tribunal removed from the war cannot judge decisions made in the brutal conditions of a POW camp. But the prosecutor says that if Hall is acquitted, "From that second on, no member of an armed force would have any compunctions about dealing with an enemy. We set a precedent that says, if a man must break, he must break—that's all there is to it. And why? Because in that court-martial we excused a man for collaboration and maybe worse. We're not crucifying a man. We're trying to put a little muscle into every other man who may have to face the same things he did."[32] In the end, Hall is convicted. His father forgives him but says, "I think the verdict just." Hall replies, "I think so too now."[33] Serling's message reiterates the quintessentially pro–Cold War theme of Herman Wouk's *The Caine Mutiny*—that the military is one of the few institutions in America that truly works and that, even if unfair, authority must be obeyed.

Serling's penchant for moral ambiguity was further realized in his brilliant teleplay "Patterns,"[34] which concerns the brutal office politics in a major New York corporation. Fred Staples is a young executive brought into the firm by the ruthless and successful CEO, Ramsey. Unbeknownst to Staples, Ramsey intends to use him to squeeze out an older vice president, Andy Sloan. In Ramsey's view, Sloan's business instincts are anachronistic, tempered too strongly by such concerns as how corporate restructuring will affect workers and their families. Staples develops a friendship with Sloan but also inexorably finds himself serving Ramsey's purpose of ruining Sloan. Eventually Sloan dies of a heart attack, and Staples, disgusted with Ramsey, tells him, "It's a tragic renunciation of pride to lick a man's boots. But it's a lot more pitiable to be the man who has to have his boots licked." Just as Serling appeared headed for a clichéd ending, he reversed course. Ramsey refuses to atone for his sin, dismissing Sloan as too weak. He invites Staples to remain with the firm, telling him that only in such a competitive environment will he be able to reach his potential. "I need help on my level," Ramsey says, "and you're the only one good enough to function there. You don't like me. I'm not a 'nice person' in your mind. But you will learn more, grow more, do more with me than anywhere else because I'll beat you ragged until you do. I don't ask to be liked—fight me, take over if you can.

And watch the business grow from your efforts beyond even our dreams."[35] Staples agrees but warns Ramsey to always cover himself to the rear.

"Patterns" simultaneously regrets the passing of an older, more humanized capitalism and celebrates the accomplishments of a newer, vaster, bureaucratized system. Such a jaundiced examination of American business was uncommon in mainstream cultural forms in the postwar era. But Serling made clear that the play was not intended as a criticism of capitalism. Two years after it aired, he wrote, "'Patterns' is a story of power. There is no single character within it who could be considered a prototype of an economic system. I couched it in terms of big business because there is an innate kind of romance in the big, the blustering, the successful. But there is, in the final analysis, nothing Marxist in the message of this play. It is not an indictment of our capitalistic system nor an exposé of the evils of big money."[36] To show his even-handedness, four years later Serling addressed the corruption and abuse of power in the labor movement in "The Rank and File," a story of a Jimmy Hoffa–type union leader.[37]

Though Serling denied any fundamental critique of big business in his work, he was fascinated with the various permutations the success ethic could take. In "Requiem for a Heavyweight" he cast a sympathetic eye on Mountain McClintock, a one-time contender for the heavyweight boxing crown who finds himself washed up at thirty-two, unprepared to do anything else with his life.[38] To Serling, McClintock symbolized the superfluous people in the American social system, cast aside when no longer useful (much like the workers in the plant Sloan pleads with Ramsey not to close down in "Patterns"). McClintock seemingly has little option but to use his former celebrity to get work as a professional wrestler.

In "The Comedian," Serling showed the corrupting nature of power in the story of Sammy Hogarth, a popular television performer who delights in viciously browbeating all those around him.[39] And in the partly autobiographical "The Velvet Alley," Serling used his own experiences to underline the fundamental insecurity of success in the story of a television writer who dumps his long-time agent and moves to California, where he is seduced by the opulent lifestyle.[40] But as one character warns him, "You know how they do it . . . ? They give you a thousand dollars a week and they keep giving it to you until you can't live without it. Then they start to talk about taking it away, and there isn't anything you won't do to keep that thousand dollars a week."

In Search of an Exit

Serling's decision to begin working on his own series in 1959 was widely derided as a sellout. Though all but the willfully blind accepted that the era of live drama was in its dying throes, few serious television writers were willing to accept what was replacing it—the half-hour taped series. Worthington Miner told the Federal Communications Commission in 1960 that series television "really doesn't take much writer to do it, and no self-respecting writer will do it, certainly won't do it over his own name." Chayefsky told the same panel, "No writer who takes himself seriously wants to write the sort of thing that passes for a television series."[41] That same year, Barnouw complained, "The author of 'Requiem for a Heavyweight' now writes formula mysteries of the supernatural and even wins prizes for them, a symptom of the low estate to which television drama has fallen in just a few years."[42]

In defending his decision to begin working on a series, Serling claimed he had grown tired of his constant battles with censors. "I'm tired of fighting the fight," he said in 1959. "It's a fight against advertisers where we can't say certain things. . . . We tilted at the same dragons for seven or eight years and after the smoke cleared the dragons won."[43] But as both Lawrence Venuti and Joel Engel have argued, in retrospect *The Twilight Zone* was a natural outgrowth of Serling's earlier career. During the Golden Age, Venuti has written, Serling perfected the art of telling the truth at a slant, of using indirection in writing his reformist dramas. Serling explained: "From experience I can tell you that the drama—at least in television—must walk on tiptoe and in agony lest it offend some cereal buyers in Mississippi. Hence we find in this mass medium a kind of ritual track-covering in which we attack, quite obliquely, the business of minority problems. The television writer turns his literary guns on certain minority hangups that are allowed. So instead of a Negro, he gives battle against that prejudice visited on American Indians or Alaskan Eskimos or Armenian peasants under the Czar."[44] In *The Twilight Zone,* Serling merely worked a new variation on this track-covering, using fantasy fables to convey his messages. According to Venuti, "He had acquired much experience with this sort of indirection from his numerous confrontations with the censors who often forced him to 'cover the tracks' of his social commentary."[45]

Engel pointed out that Serling had long toyed with the idea of using fantasy elements to mask his social criticism. As early as 1954, he had proposed a science fiction script for *Studio One,* prompting this response from the show's story editor: "NO NO NO NO NO NO NO NO NO NO. Never. Fantasy in any form is out. And irony."[46] Similarly, in discussing the censorship of his political drama "The Arena" in 1957, Serling commented, "In retrospect, I probably would have had a much more adult play had I made it science fiction, put it in the year 2057, and peopled the Senate with robots."[47]

Thematically, Serling had also broached the concept of a world in which basic assumptions are undermined and everyday rules overthrown before *The Twilight Zone.* In "The Strike," he portrayed war as a time of psychic chaos, in which morality is the opposite of what it is in the real world, in which the center cannot hold. Major Gaylord, explaining to a chaplain why the Bible does not provide much comfort in wartime, says, "I suppose it's because order is suddenly turned upside down and we find ourselves without any base. Things we thought were true aren't any more."[48] This type of subversion of everyday assumptions was the basic concept of *The Twilight Zone.*

But the new series did more than change the form of Serling's polemical works; it forced him into a deeper, more fundamental critique of postwar culture, beyond even his own conscious political temperament. In many ways, Serling remained a consensus liberal throughout his career. He was deeply committed to civil rights, writing, for instance, an embarrassingly bad antisegregation novella, "Color Scheme" (1967);[49] a heartfelt plea for tolerance in a letter to the *Los Angeles Times* immediately after Martin Luther King's assassination;[50] and the screenplay to an adaptation of Irving Wallace's bestseller *The Man* (1972), about a black politician accidentally thrust into the office of president of the United States. He publicly opposed the nuclear arms race (joining SANE in the late fifties) and, somewhat belatedly, the war in Vietnam. But he always remained firmly within the American political system, celebrating American-style democracy as the last, best hope in his screenplay for *Seven Days in May.* And in 1964, he also wrote the screenplay for "Let Us Continue," a United States Information Agency documentary for international audiences pleading for a smooth transition of power after the Kennedy assassination.[51]

With *The Twilight Zone,* however, Serling deconstructed the most commonly held assumptions that even he seemed to uphold in other venues. For the basis of the show was, in the words of the Firesign Theater (in a different context), "Everything you know is wrong." If nothing is certain, and all the supposedly immutable laws that we assume govern us can be arbitrarily and capriciously repealed, then the official certainties of the dominant Cold War culture appear much less stable.

The critique of the dominant cultural vision that Serling presented in *The Twilight Zone* differed fundamentally from anything that had been done before on television. The situation in television in the fifties and early sixties was an exaggerated version of the contemporary scene in theater. As drama critic Martin Gottfried wrote in 1967, American theater in the postwar era was split into two separate traditions, with virtually no interaction between the two. Gottfried labeled these traditions right-wing and left-wing, though in his view he was not necessarily using the terms in their political sense, referring instead to the off-stage area, or wing, in a theater.[52] In the postwar United States, according to Gottfried, the right-wing dominated. This wing featured professionalism, commercialism, and straightforward narrative. The right-wing tradition, Gottfried wrote, "means a belief in God, a respect for law, a love of country, a need for order, a sense of family, a concern with appearance, a willingness to be organized, a recognition of the good in social responsibility. It means an interest in melodic music, representational art, story fiction, rhymed poetry. It means an acceptance of the various interdenominational nonsectarian, middle-class values, ranging from the Ten Commandments to the Boy Scout oath."[53] Conversely, the left-wing theater was less professional and commercial and more experimental, less interested in delivering a specific message than in raising more fundamental questions. "For the left wing," Gottfried said, "the theater is a sacred place where great and wonderful things happen. It seeks the what-is-the-point?, the where-am-I-going?, the what-is-my-identity? Childish? Usually. In most cases, the playwright dipping for depth will come up with a handful of warmed-over Kafka leaking through his fingers."[54]

In adapting Gottfried's schematic to Golden Age television, Kenneth Hey has argued that television drama lay entirely within the right wing. "The major conflict in television dramatists' works," he wrote, "revolved less around illusion versus reality and more around tradition versus modernity." This trait showed the marked influence of such right-wing playwrights as Arthur Miller, but commercial considerations forced television writers to adopt a much more upbeat tenor than did those writing for the stage.[55]

In *The Twilight Zone,* Serling moved beyond the moralistic, right-wing concerns of his live dramas and began raising such left-wing issues as "What is real?" and "What is the nature of identity?" Specific reformist messages occasionally did come through, but they were secondary to the central vision of the show—a world steeped in paranoia with humans at the mercy of vast forces beyond their control, a universe marked by absurdity and governed by a strong sense of irony. It was a world both recognizable and frighteningly unfamiliar, and the cumulative effect was a subversion of the dominant cultural assumptions.

The Twilight Zone contains multitudes. It is contradictory and discordant. Alien invaders in the show are, variously, good, bad, and nonexistent; they appear as giants, midgets, two-headed freaks, leather-jacketed hoodlums, and messianic strangers; nostalgia is, at different times, positive, negative, and self-deceptive; death is alternately terrifying and comforting; and conformity is, by turns, humanizing and dehumanizing. Partly these multitudes arose from the show's format. Serling was the chief writer, eventually scripting 92 of the 155 episodes. But as the show's executive producer (and half owner), he was responsible for hiring other writers, and he built up a small coterie of talented authors, especially Richard Matheson and Charles Beaumont. The variety of contributors helped create a range of visions. More fundamentally, though, the contradictory nature of the show heightened the sense of dislocation it created. Because there are no recurring characters (except the narrator, Serling), literally anything can happen, and no one, not even the main character, is safe. In a series, to the contrary, the viewer knows that the main characters will survive, no matter how bleak the outlook.

Though its settings varied—ranging through the past, present, and future, earthly and alien—*The Twilight Zone* is firmly situated in the postwar context. In Beaumont's "The New Exhibit,"[56] the curator of a wax museum featuring a grisly murderers' row explains his decision to close down, saying the "ovens at Dachau have made our horror museum blasé." In Serling's classic episode "To Serve Man,"[57] the narrator explains that such contemporary events as the Berlin crisis and the Algerian war "had lost their horror because we were so accustomed to them." In "No Time Like the Past,"[58] the inventor of a time machine wants to escape the twentieth century. Referring to the presence of Strontium 90 in milk, he says, "We live in a cesspool, a septic tank, a gigantic sewage complex in which runs the dregs, the filth, the misery-laden slop of the race of man. Everything he designs as an art for dying is his excuse for living. We live in an exquisite bedlam, made all the more grotesque by the fact we don't recognize it as insanity."

A strong urban sensibility also runs throughout *The Twilight Zone,* helping locate it in a modern context. As Marc Scott Zicree commented, the show "was the first, and possibly only, TV series to deal on a regular basis with the theme of alienation—particularly urban alienation."[59] Numerous episodes used the chaos of modern urban society as a starting point for exploring questions of paranoia, isolation, and reality. "The Four of Us Are Dying,"[60] for example, begins with a shot of a city street at night. Wild and discordant jazz music, flashing neon lights, and odd camera angles accentuate the alienation and dislocation of modern life in this story of a man who can change his appearance at will, thereby making his own identity problematic. Similarly, Beaumont's "Perchance to Dream"[61] opens with a strangely angled and disconcerting shot of a sky-scraper then switches to a busy sidewalk outside the building, while a sick and haggard man watches the human traffic file by, creating a strong sense of isolation and alienation.

The show used this urban setting in other, equally unsettling ways. In Serling's premiere episode, "Where Is Everybody?"[62] a lone man wanders through a town with all the signs of being inhabited—smoldering cigarettes, ringing telephones, blaring radios—but no one in sight. The overwhelming effect is eerily disturbing as the man's loneliness drives him further and further into insanity. Even more terrifyingly disconcerting is the main character in "Time Enough at Last,"[63] who wanders through a postapocalyptic New York City, absolutely calm and still, in which the magnificent skyline has been reduced to rubble.

Serling frequently placed this urban anomie in the context of work in the modern, corporate economy. "The Brain Center at Whipples"[64] begins with an industrial film for stockholders proclaiming that a new machine will eliminate over sixty thousand jobs and totally automate the factory. When someone protests putting so many people out of work, Whipple responds, "When it comes to progress, you're a foot-dragger." Whipple is undeterred by complaints about the decline of craftsmanship or the fact that, with so many people unemployed, no one will be able to buy his products. In the end, Whipple's automated factory decides he too is superfluous and fires him. In other episodes, the modern office serves as a symbol of conformity, designed to identify and alienate those who are different. Charlie Parks, the main character in "Miniature," is fired by his boss, who explains that an office is a "team or platoon" and that Parks is not a "team player" but a "square peg" who does not "fit in."[65]

Other *Twilight Zone* characters seek to escape the pressures of their jobs by fleeing to some simpler, pre-urban existence. In Serling's short story adaptation of his script "Walking Distance,"[66] the protagonist, Martin Sloan, is a young, successful advertising executive. "He knew panic a dozen times a day—that convulsive, breath-stopping, ice-cube feeling of doubt and indecision; of being second-guessed, of being wrong; the effort to make his voice firm, his decisions sound irrevocable, when deep inside his gut—worse as each day passed—he felt a vague slipping away of all the props he conjured up and took on the stage with him when he faced the president of the agency, the clients, or the other account execs."[67] Sloan magically returns to his hometown, unchanged since his childhood, to find refuge from the oppressiveness of his life. In Serling's "A Stop at Willoughby,"[68] Gart Williams, an advertising executive whose career seems to be crumbling before his eyes, symbolizes the fundamental insecurity of the success ethic. After a brief introduction, in which Williams is publicly berated by his boss for losing a major account, Serling says in his voice-over narration, "This is Gart Williams, age thirty-eight, a man protected by a suit of armor all held together by one bolt. Just a moment ago, someone removed the bolt, and Mr. Williams' protection fell away from him and left him a naked target. He's been cannonaded this afternoon by all the enemies of his life. His insecurity has shelled him, his sensitivity has straddled him with humiliation, his deep-rooted disquiet about his own worth has zeroed in on him, landed on target, and blown him apart." Like Sloan, Williams escapes to the peaceful, non-competitive life of a small, quiet, late–nineteenth-century village.

The Twilight Zone depicts an absurdist universe that in many ways mirrors the vision of such black humorists as Kurt Vonnegut, Richard Condon, and Thomas Pynchon. Several episodes are done as comedies, but they tend to be the less successful shows. But the ironic twists at the end of each story are usually grimly humorous, reflecting a mordant and sardonic worldview. In "Time Enough at Last," for instance, a timid bank clerk who wants nothing more than some time to read is prevented from doing so by his bullying boss and shrewish wife. Hiding in a vault at lunch time to surreptitiously read, he is the lone survivor of a nuclear war. Wandering the ruins of the city, he discovers the library, where many books have been left undamaged. As he finally sits down to read with no interruptions, his glasses fall off and break.

Often the stories are crude existential parables—if not warmed-over Kafka, then at least warmed-over Beckett. In "Where Is Everybody?" a man finds himself existing with no memory and no idea of who or where he is. In "Five Characters in Search of an Exit,"[69] five people, identifiable only by the costumes they wear (clown, hobo, ballet dancer, bagpiper, and soldier), find themselves together in a setting devoid of any distinguishing characteristics except a high wall surrounding them. The ballet dancer says, "Each of us woke up one moment. Here we were in the darkness. . . . No knowledge of who we are. No knowledge of what will be." "We are in hell," the soldier concludes. They work together to escape, only to discover that they are dolls in a metal can at a Girl Scouts' Christmas giveaway, whereupon they are picked up and tossed back into the can.

Other episodes show characters in their own private hells, from which there is no exit. In Beaumont's "Shadow Play,"[70] Adam Grant, a man on death row, tells people they are merely characters in his recurring nightmare. Everything that is happening to him has happened countless times before in slightly different form, he says, and as soon as he wakes up (that is, when he is electrocuted), everyone will cease to exist. Only one reporter believes Grant, and he tries to get the governor to stay the execution, but the call is too late, Grant is executed, and everyone vanishes, only to reappear in a reprise of the opening scene—with some different characters—and pronounce a death sentence on Grant.[71]

As Gordon Sander has pointed out, Serling's live drama often involved individuals faced with large, impersonal forces beyond their control. In "Patterns" and "Requiem for a Heavyweight," the characters are at the mercy not so much of evil individuals, but of economic forces, while in "The Strike" and "The Rack," individuals are powerless when confronted by military/bureaucratic imperatives.[72] With *The Twilight Zone,* Serling made this theme more explicit. The tendency to view humans as victims of vast and impersonal powers was also a common theme for literary black humorists. Like Condon's world, Serling's is marked by extreme paranoia, which, at one level, reflects the official paranoia of Cold War mentality. But Serling's vision also worked at a deeper level, the reductio ad absurdum of the dominant ideology, in which everything—animate and inanimate, earthly and extraterrestrial—can conspire against someone. In "To Serve Man," giant aliens come to Earth preaching peace. These advanced beings end world hunger by irrigating deserts and render war obsolete by setting up protective force fields around countries. When Chambers, a U.S. government cryptographer, deciphers the title of a book left at the United Nations building by an alien as *To Serve Man,* he remarks, "I call that a reasonably optimistic sentiment." Humans quickly settle into a comfortable complacency and begin signing up in droves to travel to the aliens' planet. Only too late does Chambers discover that *To Serve Man* is a cookbook. Conversely, people might be convinced there is a conspiracy when there is none (or, at least, not the one they imagine). In "The Monsters Are Due on Maple Street,"[73] the neighbors on a quiet suburban street quickly transform themselves into a howling mob when, after an unexplained power outage, they become convinced someone in the neighborhood is an alien.[74]

Characters in *The Twilight Zone* also fight a never-ending battle against a conspiracy of machines and technology. In "You Drive,"[75] a hit-and-run driver's car continues to haunt him until it literally drives him to the police station. In the haunting "Living Doll,"[76] a child's talking doll designed to say "I love you" says instead to the girl's stepfather (when no one else is around), "I hate you." The stepfather tries to destroy the doll, but in the dark the doll trips the man, who falls down the stairs and breaks his neck. Lying at the foot of the stairs beside the dead man, the doll says to the girl's mother, "You'd better be nice to me."[77]

As science fiction, much of *The Twilight Zone* is not very good.[78] According to Engel, Serling always recognized he was a latecomer to science fiction and felt insecure in the presence of such masters of the genre as Matheson, Beaumont, and Ray Bradbury.[79] Nevertheless, Serling dealt with issues normally associated with such avant-garde science fiction authors as Philip Dick. Like Dick, Serling frequently asked the question, "What is real?" and hypothesized the existence of alternative realities. In Serling's "Mirror Image,"[80] Millicent Barnes, a young woman traveling alone, waits at a bus station at night where she is told by everyone that she has done things she knows she has not done. When she looks in a mirror, Barnes sees herself sitting on the far side of the station. She wonders if there are "different planes of existence . . . parallel worlds that exist side by side." Each person has a counterpart in the other world who sometimes, by a fluke, enters this world and, to survive, must take over its alter ego. A kindly man tries to help her by calling the police, who take her to a mental hospital, but the viewer knows Barnes is not mad and that, by taking her away, the authorities have allowed her counterpart to take her place.[81] Both Serling and Dick utilized this concept to articulate a radical critique of the dominant paradigm. According to Dick's biographer Lawrence Sutin, Dick believed that "things are not as they seem, but those in power are anxious to dispense with questions."[82] In Serling's world, too, those with power—police, physicians, politicians, academics, adults, the military—are quick to put a clamp on the imagination, fearing the destabilizing effect it can have on their power. A particularly malevolent example of the subversive power of imagination over authority occurs in "It's a Good Life,"[83] in which a six-year-old boy, with the power to make his desires reality, terrifies the adults in his community by destroying them, turning one into a giant jack-in-the-box and generally wreaking havoc on all who refuse to do his bidding.

The Velvet Alley

After *The Twilight Zone*'s cancellation, Serling never regained the form that had made him the best in his profession. Between 1964 and his death in 1975, his artistic and commercial successes were few and far between. To maintain the style of living he had grown accustomed to, he was reduced to shilling Anacin, Crest, Echo Floor Wax, and other goods and hosting a television game show, *Rod Serling's Liar's Club.* The image of the outspoken critic of television commercialism becoming the medium's most recognizable commercial spokesman seemed an irony right out of *The Twilight Zone.*

Partly Serling's eventual failure was personal, the result of burnout from the exhausting pace he had maintained since entering television in 1951. But the failure was also partly a result of the industry's domestication of the fantasy genre. *The Twilight Zone* first convinced the networks that science fiction and fantasy shows could work in formats other than children's shows. After Serling's success, though, the networks created several new fantasy programs, from *The Outer Limits* to *The Sixth Sense.* With few exceptions, these shows were formulaic horror stories, less interested in thought-provoking, quality scripts than in simple shock value. Most disturbing of all was *Rod Serling's Night Gallery* (1970–1972), a show that banked on Serling's name and used him as narrator but lacked the intelligence of *The Twilight Zone.* Unlike the earlier series, Serling had no part in the production of *Night Gallery* and no say in the selection of scripts. Before long, Serling's own scripts were being passed over for those with more violence and horror. By all accounts it was Serling's worst professional experience.[84] The television industry had finally succeeded in eviscerating one of its most creative geniuses.

Conclusion

The Emancipation of Dissonance

One prominent history of the period 1945–1960 is subtitled "The Years of Confidence." Another study of the forties is called *The Age of Doubt*.[1] As these titles indicate, Americans in the postwar era experienced a dual consciousness, in which the outward optimism and certainty with which they encountered the threat of international communism and the bounty of their consumer culture were based on cultural repression of fundamental tensions and anxieties. Part of the difference in the books' titles is also a result of their slightly different periodization. Through the fifties there occurred a concerted effort to drive dissenting voices, which had marked the period immediately after World War II, out of the realm of public discourse and assert a more affirmative and certain worldview. As the existence of the underground culture shows, such doubts persisted and, when denied access to mainstream channels of debate, found voice in less traditional, more culturally disreputable forms.

To state the obvious, our view of culture and intellectual life is given depth, complexity, and context if we look beneath the dominant, elite culture. To understand postwar culture, for instance, it is necessary to look beyond the "New York intellectuals." Elite critics do play a major role in the nation's intellectual life, but their ideas filter into public debate indirectly, and frequently that indirection and mediation drastically change their meaning. By reconstructing the broader cultural milieu, the twisted and often tortuous paths of intellectual influence emerge. Ideas from elite critics enter the public discourse, where they are interpreted (or misinterpreted) by others, who may have somewhat different agendas.

Artists in the underground culture played off dominant cultural ideas and images but frequently provided them with new and ironic twists. Patricia Highsmith used the era's official homophobia as a point of reference against which to discuss the nature of American masculinity. Richard Condon played off liberal intellectuals' concerns over the "paranoid style in American politics" but turned the concept against itself by claiming that the style is not peculiar to conservatives but inhabits the political mainstream. Chester Himes worked fascinating variations on the Cold War emphasis on racial integration by arguing that the absurdity of racism had perverted the American character—both black and white—making integration problematic. Several artists in the underground culture shared the concerns of the elite critics, especially regarding the effects of mass culture. Ray Bradbury and Charles Beaumont, for instance, warned that postwar America's hunger for physical pleasure and happy consciousness threatened to extirpate people's ability to think critically and quash social and political deviance, leading to new forms of totalitarianism. This view reflected the opinions of such intellectuals as Dwight Macdonald and Clement Greenberg. But Bradbury and Beaumont made their criticisms in some of the most debased cultural forms—science fiction and fantasy writing for paperbacks and pulp magazines. In using such vehicles to attack the effects of mass culture, underground artists transformed the nature of the criticism, giving it a thick layer of irony.

The influence of elite critics and intellectuals, then, is not a simple trickle-down process in which high-culture ideas filter into the mainstream in unadulterated form. Public discourse is contested, and such ideas are often refuted, undermined, or given new wrinkles and interpretations. Neither should the movement of ideas be viewed as going in only one direction. Ideas sometimes appear first—or at least are encountered first by an audience—in popular forms before being formulated into an intellectually coherent theory. Many people in the postwar period who read *Fahrenheit 451* as teens may have read *One-Dimensional Man* as graduate students and felt a glimmer of recognition that they had encountered these concepts before. To a large extent, then, the underground culture worked at the level of what Raymond Williams called a "structure of feeling," a constellation of attitudes and experiences just beneath the level of conscious awareness.

In the power struggles that marked the immediate postwar period, critical political and cultural voices were gradually either integrated into the consensus or ostracized from the realm of public debate. An official policy of suppression of political radicalism triumphed in such forms as the Taft-Hartley Act, the activities of HUAC, and the ascendancy of Joseph McCarthy. Accompanying and reinforcing this attack on political deviance was an official policy of suppression of various forms of cultural deviance, such as congressional investigations of the effects of comic books on children or the security risks posed by homosexuals in government. Even more fundamentally, the binary oppositions marking the official Cold War paradigm—between, for instance, communism and democracy, good and evil, totalitarianism and freedom—drove out of public discourse darker and more morally ambiguous visions, such as film noir. At the same time, the dominant culture worked to incorporate many previously dissenting voices. Modernist authors like John Dos Passos vigorously defended the status quo, while modernist artists like Jackson Pollack sold their critical birthright for the pottage of recognition as a symbol of Western freedom.

By the early fifties, political and cultural dissent had been largely "contained," or at least so most people thought. In fact, this dissent had merely been transformed. While in the face of official suppression many people learned to censor themselves, artists in the underground culture learned to speak through indirection. To make palatable his criticism of American imperialism, for example, Ray Bradbury had to articulate it in the form of a fantasy story about the colonization of Mars. Similarly, Charles Beaumont wrote his brilliant attack on Western imperialism and ethnocentrism, "The Jungle," as a futuristic fantasy. Jim Thompson disguised his attacks on the devastating effects of American capitalism on society's marginal people behind the mask of a series of crime thrillers. And in an artist like Rod Serling, we can see the process by which dissent was driven underground. Serling set out to confront directly the political issues of the day with his early realistic morality tales. In doing so, he kept encountering the power of the dominant culture, which was determined to stifle controversy and dissent. Driven to the point of distraction, Serling finally created his fantasy series, *The Twilight Zone,* which raised the issues of nuclear war, racism, blacklisting, and the dehumanizing nature of modern work through allegory and parable, transforming, for instance, minority groups into aliens. In this way, Serling not only escaped the wrath of television's official censors but actually deepened the nature of his critique of postwar culture as he advanced beyond the liberal reformism of his earlier work to pose such fundamental questions as "What is truth?" and "What is the nature of reality?"

Modernism in the Streets

In an oft-quoted comment, Lionel Trilling once characterized the political and cultural upheavals of the sixties as "modernism in the streets."[2] The underground culture helps explain the path of modernism from academic halls and museum walls to the street. Modernism had arisen in the early twentieth century as a revolt against the dichotomous paradigm of the earlier Victorian culture. Whereas in the dominant nineteenth-century view the world could be seen in terms of such polar opposites as civilization and primitivism, rationality and irrationality, consciousness and unconsciousness, and morality and immorality, modernism worked to break down such dichotomies. Fueled by changing paradigms in such fields as psychology, anthropology, and physics, modernism placed such concepts as civilization and primitivism on a continuum and, furthermore, refused to grant the former greater legitimacy. In such works as Picasso's African motifs, Stravinsky's *Rite of Spring,* and the jazz of African Americans, modernist artists sought to integrate primitive elements into their work. In its earliest forms, then, modernism, by definition, contained a strong critical impulse as it attacked the binary oppositions on which the dominant culture was built.[3]

By the postwar period, modernism had lost much of its critical element. It had been canonized and turned into a weapon of the Cold War, used to give intellectual support to the rigid dichotomies of the official culture. At the same time, defenders of modernism like Macdonald and Harold Rosenberg advocated erecting walls around canonized modernism to prevent its contamination by popular culture. Thus modernism—or at least the dominant strain of it—in Andreas Huyssen's words, "was no longer felt to be an adversary culture. It no longer opposed a dominant class and its worldview, nor had it maintained its programmatic purity from contamination by the culture industry." Modernism, in other words, had succeeded too well and had "been perverted into a form of affirmative culture."[4]

The critical impulse that originally marked modernism, but which had been largely lost by the postwar period, was maintained and even extended by artists in the underground culture. As Daniel Joseph Singal said, "In its ideal form at least, Modernism . . . eschews innocence and demands instead to know 'reality' in all its depth and complexity, no matter how painful."[5] In the postwar period, the canonized, pro-West, high modernism increasingly failed to raise such questions. But working at a different level, the underground culture did not. It plumbed the depths of the fundamental contradiction of the dominant liberal consensus, which Irving Howe had raised in his contribution to *Partisan Review*'s "Our Country and Our Culture" symposium: how can the modest reform program advocated by liberal intellectuals be adequate to deal with a world marked by chaos, anxiety, and absurdity, whose most effective chronicler was Kafka? On occasion, artists in the underground culture like Serling, Bradbury, and Beaumont would create liberal morality tales. But more fundamentally, the underground culture stressed the unsettling, ambiguous, Kafkaesque nature of society, making clear the inadequacy of liberal reformism.

Avant-Garde

While artists in the underground culture tended to look with suspicion at the effects of mass culture, unlike such traditional intellectuals as Macdonald and Greenberg, they did not hearken back to some unadulterated high culture as an ideal type. Rather they looked to earlier popular-culture forms as a model. Often this attitude was suffused with nostalgic sentimentalism, but it also contained a telling critique of postwar popular culture. Charles Beaumont confronted this issue most directly in his collection of essays, *Remember? Remember?* in which he celebrated earlier forms of popular culture as more authentic and exuberant, less homogenized and sterile, than in the postwar era.[6] The older entertainments, from movie serials and pulp magazines to amusement parks, may have been generally awful, but at least they expressed something of the creator's sensibility. The mass-produced culture of the postwar period, on the other hand, was safe and predictable, routinized, and devoid of personality. This impulse partly explained Beaumont's fascination with jazz and its emphasis on improvisation. Unable to be replicated, jazz stands against the commodification of culture. It must be experienced as it happens, and the process of creation is directly connected to the product created. Many of the artists working in the underground culture sought to create their own equivalents of jazz. Thompson churned out his pulp novels in ten days, while Bradbury tried to write a story a week. Corman seemingly improvised entire films and set nearly impossible shooting schedules, while Fuller built improvisation into the making of his movies through such tactics as rearranging the set just before filming or shooting ten-minute, single-take tracking shots. For Serling, the chaos of live television placed a premium on improvisation and adaptability, while the experience of shooting a series (in the days when there were thirty-six episodes in a season) was hardly any less hectic. Thus the underground critique did not focus only on the quality of the dominant culture, but also on the manner in which it was produced.

Underground artists specialized in breaking down barriers between high and popular culture. Roger Corman included homages to European cinematic masters in his tawdry B-movies, while Samuel Fuller referred to Shakespeare, Baudelaire, and Beethoven in his lurid melodramas. Charles Willeford's psychopathic narrators constantly read Eliot, Joyce, or Kafka or listen to Mussorgsky or Tchaikovsky. This radical juxtaposition served a variety of purposes: it deconstructed the belief in the civilizing influence of high culture by placing it in context of a violent, amoral, chaotic universe; it reestablished links between elite and mass culture that many intellectuals wanted to sever permanently; and it allowed a running inside joke for audiences as they sought to catch all the references. In other ways, underground artists created pastiches of intertextual references. Fuller's and Corman's films often drew inspiration from a wide variety of cultural sources: comic books, tabloid journalism, television sitcoms, other films, and Brechtian theater. Similarly, Condon's novels were often parodies of popular genres, such as spy thrillers and westerns. Artists in the underground culture culled their ideas and language directly from the rhythms of everyday life, from Corman's exploitation movies, to Condon's story ideas, taken from the front pages of newspapers, to Thompson's and Himes's intimate knowledge of the daily existence of their marginal subjects. The underground culture used as its subject the found material and cultural detritus of postwar American culture.

In keeping the critical impetus of modernism alive by transforming it into popular-cultural forms (and drawing inspiration from other popular-cultural forms), the underground culture pioneered in a new sensibility that would later come to be labeled "postmodernism."[7] A cultural style that has emerged since the early sixties, postmodernism ("a buzz word," as J. Hoberman has put it, "which, to put it mildly, has no fixed meaning")[8] involves the breaking down of traditional distinctions between high and popular culture, a pastiche of cultural references emphasizing radical juxtapositions, and an attitude of (somewhat detached) irony on the part of the viewer. Critics like Fredric Jameson have argued that postmodernism represented a dramatic break with modernism.[9] But in looking at the underground culture, one can see the process by which modernism was transformed into postmodernism. As the dominant strain of modernism increasingly assumed quasi-official status in the postwar period, artists working in popular forms, who were beneath the notice of serious intellectuals (except as they fell under the general heading of mass culture), found themselves freer to maintain a critical stance vis-à-vis the Cold War state. Self-consciously working the terrain between the critical spirit of prewar modernism and the intellectually disreputable popular culture, underground artists delighted in deconstructing the most fundamental beliefs on which the postwar consensus was founded, from the United States' fitness to lead the postwar world to the benevolence of American capitalism and the sanctity of the suburban family.

Prediction

Historian John Patrick Diggins has commented that "the New Left [of the sixties] was one of the great political surprises of the mid-twentieth century."[10] Coming out of a seemingly staid, conservative, conformist era, the movement appeared to lack direct political antecedents. The underground culture helps explain the sudden emergence of political dissent in the sixties. This culture had been marked by a vaguely leftist sensibility, proffering at various times critiques of capitalism and the modern culture of work, imperialism and Americans' view of themselves as world leaders, the family, mass culture, and race relations. But overall, the emergent culture had not really possessed any well-defined political vision. Underground artists, though, had developed an alternative paradigm built on such concepts as irony, absurdity, satire, authenticity, and a dark existentialism, which would reverberate through the sixties in such forms as the movie *Dr. Strangelove;* the song "Alice's Restaurant"; the student movement at the University of Texas, leading a fight to integrate toilet facilities under the slogan "Let my people go"; or Jerry Rubin's 1966 appearance before HUAC in the costume of a revolutionary war soldier.[11] The underground culture pioneered in the antipolitical politics and anti-ideological ideology that would characterize the New Left, marking it as different from previous political systems of thought and more appropriate to the nature of American politics in the sixties. Such an absurdist worldview was ideal for creating opposition to the Vietnam war, much more so than any standard Marxist critique, because, as Dwight Macdonald stated, "It's hard to fit Vietnam into Marxist—or any rational—categories."[12]

The politicization of the underground culture in the sixties opened up the left by freeing it from the rigid dogmas of traditional Marxism. But this new, anti-ideological radicalism presented a variety of new problems that reverberate down to the present. In the first place, a vision based on absurdity works better for those on the inside than those on the outside. People who are part of a system have the luxury of being able to view it as meaningless and ridiculous, but those fighting for inclusion are less able to see the object of their struggle as absurd. For instance, whites working in the civil rights movement often entered with entirely different assumptions than blacks, and the eventual racial split partly developed out of these different paradigms. For this reason there were relatively few minority artists working in the underground culture. Second, though most underground artists sought to maintain a fundamental core of humanism, in their dark pessimism there always existed the temptation to slide into nihilism. In the same way, as the official violence of the state increased in the late sixties, some New Leftists responded by escaping into a violent and paranoid nihilism, an apocalyptic act of self-destruction worthy of a Jim Thompson or Chester Himes character (Himes, in fact, wrote about just such a character in his short story "Prediction").[13]

Finally, just as modernism was incorporated into the postwar consensus, so the underground culture in its postmodern form has been integrated into the post-Vietnam dominant culture and its critical element largely eviscerated. Whereas, for instance, directors like Samuel Fuller and Roger Corman formed pastiches of cultural references to subvert Hollywood formulas and undermine dominant cultural assumptions, a new generation of filmmakers, led by Stephen Spielberg and George Lucas, use similar tactics to create a seamless and harmonious universe.[14] At the same time, underground artists like Thompson, Himes, and Fuller have been "rediscovered" and elevated to postmodern canonical status. In the process, though, they have been divorced from their historical contexts and the social and cultural struggles that formed them.

Notes

Preface: Mapping the Underground Culture

1. Manny Farber, "Underground Films," in *Negative Space: Manny Farber on the Movies* (New York: Praeger, 1971), 14.
2. Farber, 16.
3. Farber, 17.
4. Dwight Macdonald, "Masscult and Midcult," in *Against the American Grain: Essays on the Effects of Mass Culture* (New York: Da Capo, 1983 [1962]), 6.
5. Like Farber, I use "underground culture" to refer to artists working in culturally disreputable genres and media forms, producing work that offered a darker, more critical vision than was common in the dominant culture, not to the self-consciously avant-garde, experimental art of such people as Stan Brakhage, Jonas Mekas, William S. Burroughs, or Yoko Ono.
6. These artists are certainly not the only ones whose work illustrates the emergence of the underground culture. Philip K. Dick, Ursula LeGuin, Theodore Sturgeon, Roger Zelazny, Harlan Ellison, Richard Matheson, David Goodis, Peter Rabe, John D. MacDonald, Ross Macdonald, Edgar Ulmer, and Robert Aldrich, to name a few, would probably work equally well.
7. Lionel Trilling, *The Liberal Imagination: Essays on Literature and Society* (Garden City, N.Y.: Anchor, 1950), 7.

Introduction: Within the Shell of the Old

1. Editorial comment, "Our Country and Our Culture," *Partisan Review* 19, no. 3 (May–June 1952): 284–85.
2. Sidney Hook, "Our Country and Our Culture," *Partisan Review* 19, no. 5 (September–October 1952): 574.
3. On the variety of alternatives to the dominant Cold War policies, see Thomas Paterson, "Resisting Exaggerations of the Threat: Critics of the Early Cold War," in *Meeting the Communist Threat* (New York: Oxford University Press, 1988), 95–113; and the essays in *Cold War Critics: Alternatives to American Foreign Policy in the Truman Years,* ed. Thomas Paterson (Chicago: Quadrangle, 1971).
4. George Lipsitz, *Rainbow at Midnight: Labor and Culture in the 1940s* (Urbana: University of Illinois Press, 1994).
5. William Graebner, *The Age of Doubt: American Thought and Culture in the 1940s* (Boston: Twayne, 1991), 19.
6. Cited in Stephen Whitfield, *The Culture of the Cold War* (Baltimore: Johns Hopkins University Press, 1990), 129–31.
7. A few films noirs were made after the early fifties, though they were usually directed by such self-consciously independent auteurs as Robert Aldrich (e.g., *Kiss Me Deadly,* 1955) and Orson Welles (e.g., *Touch of Evil,* 1957). On film noir, see Lipsitz, *Rainbow at Midnight,* 279–302; and Alain Silver and Elizabeth Ward, eds., *Film Noir: An Encyclopedia Reference to the American Style,* 3d ed. (Woodstock, N.Y.: Overlook Press, 1992).
8. Arthur Schlesinger Jr., *The Vital Center: The Politics of Freedom* (Boston: Houghton Mifflin, 1949), 39.
9. The ad is reprinted in its entirety in Victor Navasky, *Naming Names* (New York: Viking, 1980), 204–6.
10. Dwight Macdonald, "I Choose the West," in *Memoirs of a Revolutionist: Essays in Political Criticism* (New York: Farrar, Strauss and Cudahy, 1957), 198.
11. On Rosenberg, see J. Hoberman, "Harold Rosenberg's Magic Act," in *Vulgar Modernism: Writings on Movies and Other Media* (Philadelphia: Temple University Press, 1991), 107–20.
12. John Steinbeck, *East of Eden* (New York: Penguin, 1952), 171–72.
13. Serge Guilbaut, *How New York Stole the Idea of Modern Art: Abstract Expressionism, Freedom, and the Cold War* (Chicago: University of Chicago Press, 1983).
14. Frances K. Pohl, *Ben Shahn: New Deal Artist in a Cold War Climate, 1947–1954* (Austin: University of Texas Press, 1989).
15. In a series of 1949 speeches and articles, one of the leading conservative opponents of modern art, Representative George Dondero, a Michigan Republican, claimed modernism was part of a communist plot to undermine American values in the following ways: "Cubism aims to destroy by designed disorder. Futurism

aims to destroy by the machine myth. . . . Dadaism aims to destroy by ridicule. Expressionism aims to destroy by aping the primitive and insane. Abstractionism aims to destroy by the creation of brainstorms. Surrealism aims to destroy by the denial of reason" (quoted in Pohl, 75; see also 72–77 passim).

16. Godfrey Hodgson, *America in Our Time* (New York: Vintage, 1976), 12, 76.

17. See, for instance, Lionel Trilling, "Reality in America," in *The Liberal Imagination: Essays on Literature and Society* (Garden City, N.Y.: Anchor, 1950), 1–19.

18. Max Lerner, "Our Country and Our Culture," *Partisan Review* 19, no. 5 (September–October 1952): 583.

19. Schlesinger, *Vital Center,* 150–53.

20. Daniel Boorstin, *The Genius of American Politics* (Chicago: University of Chicago Press, 1953).

21. Eric Hoffer, *The True Believer* (New York: Harper and Row, 1951).

22. Schlesinger, *Vital Center,* 56.

23. Graebner, *Age of Doubt,* 69.

24. Henry Steele Commager, *The American Mind* (New York: Bantam, 1950).

25. See, for example, Richard Hofstadter, *The American Political Tradition* (New York: Vintage, 1948); Louis Hartz, *The Liberal Tradition in America: An Interpretation of American Political Thought since the Revolution* (New York: Harcourt, Brace, 1955); and Boorstin, *Genius.*

26. See, for example, Henry Nash Smith, *Virgin Land: The American West as Symbol and Myth* (New York: Vintage, 1950); R. W. B. Lewis, *The American Adam: Innocence, Tragedy, and Tradition in the Nineteenth Century* (Chicago: University of Chicago Press, 1955); and Leo Marx, *The Machine in the Garden: Technology and the Pastoral Ideal in America* (New York: Oxford University Press, 1964).

27. Schlesinger, *Vital Center,* 52, 57.

28. Irving Howe, "Our Country and Our Culture," *Partisan Review* 19, no. 5 (September–October 1952): 580.

29. Daniel Bell, "America as a Mass Society," in *The End of Ideology* (New York: Free Press, 1962), 34.

30. David Manning White, "Mass Culture in America: Another Point of View," in *Mass Culture: The Popular Arts in America,* ed. Bernard Rosenberg and David Manning White (New York: Free Press, 1957), 13–21.

31. Clement Greenberg, "Avant-Garde and Kitsch," reprinted in Rosenberg and White, 98–107, quoted on 102.

32. Greenberg, 105.

33. Bernard Rosenberg, "Mass Culture in America," in Rosenberg and White, *Mass Culture,* 9.

34. Jacques Barzun, "Our Country and Our Culture," *Partisan Review* 19, no. 4 (July–August 1952): 428.

35. Irving Howe, "Notes on Mass Culture," in Rosenberg and White, *Mass Culture,* 497.

36. Leo Lowenthal, "Historical Perspectives of Popular Culture," in Rosenberg and White, *Mass Culture,* 55.

37. Dwight Macdonald, "Masscult and Midcult," in *Against the American Grain: Essays on the Effects of Mass Culture* (New York: Da Capo, 1983 [1962]), 4.

38. Macdonald, "Masscult," 12–13.

39. Andrew Ross, "Containing Culture in the Cold War," in *No Respect: Intellectuals and Popular Culture* (New York: Routledge, 1989), 42–64.

40. Harold Rosenberg, "Pop Culture and Kitsch Criticism," *Dissent* 5, no. 4 (winter 1958): 16.

41. Clement Greenberg, "The Plight of Our Culture," *Commentary,* June 1953, 564.

42. Macdonald, "Masscult," 3–75, especially 37, 47.

43. Greenberg, "Plight of Our Culture," 566.

44. Howe, "Our Country and Our Culture," 578.

45. Macdonald, "Masscult," 61.

46. Macdonald, "Masscult," 50.

47. Macdonald, "Masscult," 57.

48. Clement Greenberg, "Work and Leisure under Industrialism," *Commentary* 16 (July 1953): 55.

49. Norman Mailer, "The White Negro," in *Advertisements for Myself* (New York: G. P. Putnam's Sons, 1959), 311–31.

50. James Gilbert, *A Cycle of Outrage: America's Reaction to the Juvenile Delinquent in the 1950s* (New York: Oxford University Press, 1986), 94–97.

51. Frederick Wertham, *Seduction of the Innocent* (New York: Rinehart, 1954), 15.

52. C. Wright Mills, "Nothing to Laugh At," *New York Times Book Review,* April 25, 1954, 20.

53. Gilbert, *Cycle of Outrage,* 101.

54. William W. Savage Jr., *Comic Books and America, 1945–1954* (Norman: University of Oklahoma Press, 1990), 95–103.

55. Wertham, *Seduction,* 95.

56. Savage, *Comic Books,* 99–100; Frank Jacobs, *The Mad World of William Gaines* (Secaucus, N.J.: Lyle Stuart, 1972), 99–115. Entertaining Comics was ruined by the establishment of the Comic Code Authority, but Gaines recouped his fortune by changing his comic *Mad* into a magazine (and thereby escaping the CCA's authority). He discovered among American youth a much greater appreciation of satire than in the dominant culture.

57. Gilbert, *Cycle of Outrage,* 93.

58. Gilbert, 109.

59. Quoted in Nat Hentoff, *Free Speech for Me, but Not for Thee: How the Left and Right Relentlessly Censor Each Other* (New York: Harper Collins, 1992), 5–6.

60. On Bruce's legal troubles, see Hentoff, 315–35.

61. Geoffrey O'Brien, *Hardboiled America: Lurid Paperbacks and the Masters of Noir* (New York: Da Capo, 1997), 16.

62. Macdonald, "Masscult and Midcult," 49.

63. Paul Fussell, *Wartime: Understanding and Behavior during the Second World War* (New York: Oxford University Press, 1989), 83.

64. Raymond Williams, *Marxism and Literature* (New York: Oxford University Press, 1977), 128–35, quoted on 130.

Chapter 1: Jim Thompson's Theology of Absurdity

1. Jim Thompson, *Texas by the Tail* (New York: Vintage, 1965), 169–74.

2. Jim Thompson, *Bad Boy* (New York: Mysterious Press, 1953), 122–23.

3. Thompson, 204.

4. Quoted in Robert Polito, *Savage Art: A Biography of Jim Thompson* (New York: Vintage, 1995), 211.

5. On this period of Thompson's life, see Polito, 201–68; and Michael McCauley, *Jim Thompson: Sleep with the Devil* (New York: Mysterious Press, 1991), 48–83.

6. Jim Thompson, *Now and on Earth* (New York: Vintage, 1942), 140–41.

7. Thompson, 26–27.

8. For a complete bibliography of Thompson's work, see McCauley, *Jim Thompson,* 309–15.

9. This material is drawn from the biographies by Polito and McCauley.

10. Geoffrey O'Brien, "Afterword," in Jim Thompson, *After Dark, My Sweet* (Berkeley, Calif.: Black Lizard Press, 1955), unpaginated. O'Brien's afterword was copyrighted in 1985.

11. Lawrence Block, "A Tale of Pulp and Passion: The Jim Thompson Revival," *New York Times Book Review,* October 14, 1990, 37–38; Geoffrey O'Brien, untitled review of several Thompson novels, *Voice Literary Supplement,* February 1982, 19; Meredith Brody, "Killer Instinct: Jim Thompson," *Film Comment* 20, no. 5 (September/October 1984): 46–47; David Thomson, "The Whole Hell Catalogue," *New Republic,* April 15, 1985, 37–41; Malcolm Jones Jr., "Furtive Pleasures from a Pulp Master," *Time,* February 4, 1991, 71; Peter Prescott, "The Cirrhosis of the Soul," *Newsweek,* November 17, 1986, 90.

12. Block, "Tale of Pulp," 38.

13. Quoted in Jones, "Furtive Pleasures," 71. Westlake wrote the screenplay to the 1991 film version of *The Grifters.*

14. Jim Thompson, *The Criminal* (New York: Vintage, 1953), 59.

15. Jim Thompson, "This World, Then the Fireworks," in *Fireworks: The Lost Writings* (New York: Mysterious Press, 1988), 229. Though written in the mid-fifties, this story was not published until 1988.

16. Jim Thompson, *The Alcoholics* (New York: Vintage, 1953), 16.

17. Jim Thompson, *Recoil* (New York: Vintage, 1953), 5.

18. Jim Thompson, *Nothing More than Murder* (Berkeley, Calif.: Black Lizard Press, 1948), 78.

19. Thompson, 65.

20. Thompson, *Alcoholics,* 122.

21. Jim Thompson, *Savage Night* (New York: Vintage, 1953), 70–71.

22. Thompson, 72. Emphasis in original.

23. Jim Thompson, "'Hell' from *Ironside,*" in *Fireworks: The Lost Writings,* 195.

24. Thompson, *After Dark,* 130–31. Thompson used a similar strategy in *Savage Night,* 149, and *A Hell of a Woman* (New York: Vintage, 1954), 184–85.

25. Thompson, *Nothing More than Murder,* 210.

26. Jim Thompson, *The Killer inside Me* (New York: Vintage, 1952), 240.

27. Thompson, *Texas by the Tail,* 85. See the similar attitude of Doctor Murphy toward his patients in *Alcoholics,* 70.

28. Thompson, *Savage Night,* 105–7.

29. Jim Thompson, *Pop. 1280* (New York: Vintage, 1964), 183.

30. Morris Dickstein, *Gates of Eden: American Culture in the Sixties* (New York: Penguin, 1977), 97.

31. Richard Pells, *Radical Visions and American Dreams: Culture and Social Thought in the Depression Years* (Middletown, Conn.: Wesleyan University Press, 1973), 362.

32. Irving Howe, "Mass Society and Post-Modern Fiction," in *A World More Attractive: A View of Modern Literature and Politics* (Freeport, N.Y.: Books for Libraries Press, 1970), 89.

33. According to Alberta Thompson, Jim's wife, Faulkner was Thompson's favorite author. Polito, *Savage Art,* 226.

34. Jim Thompson, *The Nothing Man* (New York: Mysterious Press, 1953), 3.

35. Thompson, 39.

36. Thompson, *Savage Night,* 33.

37. Thompson, *Killer inside Me,* 215–17.

38. Thompson, 118.

39. Thompson, *Pop. 1280,* 11, 155.

40. Jim Thompson, *A Swell-Looking Babe* (New York: Vintage, 1954), 20.

41. Thompson, *Recoil,* 78.

42. Macdonald's criticism of Marxist theory is briefly discussed in Peter Novick, *That Noble Dream: The "Objectivity Question" and the American Historical Profession* (Cambridge: Cambridge University Press, 1988), 480.

43. Jim Thompson, *Heed the Thunder* (New York: Vintage, 1946), 272–73. Ellipsis in original. For similar discussions of the effects of capitalist agricultural methods on the land, see Thompson, *Heed the Thunder,* 136; *The Killer inside Me,* 236; and Jim Thompson, *Cropper's Cabin* (New York: Vintage, 1952), 12.

44. Jim Thompson, *South of Heaven* (New York: Vintage, 1967), 208–9.

45. Warren Susman, "'Personality' and the Making of Twentieth Century Culture," in *Culture as History: The Transformation of American Society in the Twentieth Century* (New York: Pantheon, 1984), 280, 271–85 passim.

46. Thompson, *Nothing Man,* 12.

47. Jim Thompson, *The Getaway* (New York: Bantam, 1958), 7.

48. Thompson, 24.

49. Thompson, 41.

50. Thompson, 126.

51. Jim Thompson, *The Grifters* (New York: Vintage, 1963), 14.

52. Thompson, 164.

53. Thompson, 127.

54. Elaine Tyler May, "Explosive Issues: Sex, Women, and the Bomb," in *Recasting America: Culture and Politics in the Age of Cold War,* ed. Lary May (Chicago: University of Chicago Press, 1989), 154–70. See also Elaine Tyler May, *Homeward Bound: American Families in the Cold War Era* (New York: Basic Books, 1988).

55. Thompson, *Swell-Looking Babe,* 60–61.

56. Philip Wylie, *Generation of Vipers* (New York: Farrar and Rinehart, 1942), 184–204.

57. Thompson, *Swell-Looking Babe,* 68. See also the ironic twist on the Oedipal saga in *Grifters,* 41, 187.

58. For a general discussion of the role of religion in Cold War culture, see Stephen Whitfield, *The Culture of the Cold War* (Baltimore: Johns Hopkins University Press, 1991), 77–100.

59. Thompson, *Now and on Earth,* 27; Thompson, *Nothing Man,* 39.

60. Thompson, *Savage Night,* 71; see also *Heed the Thunder,* 270, and *Pop. 1280,* 179.

61. Thompson, *Savage Night,* 144–49.

62. Thompson, *Hell of a Woman,* 183–85. This section indicates the split narrative by having every other line italicized. Here is a brief excerpt:

> Making him feel like a bastard because he didn't have what
> *she was and the room was and I was. It was like it ought*
> he couldn't get. Making him hate himself, and if a guy
> *to be at the end if it's never been that way before. and*
> hates himself how can he love anyone else? Helene came home,
> *we kept digging into the mattress, and the porter kept*
> my fairy princess, and she saw I was feeling low so she fixed
> *bringing in the stuff. helene started vomiting a lot, but*
> me a big drink. And right after that I began to get drowsy.

63. Thompson, *Getaway,* 170–71.

64. Thompson, 175.

65. Barry Gifford, "The Godless World of Jim Thompson," introduction to *Nothing More than Murder,* v.
66. Thompson, *Criminal,* 46–50.
67. Thompson, *Savage Night,* 55–56.
68. Thompson, 143.
69. Thompson, *Getaway,* 171–72.
70. Thompson, 177–78. A similar character is the serial killer (simply called The Killer) in *Ironside.* See Jim Thompson, "'Hell' from in *Ironside,*" in *Fireworks,* 190–200.
71. Thompson, *Pop. 1280,* 198.
72. Thompson, *Savage Night,* 123.
73. There is a good discussion of this point in Thompson, *Nothing More than Murder,* 138–40.
74. Thompson, *Alcoholics,* 3–4.
75. Thompson, 34.
76. Thompson, 75.
77. Thompson, 108.
78. Thompson, 54.
79. Jim Thompson, *The Kill-Off* (Mysterious Press, 1957), 78–79.
80. Thompson, *Swell-Looking Babe,* 45.
81. Thompson, *Cropper's Cabin,* 105.
82. Thompson, *Criminal,* 105–6.
83. Thompson, *Swell-Looking Babe,* 142, 144.
84. Jim Thompson, *Wild Town* (New York: Vintage, 1957), 119.
85. Thompson, 190.

Chapter 2: The Paperback Worldview of Charles Willeford

1. Charles Willeford, *High Priest of California* and *Wild Wives* (San Francisco: Re/Search, 1987 [1953]), 49.
2. Sybil Steinberg, "PW Interview: Charles Willeford," *Publishers Weekly,* February 6, 1987, 79.
3. Steinberg, 79. For a more detailed account of Willeford's early life, see the first volume of his autobiography, *I Was Looking for a Street* (Woodstock, Vt.: Countryman Press, 1988).
4. On Willeford's military experiences before World War II, see the second volume of his autobiography, *Something about a Soldier* (New York: Random House, 1986).
5. Steinberg, "PW Interview," 78.
6. Will Charles [Charles Willeford], *The Hombre from Sonora* (Lenox Hill Press, 1971), 53–54.

7. Quoted in Lou Stathis, "Charles Willeford: New Hope for the Living," introduction to Willeford, *High Priest of California* and *Wild Wives,* 9.

8. Stathis, 9–10.

9. Steinberg, "PW Interview," 78.

10. Charles Willeford, *Proletarian Laughter* (Yonkers, N.Y.: Alicat Bookshop Press, 1948).

11. Charles Willeford, *Miami Blues* (New York: Ballantine, 1984); *New Hope for the Dead* (New York: Ballantine, 1985); *Sideswipe* (New York: Ballantine, 1987); *The Way We Die Now* (New York: Ballantine, 1988).

12. For a brief history of *Black Mask* and its influence on noir writing, see Philip Durham, "The 'Black Mask' School," in *Tough Guy Writers of the Thirties,* ed. David Madden (Carbondale: Southern Illinois University Press, 1968), 51–79; and Ron Goulart, *Cheap Thrills: An Informal History of the Pulp Magazines* (New Rochelle, N.Y.: Arlington House, 1972), 113–33.

13. Charles Willeford, *High Priest of California* and *Wild Wives* (San Francisco: Re/Search, 1987 [1956]), 60.

14. Stathis, "Charles Willeford," 11. For a complete publishing history of Willeford's work, see *Wild Wives,* 7. In this chapter, I use the books' titles in their most recent printing.

15. Reprinted in Stathis, "Charles Willeford," 3. Also in large letters, Willeford's name is misspelled "Williford."

16. Geoffrey O'Brien, *Hardboiled America: Lurid Paperbacks and the Masters of Noir* (New York: Da Capo, 1997), 15–18.

17. Steinberg, "PW Interview," 78.

18. Except, of course, for his unprovoked assaults on the parking lot attendant and the stranger in the bar. Willeford, *High Priest,* 22, 49.

19. Willeford, *Wild Wives,* 25–26.

20. Stathis, "Charles Willeford," 8.

21. Willeford, *High Priest,* 35.

22. Willeford, 43.

23. Charles Willeford, *The Black Mask of Brother Springer* (Berkeley, Calif.: Black Lizard Press, 1958), 129. See also Willeford's similar discussion of the benefits of the Toastmasters in *The Woman Chaser* (New York: Carroll & Graff, 1960), 66.

24. Willeford, *High Priest,* 122.

25. Willeford, *Woman Chaser,* 63.

26. Willeford, 175–76.

27. Willeford, *Wild Wives,* 64.

28. Willeford, *Black Mask of Brother Springer,* 5.

29. Willeford, 7.

30. Willeford, *Woman Chaser,* 69.

31. Willeford, 70.
32. Charles Willeford, *Pickup* (New York: Vintage, 1954), 52.
33. Willeford, *Woman Chaser,* 154.
34. Irving Howe, "Mass Society and Post-Modern Fiction," in *A World More Attractive: A View of Modern Literature and Politics* (Freeport, N.Y.: Books for Libraries Press, 1970 [1963]), 87–89.
35. Willeford, *Wild Wives,* 38.
36. Willeford, *Woman Chaser,* 24–26.
37. Willeford, *High Priest,* 65–66.
38. Willeford, *Black Mask,* 141–42.
39. Willeford, *Woman Chaser,* 74–84.
40. Willeford, 147–49.
41. Willeford, 169.
42. Willeford, *Pickup,* 20.
43. Willeford, 26, 41.
44. Willeford, 135.
45. Willeford, 42.
46. Willeford, 104.
47. Willeford, 166.
48. Richard Wright, *Native Son* (New York: Harper, 1940).
49. Frankie Bailey, *Out of the Woodpile: Black Characters in Crime and Detective Fiction* (New York: Greenwood Press, 1991), x, 90. Interestingly, considering her topic, Bailey ignored Willeford in her study.
50. Dorothy Hughes, *The Expendable Man* (New York: Random House, 1963).
51. See Charles Willeford, "Chester Himes and His Novels of Absurdity," *American Visions,* August 1988, 43–44. For more on Himes, see chapter 5.
52. Albert Camus, *The Myth of Sisyphus and Other Essays* (New York: Vintage, 1955), 3.
53. Willeford, *Pickup,* 162.
54. Erich Fromm, *Escape from Freedom* (New York: Avon, 1941).
55. Morris Dickstein, *Gates of Eden: American Culture in the Sixties* (New York: Penguin, 1989), 36.
56. Herbert Marcuse, *One-Dimensional Man* (Boston: Beacon Press, 1964), 256–57.
57. Willeford, *Black Mask,* 26–27.
58. Willeford, 66.
59. Willeford, 82–85.
60. Willeford, 90.
61. Willeford, 161.
62. Marcuse, *One-Dimensional Man,* 257.

Chapter 3: The Fantastic World of Ray Bradbury

1. "Allegory of Any Place," *Time,* October 30, 1964, 85–86. "Special Delivery" aired on November 29, 1959. "Come into My Cellar" appears in Ray Bradbury, *S Is for Space* (New York: Bantam, 1966).

2. The advertisement appeared in *Variety* on November 6, 1952, and is reprinted in its entirety in *The Nation,* November 29, 1952, 481.

3. Dwight Macdonald, "Too Big" (1946), in *Memoirs of a Revolutionist: Essays in Political Criticism* (New York: Farrar, Strauss and Cudahy, 1957), 373–74.

4. George Orwell, "Politics and the English Language," in *In Front of Your Nose, 1945–1950: The Collected Essays, Journalism and Letters of George Orwell,* vol. 4, ed. Sonia Orwell and Ian Angus (New York: Harcourt, Brace, Jovanovich, 1968), 136.

5. Kingsley Amis, *New Maps of Hell: A Survey of Science Fiction* (New York: Harcourt Brace, 1960), 105.

6. Damon Knight, "When I Was in Kneepants: Ray Bradbury," in *In Search of Wonder: Essays on Modern Science Fiction* (Chicago: Advent Publishers, 1967), 109.

7. Russell Kirk, "Count Dracula and Mr. Ray Bradbury," *National Review* 19, no. 13 (April 4, 1967): 365.

8. Harlan Ellison, "Introduction to Ray Bradbury's 'Christ, Old Student in a New School,'" in *Again, Dangerous Visions,* ed. Ellison (New York: Signet, 1972), 188–89.

9. For a brief autobiographical sketch, see Ray Bradbury, "Afterword: Fifty Years, Fifty Friends," in *The Bradbury Chronicles: Stories in Honor of Ray Bradbury,* ed. William F. Nolan and Martin H. Greenberg (New York: Penguin, 1991), 324–35.

10. On science fiction's Golden Age, see Lester del Rey, *The World of Science Fiction* (New York: Ballantine, 1979), 91–157; and Thomas Clareson, *Understanding Contemporary American Science Fiction: The Formative Period, 1926–1970* (Columbia: University of South Carolina Press, 1990), 5–129.

11. Isaac Asimov, "Ray: An Appreciation," in *The Bradbury Chronicles,* ed. Nolan and Greenberg, 12.

12. Ray Bradbury, "How to Keep and Feed a Muse," *The Writer,* July 1961, 11.

13. "Allegory of Any Place," 85–86; Asimov, "Ray," 12–13.

14. Ray Bradbury, *Dandelion Wine* (New York: Bantam, 1957), 35.

15. Ray Bradbury, "Pillar of Fire," in *S Is for Space,* 38.

16. Ray Bradbury, "The Small Assassin," in *The October Country* (New York: Ballantine, 1955), 142.

17. Ray Bradbury, "The Winds," in *October Country,* 205.

18. Ray Bradbury, "The Crowd," in *October Country,* 154–55.

19. Ray Bradbury, "Zero Hour," in *The Illustrated Man* (New York: Bantam, 1951), 39–42.

20. Bradbury, "Come into My Cellar," 127–44.

21. Pete Biskind, *Seeing Is Believing: How Hollywood Taught Us to Stop Worrying and Love the Fifties* (New York: Pantheon, 1983), 149.

22. Ray Bradbury, "The City," in *Illustrated Man,* 162–69.

23. Ray Bradbury, "Perhaps We Are Going Away," in *The Machineries of Joy* (New York: Bantam, 1964), 71–74.

24. Ray Bradbury, "—And the Moon Still Be as Bright," in *The Martian Chronicles* (New York: Bantam, 1950), 59.

25. Ray Bradbury, "The Wilderness," in *The Golden Apples of the Sun* (New York: Bantam, 1953), 30–31.

26. Bradbury, *Martian Chronicles,* 87.

27. Bradbury, 54.

28. Bradbury, 102–3.

29. Ray Bradbury, "Here There Be Tygers," in *R Is for Rocket* (New York: Bantam, 1962), 97–109.

30. Ray Bradbury, "A Piece of Wood," in *Long after Midnight* (New York: Alfred A. Knopf, 1976), 49–54.

31. Ray Bradbury, "There Will Come Soft Rains," in *The Martian Chronicles,* 166–72.

32. Ray Bradbury, "The Garbage Collector," in *Golden Apples,* 145–49.

33. Knight, "When I Was in Kneepants," 108–13.

34. Bradbury, *Dandelion Wine,* 158–76.

35. Bradbury lived in Ireland for several months while writing the screenplay for *Moby Dick.* For a brief discussion of his period in Ireland, see Ray Bradbury, "The Queen's Own Evaders: An Afterword," in *The Anthem Sprinters and Other Antics* (New York: Dial, 1963), 151–59. Among his Irish stories are, from *I Sing the Body Electric* (New York: Bantam, 1969), "The Terrible Conflagration up at the Place," 13–29, "The Cold Wind and the Warm," 100–119, "The Haunting of the New," 133–50; from *The Machineries of Joy,* "The Beggar on O'Connell Bridge," 142–56, and "The Anthem Sprinters," 203–13; from *A Medicine for Melancholy* (New York: Bantam, 1959), "The First Night of Lent," 116–23, and "The Great Collision of Monday Last," 141–47; and from *Long after Midnight,* "Getting through Sunday Somehow," 100–9.

36. Among Bradbury's Mexico stories are, from *A Memory of Murder* (New York: Dell, 1984), "The Candy Skull," 175–92; from *October Country,* "The Next in Line," 16–51; from *Machineries of Joy,* "El Dia de Muerte," 83–92, and "The Lifework of Juan Diaz," 183–92; and from *Long after Midnight,* "Interval in Sunlight," 124–52.

37. Bradbury's stories set in monasteries or dealing with priests include, from *Machineries of Joy,* "The Machineries of Joy," 1–13; from *Illustrated Man,* "Fire Balloons," 75–90; and from *Long after Midnight,* "The Messiah," 55–66.

38. Ray Bradbury, "The Dwarf," in *October Country,* 3–15.

39. Ray Bradbury, "Uncle Einer," in *October Country,* 191–98.

40. Ray Bradbury, "The Foghorn," in *Golden Apples,* 1–8.

41. Ray Bradbury, "The Big Black and White Game," in *Golden Apples,* 77–87.

42. Ray Bradbury, "Way in the Middle of the Air," in *Martian Chronicles,* 89–102.

43. Ray Bradbury, "The Other Foot," in *Illustrated Man,* 27–38.

44. Ray Bradbury, "The Long Night," in *Memory of Murder,* 67–82.

45. Ray Bradbury, "I See You Never," in *Golden Apples,* 69–72.

46. Ray Bradbury, "The Wonderful Ice Cream Suit," in *Medicine for Melancholy,* 27–50.

47. Ray Bradbury, "The Joy of Writing," *The Writer,* October 1956, 294.

48. Ray Bradbury, "Sun and Shadow," in *Golden Apples,* 125–31.

49. Dwight Macdonald, for instance, made a similar criticism of *Life* in his essay "Masscult and Midcult," in *Against the American Grain: Essays on the Effects of Mass Culture* (New York: Da Capo, 1983 [1962]), 14–15.

50. Ray Bradbury, "The Concrete Mixer," in *Illustrated Man,* 144–45.

51. Bradbury, 148.

52. Bradbury, 150.

53. Bradbury, 152–55.

54. Ray Bradbury, *Fahrenheit 451* (New York: Ballantine, 1953), 24. Throughout Bradbury's oeuvre, psychiatry is viewed as a tool of the state to impose conformity on heretics and eccentrics.

55. Bradbury, 31.

56. Bradbury, 31–32.

57. Bradbury, 15–16.

58. Bradbury, 58.

59. Bradbury, 63.

60. Herbert Marcuse, *One-Dimensional Man* (Boston: Beacon, 1964), 79.

61. Marcuse, 23.

62. Bradbury, *Fahrenheit 451,* 79–80.

63. Marcuse, *One-Dimensional Man,* 10.

64. Bradbury, *Fahrenheit 451,* 85–86. Compare Kurt Vonnegut's 1961 short story, "Harrison Bergeron," in which in the future everyone has been made completely equal, so that no one is smarter or more beautiful or more athletic than anyone else. To prevent intelligent people from having an unfair advantage, small sirens have been inserted in their ears to go off periodically to scatter their thoughts. *Welcome to the Monkey House* (New York: Dell, 1970), 7–13.

65. Christopher Lasch has made a similar point regarding contemporary education, arguing that "the censorship of fairy tales, like the attack on 'irrelevant' literature in general, belongs to a general assault on fantasy and imagination." *The Culture of*

Narcissism: American Life in an Age of Diminishing Expectations (New York: Warner, 1979), 261.

66. Ray Bradbury, "Usher II," in *Martian Chronicles,* 105.

67. Bradbury, 103–18. A similar story is "The Exiles" (1950), in *The Illustrated Man,* 94–105.

68. Ray Bradbury, "The Pedestrian," in *Golden Apples,* 9–13.

69. Ray Bradbury, "The Murderer," in *Golden Apples,* 56–63.

70. Ray Bradbury, "To the Chicago Abyss," in *Machineries of Joy,* 193–202.

71. Bradbury, *Fahrenheit 451,* 129–30.

72. Bradbury, "Pillar of Fire," 27–67.

73. Bradbury, "—And the Moon," 48–72.

74. Ray Bradbury, "The Scythe," in *October Country,* 175–90.

75. Ray Bradbury, "A Sound of Thunder," in *Golden Apples,* 88–89.

76. Bradbury, 91.

77. Bradbury, 98–99.

78. For a good introduction to chaos theory, see James Gleick, *Chaos: Making a New Science* (New York: Viking, 1987). On the so-called butterfly effect, see 9–31.

79. Arthur Schlesinger Jr., *The Vital Center: The Politics of Freedom* (Boston: Houghton Mifflin, 1949), 52.

80. Irving Howe, "Our Country and Our Culture," *Partisan Review* 19, no. 5 (September–October 1952): 580.

Chapter 4: The Devil and Charles Beaumont

1. Charles Beaumont, "Gentlemen, Be Seated," in *The Howling Man,* ed. Roger Anker (New York: Tor, 1988), 273–92.

2. According to Harlan Ellison, an editor at *Rogue* at the time, because of Beaumont's contract with *Playboy,* he wrote for *Rogue* as C. B. Lovehill, a pen name Ellison invented. Ellison commented, "The C and the B are obvious; *beau* I twisted out the French to get *love,* though idiomatically it was a stretch; and *mont* became *hill.*" See Ellison, "The Howling Man: Introduction by Harlan Ellison," in *Howling Man,* 135. For a complete publishing history of Beaumont's work, see William F. Nolan, *The Work of Charles Beaumont: An Annotated Bibliography and Guide* (San Bernardino, Calif.: Borgo Press, 1986).

3. For Corman, Beaumont wrote the screenplays for his own *The Intruder* (1961) as well as for *The Premature Burial* (1962), *The Haunted Palace* (1963), and *The Masque of the Red Death* (1964, coauthored with R. Wright Campbell).

4. For biographical information, see Marc Scott Zicree, *The Twilight Zone Companion* (New York: Bantam, 1989), 74–77, 353–56; Lee Prosser, *Running from the Hunter: The Life and Works of Charles Beaumont* (San Bernardino, Calif.: Borgo

Press, 1996), 5–28; and the reminiscences by family, friends, and colleagues in Beaumont, *Howling Man.*

5. Charles Beaumont, *Remember? Remember?* (New York: Macmillan, 1963), 39.

6. Beaumont, 39.

7. Beaumont, 178–79.

8. Beaumont, 211–12,

9. Beaumont, "Gentlemen, Be Seated," 284.

10. Beaumont, 289. On the effort to drive *Amos 'n' Andy* off the air, see Melvin Patrick Ely, *The Adventures of Amos 'n' Andy: A Social History of an American Phenomenon* (New York: Free Press, 1991), 160–244; Mel Watkins, *On the Real Side: Laughing, Lying, and Signifying: The Underground Tradition of African-American Humor That Transformed American Culture from Slavery to Richard Pryor* (New York: Simon & Schuster, 1994), 321–22. Beaumont did not specifically name the *Amos 'n' Andy* show, but he clearly referred to it by portraying characters in blackface speaking in a heavy, pseudo-black dialect and mentioning television censorship and the decline of racial humor.

11. Beaumont, *Remember?* 21.

12. Beaumont, 3–4.

13. Beaumont, 7–8.

14. Beaumont, 16–17. Beaumont portrayed a similar theme in his short story "The Dark Music" (1956), about a puritanical high school biology teacher who uses her position to crack down on her students' budding sexuality. Charles Beaumont, "The Dark Music," in *The Magic Man and Other Science-Fantasy Stories* (Greenwich, Conn.: Fawcett, 1965), 162–76.

15. Beaumont, *Remember?* 52. In his screenplay for the *Twilight Zone* episode "Static," Beaumont celebrated the days of radio drama, even having one character repeat the line, "Radio is a world that has to be believed to be seen." "Static" aired March 10, 1961. Beaumont's script was based on an unpublished short story by Ocee Ritch.

16. Beaumont, 95.

17. Beaumont, "The Magic Man," in *Howling Man,* 176–98.

18. Beaumont, *Remember?* 81–82.

19. Beaumont, 150.

20. Beaumont, 154. In his short story "Perchance to Dream" (1958), Beaumont portrayed the potentially terrifying nature of older-style amusement parks by setting the climax on a roller coaster ("Perchance to Dream," in *Howling Man,* 347–58), while in the *Twilight Zone* episode "The New Exhibit," he set his horror story among the anachronistic figures of a wax museum's murderers' row, which has been closed due to dwindling attendance. "The New Exhibit" aired April 4, 1963; Beaumont cowrote the story with Jerry Sohl, but Beaumont received sole credit.

21. Beaumont, "The Monster Show," in *Magic Man,* 74–80.
22. Charles Beaumont, "The Beautiful People," in *The Twilight Zone: The Original Stories,* ed. Martin H. Greenberg et al. (New York: Avon, 1985), 515.
23. Beaumont, 517–18.
24. "Number Twelve Looks Just Like You" aired January 24, 1964. Though credited to Beaumont, it was written by John Tomerlin.
25. Beaumont, "Beautiful People," 525.
26. Charles Beaumont, "Buck Fever," in *Night Ride and Other Journeys* (New York: Bantam, 1960), 48.
27. Beaumont, "The Trigger," in *Night Ride,* 98–110.
28. Beaumont, "Night Ride," in *Night Ride,* 182–83.
29. In the futuristic world of "Gentlemen, Be Seated," such lack of humanity is seen as characteristic of a model employee. "Gentlemen, Be Seated," 274–75.
30. "Miniature" aired February 21, 1963.
31. Charles Beaumont, "The Vanishing American," in *Magic Man,* 69.
32. George Orwell, "Wells, Hitler and the World State," in *My Country Right or Left, 1940–1943: The Collected Essays, Journalism and Letters of George Orwell,* vol. 2 (New York: Harcourt Brace Jovanovich, 1968), 145.
33. Charles Beaumont, "The Neighbors," in *Night Ride,* 148–49.
34. Beaumont, 151.
35. Beaumont, 152–54. Compare the more typically Beaumontian variation on the same basic situation—a new family moving into a neighborhood and its encounter with the neighbors—in "The New People," discussed below.
36. Charles Beaumont, *The Intruder* (New York: Dell, 1962 [1959]), 90.
37. Beaumont, 206.
38. Beaumont, 220.
39. On Wylie's influence on postwar American culture, see Michael Rogin, "Kiss Me Deadly: Communism, Motherhood, and Cold War Movies," in *Ronald Reagan: The Movie, and Other Episodes in Political Demonology* (Berkeley: University of California Press, 1987), 236–71.
40. Beaumont, *The Intruder,* 176–83.
41. Eric Hoffer, *The True Believer* (New York: Harper and Row, 1951).
42. On the development of the concept of "red fascism," see Thomas G. Paterson, "Red Fascism: The American Image of Aggressive Totalitarianism," in *Meeting the Communist Threat: Truman to Reagan* (New York: Oxford University Press, 1988), 3–17.
43. Beaumont, *Intruder,* 249.
44. Beaumont, 253.
45. Beaumont, 305.
46. Beaumont, 286, 292.

47. Beaumont, 337.

48. Norman Mailer, "The White Negro," in *Advertisements for Myself* (New York: Berkeley, 1959), 313–14.

49. Mailer, 315.

50. Charles Beaumont, "Black Country," in *Magic Man,* 133.

51. Beaumont, 149–50.

52. Beaumont, "Night Ride," 170.

53. Jazz critic Stanley Crouch has termed this view "liberal racism," which "reduces the complexities of the Afro-American world to a dark, rainy pit in which Negroes sweat, suffer, dance a little, mock each other, make music, and drop dead, releasing at last a burden of torment held at bay only by drugs." Stanley Crouch, "Bird Land," *New Republic,* February 27, 1989, 25.

54. Nat Hentoff, "A Brief Note on the Romance of 'The White Negro,'" *The Jazz Life* (New York: Da Capo, 1961), 141.

55. Beaumont, "Night Ride," 172.

56. Herbert Marcuse, *One-Dimensional Man* (Boston: Beacon, 1964), 17, 23.

57. Raymond Williams, *Marxism and Literature* (New York: Oxford University Press, 1976), 130.

58. Charles Beaumont, "The Jungle," in *Twilight Zone: The Original Stories,* ed. Greenberg et al., 168.

59. Beaumont, 167.

60. Beaumont, 168–69.

61. Beaumont, 170.

62. Beaumont, 172.

63. Beaumont, 175.

64. Charles Beaumont, "The Crooked Man," in *Magic Man,* 195.

65. Beaumont, 195.

66. Charles Beaumont, "Something in the Earth," in *The Bradbury Chronicles: Stories in Honor of Ray Bradbury,* ed. William F. Nolan and Martin H. Greenberg (New York: Penguin, 1991), 112.

67. Beaumont, 117.

68. Beaumont, 120.

69. Charles Beaumont, "Place of Meeting," in *Howling Man,* 39–44.

70. Occasionally, Beaumont's parodies backfired. His first movie screenplay to be produced was *Queen of Outer Space,* starring Zsa Zsa Gabor. Beaumont commented, "I wrote the thing as a big spoof. Only trouble was the director and some of the cast didn't realize it." Quoted in Roger Anker, "Introduction," in *Howling Man,* xxv.

71. Charles Beaumont, "The Last Caper," in *Magic Man,* 32.

72. Beaumont, 34.

73. Beaumont, 39.
74. Beaumont, *Remember?* 21–22.
75. Beaumont, "Perchance to Dream," 347–58.
76. Charles Beaumont, "Traumeri," in *Yonder: Stories of Fantasy and Science Fiction* (New York: Bantam, 1958), 170–75. Beaumont adapted the story for the *Twilight Zone* episode "Shadow Play" (aired May 5, 1961).
77. Beaumont, "Dark Music," in *Magic Man*, 162–76.
78. Beaumont, "The New People," in *Magic Man*, 53.
79. Beaumont, 42–62.
80. Charles Beaumont, "The Howling Man," in *Twilight Zone*, ed. Greenberg et al., 118–20.
81. Beaumont, 124.
82. Charles Beaumont, "The Devil, You Say?" in *Twilight Zone*, ed. Greenberg et al., 362–68.
83. Beaumont, 370.
84. Beaumont, 362.
85. Beaumont, 376.
86. "Printer's Devil" aired February 28, 1963.

Chapter 5: The Black Vision of Chester Himes

1. Chester Himes, *Blind Man with a Pistol* (New York: Vintage, 1969), 176–91.
2. Himes, 5.
3. George Lipsitz, *Time Passages: Collective Memory and American Popular Culture* (Minneapolis: University of Minnesota Press, 1990), 135. Lipsitz referred specifically to postmodern culture, but the point is also true of the underground culture.
4. Lawrence Levine, *Black Culture and Black Consciousness: Afro-American Folk Thought from Slavery to Freedom* (New York: Oxford University Press, 1977), 58.
5. Clayborne Carson, *In Struggle: SNCC and the Black Awakening of the 1960s* (Cambridge, Mass.: Harvard University Press, 1981), 113.
6. Chester Himes, *My Life of Absurdity* (New York: Paragon House, 1976), 1.
7. Kenneth Stampp, *The Peculiar Institution: Slavery in the Ante-Bellum South* (New York: Vintage, 1956), vii.
8. Jules Tygiel, *Baseball's Great Experiment: Jackie Robinson and His Legacy* (New York: Vintage, 1983), 334.
9. Donald Bogle, *Toms, Coons, Mulattoes, Mammies, and Bucks: An Interpretive History of Blacks in American Films* (New York: Continuum, 1989), 147.
10. John Ball, *In the Heat of the Night* (New York: Bantam, 1965), 13.
11. For the best accounts of Himes's early years, see Edward Margolies and Michel Fabre, *The Several Lives of Chester Himes* (Jackson: University of Mississippi Press, 1997), 3–22; and Chester Himes, *The Quality of Hurt* (New York: Paragon

House, 1972) and Himes's autobiographical novel, *The Third Generation* (New York: Thunder's Mouth Press, 1954).

12. Himes, *Quality of Hurt,* 27.
13. Himes, 30–31.
14. Himes, 63. In *The Crazy Kill,* Grave Digger says, "These folks in Harlem do things for reasons nobody else in the world would think of. Listen, there were two hardworking colored jokers, both with families, got to fighting . . . and cut each other to death about whether Paris was in France or France was in Paris." Himes, *The Crazy Kill* (New York: Vintage, 1959), 56.
15. Stephen F. Milliken, *Chester Himes: A Critical Appraisal* (Columbia: University of Missouri Press, 1976), 44.
16. Chester Himes, "To What Red Hell," in *The Collected Works of Chester Himes* (New York: Thunder's Mouth Press, 1990), 286.
17. Himes, *Quality of Hurt,* 73–74.
18. See the discussion of Myrdal's book in Christopher Lasch, *The True and Only Heaven: Progress and Its Critics* (New York: W. W. Norton, 1991), 439–45.
19. Himes, *Quality of Hurt,* 75–76.
20. Chester Himes, *If He Hollers Let Him Go* (New York: Thunder's Mouth Press, 1945) and *The Lonely Crusade* (New York: Thunder's Mouth Press, 1947).
21. Ishmael Reed wrote of Himes's debut novel, "[It] is youthful, insulting, risky, brash, bad-assed, revolutionary, violent, and struts about as if to say here come cocky Chester Himes, you litterateurs, and I hope you don't like it." Ishmael Reed, "Chester Himes: Black Writer," *Black World* 21 (March 1972): 28.
22. Himes, *Quality of Hurt,* 100.
23. Himes, 103.
24. Chester Himes, "The Dilemma of the Negro Writer in the United States," reprinted in *Beyond the Angry Black,* ed. John A. Williams (New York: Cooper Square Publishers, 1966), 52–58.
25. Fred Pfeil, "Policiers Noirs," *The Nation,* November 15, 1986, 523.
26. Thomas Hill Schaub, *American Fiction in the Cold War* (Madison: University of Wisconsin Press, 1991), 95.
27. Himes, *Blind Man with a Pistol,* 187.
28. Chester Himes, *A Case of Rape* (Washington, D.C.: Howard University Press, 1984).
29. John M. Reilly, "Chester Himes' Harlem Tough Guys," *Journal of Popular Culture,* spring 1976, 935.
30. Himes, *My Life of Absurdity,* 102.
31. Reilly, "Chester Himes' Harlem Tough Guys," 935.
32. Himes, *My Life of Absurdity,* 36.
33. Chester Himes, *Run Man Run* (New York: G. P. Putnam's Sons, 1966), 36.

34. Chester Himes, *All Shot Up* (Chatham, N.J.: Chatham Bookseller, 1960), 15.

35. Chester Himes, *Cotton Comes to Harlem* (London: Alison and Busby, 1965), 107.

36. Himes, *My Life of Absurdity,* 126.

37. Chester Himes, *The Real Cool Killers* (London: Alison and Busby, 1965), 1–14.

38. John A. Williams, "My Man Himes: An Interview with Chester Himes," in *Amistad,* ed. John A. Williams and Charles F. Harris (New York: Vintage, 1970), 47.

39. Chester Himes, "Prediction," in *Collected Stories of Chester Himes,* 422.

40. Himes, *All Shot Up,* 79–85.

41. Williams, "My Man Himes," 66.

42. Williams, 48–49.

43. Himes, *Run Man Run,* 85.

44. Himes, *Crazy Kill,* 28.

45. Chester Himes, *A Rage in Harlem* (New York: Vintage, 1957), 44.

46. Himes, *Real Cool Killers,* 15–20.

47. Himes, *Rage in Harlem,* 65–66.

48. Himes, 120.

49. Himes, *Real Cool Killers,* 111.

50. Himes, *Crazy Kill,* 126–27.

51. Himes, *Rage in Harlem,* 49.

52. Ethan Mordden, *Medium Cool: The Movies of the 1960s* (New York: Alfred A. Knopf, 1990), 67.

53. Mordden, 69.

54. Himes, *Rage in Harlem,* 49.

55. Reilly, "Chester Himes' Harlem Tough Guys," 938.

56. Chester Himes, *The Heat's On* (New York: Vintage), 26.

57. Himes, 55–56.

58. Himes, *Crazy Kill,* 81–83.

59. Himes, *Real Cool Killers,* 154–59.

60. Chester Himes, *The Big Gold Dream* (Chatham, N.J.: Chatham Bookseller, 1960), 153–56.

61. Himes, *Cotton Comes to Harlem,* 150–53.

62. Himes, 116.

63. Himes, *All Shot Up,* 42.

64. Himes, 107; Himes, *Heat's On,* 77.

65. Himes, *Heat's On,* 146; Himes, *Cotton Comes to Harlem,* 101.

66. Himes, *Heat's On,* 158.

67. Michael Mok, "Chester Himes," *Publishers Weekly,* April 3, 1972, 21.

68. Himes, *Crazy Kill,* 35.

69. Himes, 125.

70. Himes, *Cotton Comes to Harlem,* 35.

71. Himes, 26.

72. Himes, *My Life of Absurdity,* 247.

73. Himes, 292.

74. Himes, *Blind Man,* 112.

75. Himes, *My Life of Absurdity,* 126. Emphasis in original.

76. Himes, 240.

77. Edward Margolies, "The Thrillers of Chester Himes," *Studies in Black Literature* 1 (June 1970): 1.

78. Himes, *Crazy Kill,* 73.

79. Himes, *Cotton Comes to Harlem,* 14–15. Ellipses in original.

80. Himes, *All Shot Up,* 21.

81. Frantz Fanon, *The Wretched of the Earth* (New York: Grove Press, 1963), 54.

82. Jackson Lears, "Uneasy Courtship: Modern Art and Modern Advertising," *American Quarterly* 39, no. 1 (spring 1987): 142–43.

83. Himes, *All Shot Up,* 17.

84. Himes, *Cotton Comes to Harlem,* 99.

85. Himes, 32.

86. Levine, *Black Culture,* 118.

87. Himes, *Rage in Harlem,* 93.

88. Himes, *Cotton Comes to Harlem,* 52.

89. Milliken, *Chester Himes,* 242.

90. Himes, *Big Gold Dream,* 69.

91. Himes, 160.

92. Himes, 159–60.

93. Himes, *Cotton Comes to Harlem,* 26.

94. Marshall Berman, *All That Is Solid Melts into Air: The Experience of Modernity* (New York: Penguin, 1988), 111.

95. Himes, "Prediction," 425.

96. Berman, *All That Is Solid,* 121.

97. Himes, *Blind Man,* 5.

Chapter 6: Patricia Highsmith and Everyday Schizophrenia

1. Patricia Highsmith, *Deep Water* (New York: Harper and Brothers, 1957), 143.

2. Highsmith, 5.

3. Highsmith, 28.

4. Highsmith, 55.

5. Highsmith, 213.

6. Jill Pearlman, "Mistress of Fright," *Harper's Bazaar,* February 1989, 52, 180.

7. Chester Himes, *The Quality of Hurt* (New York: Paragon House, 1972), 103–4.

8. Most of the relevant details of Highsmith's biography can be found in Pearlman,

"Mistress"; Joan DuPont, "Criminal Pursuits," *New York Times Magazine,* June 12, 1988, 60–66; and Russell Harrison, *Patricia Highsmith* (New York: Twayne, 1997), 1–12.

9. "The Talented Miss Highsmith," *Times Literary Supplement,* September 24, 1971, 1147.

10. Patricia Highsmith, *Plotting and Writing Suspense Fiction* (Boston: The Writer, 1972 [1966]), 141.

11. Highsmith, 142–43.

12. Highsmith, 143–44.

13. Highsmith, 1–2.

14. She rejected, for instance, the emphasis on dialogue that marks the *Black Mask* school of suspense writing, commenting, "Dialogue is dramatic and should be used sparingly, because the effect will be more dramatic when it is used." Highsmith, 65.

15. *Contemporary Literary Criticism* 2 (1974): 192.

16. Highsmith, *Plotting,* 36.

17. Patricia Highsmith, *A Game for the Living* (New York: Atlantic Monthly Press, 1958), 5.

18. Claire Morgan [Patricia Highsmith], *The Price of Salt* (New York: Arno, 1952), 4.

19. Patricia Highsmith, *The Glass Cell* (Garden City, N.Y.: Doubleday, 1964), 17.

20. Russell Harrison also has argued that within Highsmith's work there is an underlying critique of American Cold War policies, but he focuses on McCarthyite anti-communist purges. See Harrison, *Patricia Highsmith,* 55–58.

21. Patricia Highsmith, *The Talented Mr. Ripley* (New York: Penguin, 1955). Ripley would later be featured in a brilliant series of Highsmith's novels, including *Ripley under Ground* (New York: Vintage, 1970); *Ripley's Game* (New York: Vintage, 1974); *The Boy Who Followed Ripley* (New York: Vintage, 1981); and *Ripley under Water* (New York: Vintage, 1992). In these later novels, though, Ripley's character was subtly but significantly altered as he developed a strong (albeit more than a little twisted) personal moral code.

22. Highsmith, *Talented Mr. Ripley,* 14.

23. Highsmith, 66–70.

24. Anthony Channell Hilfer, "'Not Really Such a Monster': Highsmith's Ripley as Thriller Protagonist and Protean Man," *Midwest Quarterly* 25, no. 4 (summer 1984): 370.

25. Ralph Ellison, *Invisible Man* (New York: Vintage, 1952).

26. Hilfer, "'Not Really Such a Monster,'" 366.

27. Highsmith, *Talented Mr. Ripley,* 31.

28. Highsmith, 165.

29. Karen Halttenun, *Confidence Men and Painted Women: A Study of Middle-Class Culture in America* (New Haven, Conn.: Yale University Press, 1982), 204.

30. Patricia Highsmith, *The Tremor of Forgery* (Garden City, N.Y.: Doubleday, 1969), 68.
31. Highsmith, 14.
32. Highsmith, 25.
33. Highsmith, 56.
34. Highsmith, 74.
35. As Highsmith wrote in *Plotting and Writing Suspense Fiction,* "I would like to write a [suspense] novel . . . which has no murder, no crime, no violent action" (140). With *The Tremor of Forgery,* she largely succeeded.
36. Highsmith, *Tremor of Forgery,* 192.
37. Highsmith, 140.
38. Highsmith, 220, 223.
39. I. F. Stone, *The Hidden History of the Korean War* (New York: Monthly Review Press, 1952), 34.
40. Patricia Highsmith, *Those Who Walk Away* (New York: Atlantic Monthly Press, 1967), 128.
41. Patricia Highsmith, *A Suspension of Mercy* (original American title, *The Story-Teller*) (New York: Penguin, 1965).
42. Patricia Highsmith, "The Cries of Love," *The Snail-Watcher and Other Stories* (Garden City, N.Y.: Doubleday, 1970), 81–90.
43. Highsmith, *Plotting,* 144–45.
44. Patricia Highsmith, *The Two Faces of January* (Garden City, N.Y.: Doubleday, 1964), 181–82.
45. Highsmith, *Suspension of Mercy,* 133–34.
46. Highsmith, *Plotting,* 42.
47. Patricia Highsmith, *This Sweet Sickness* (New York: Harper & Brothers, 1960); Patricia Highsmith, *The Cry of the Owl* (New York: Atlantic Monthly Press, 1962).
48. Patricia Highsmith, *Strangers on a Train* (New York: Penguin, 1950), 163.
49. Highsmith, 172.
50. Highsmith, 220.
51. Highsmith, 190.
52. Highsmith, *Game for the Living,* 87.
53. Highsmith, 97.
54. Highsmith, 181–82.
55. Highsmith, *Cry of the Owl,* 8.
56. Highsmith, *This Sweet Sickness,* 36.
57. Highsmith, 123.
58. Highsmith, 239.
59. Highsmith, *Strangers on a Train,* 20–22.
60. Highsmith, 108.

61. Highsmith, 228.
62. Highsmith, 198.
63. Highsmith, 187.
64. Highsmith, *Talented Mr. Ripley,* 34.
65. Highsmith, 68–69; see also 154.
66. Highsmith, *Glass Cell,* 70–90.
67. Highsmith, *Tremor of Forgery,* 47.
68. John D'Emilio, "The Homosexual Menace: The Politics of Sexuality in Cold War America," in *Making Trouble: Essays on Gay History, Politics, and the University* (New York: Routledge, 1992), 59–60.
69. Arthur Schlesinger Jr., *The Vital Center: The Politics of Freedom* (Boston: Houghton Mifflin, 1949), 151.
70. For a good discussion of the links between communism and homosexuality in popular culture, see D'Emilio, "Homosexual Menace," 57–73.
71. Elaine Tyler May, *Homeward Bound: American Families in the Cold War Era* (New York: Basic, 1988), 94.
72. Philip Wylie, *Generation of Vipers* (New York: Farrar & Rinehart, 1942), 51–53, 191–216. For further discussion of Wylie and his influence on postwar culture, see Michael Rogin, "Kiss Me Deadly: Communism, Motherhood, and Cold War Movies," in *Ronald Reagan: The Movie* (Berkeley: University of California Press, 1987), 236–71.
73. Highsmith, *Strangers on a Train,* 14–15, 25, 56.
74. Highsmith, 37.
75. Highsmith, 14–15.
76. Highsmith, 17.
77. Highsmith, 20–22.
78. Highsmith, 56.
79. Highsmith, 96.
80. Highsmith, 82.
81. Tania Modleski, "Film Theory's Detour," *Screen 5* (November–December 1982): 76.
82. Highsmith, *This Sweet Sickness,* 86.
83. Highsmith, 66.
84. Modleski, "Film Theory's Detour," 78.
85. Highsmith, *Two Faces of January,* 11–14.
86. Highsmith, 20–23.
87. Highsmith, 35.
88. Highsmith, 83.
89. Highsmith, 97.
90. Highsmith, 105.

91. Highsmith, 200.
92. Highsmith, 202.
93. Brigid Brophy, "Highsmith," *Don't Never Forget: Collected Views and Reviews* (New York: Holt, Rinehart and Winston, 1966), 151–52.

Chapter 7: The Cinematic Vision of Samuel Fuller

1. A basic discussion of the characteristics of B-movies can be found in Charles Flynn, "The Schlock/Kitsch/Hack Movies," in *Kings of the Bs: Working within the Hollywood System,* ed. Todd McCarthy and Charles Flynn (New York: E. P. Dutton, 1975), 6.
2. Quoted in *FilmFacts* 6 (1963): 211.
3. For a discussion of the development of *la politique des auteurs,* see *Cahiers du Cinema: The 1950s: Neo-Realism, Hollywood, New Wave,* ed. Jim Hillier (Cambridge, Mass.: Harvard University Press, 1985), 5–11, 73–85.
4. See Luc Moullet, "Sam Fuller: In Marlowe's Footsteps," in Hillier, *Cahiers,* 145–55. Jean Luc Godard paid homage to Fuller by casting him (as himself) in Godard's 1965 film *Pierrot le fou,* while the German director Wim Wenders cast Fuller as a gangster in his 1977 film *The American Friend* (based on Patricia Highsmith's novel *Ripley's Game*).
5. See, for instance, Andrew Sarris, "Notes on the *Auteur* Theory in 1962," "Notes on the *Auteur* Theory in 1970," and "*Auteurism* vs. Amnesia," in his book *The Primal Screen: Essays on Film and Related Subjects* (New York: Simon and Schuster, 1973), 38–65.
6. Andrew Sarris, *The American Cinema: Directors and Directions, 1929–1968* (New York: E. P. Dutton, 1968), 93.
7. Peter Bogdanovich, "Hollywood," *Esquire,* September 1972, 14.
8. Calvin Green, untitled review of *Samuel Fuller* by Phil Hardy, *Cineaste* 4, no. 4 (spring 1971): 32.
9. Moullet, "Sam Fuller," 147–48. Moullet is not American, so he can perhaps be forgiven for not recognizing that this criticism applies to virtually all images of communism in American Cold War popular culture.
10. George Lipsitz, "The New York Intellectuals: Samuel Fuller and Edgar Ulmer," in *Time Passages: Collective Memory and American Popular Culture* (Minneapolis: University of Minnesota Press, 1990), 189.
11. See, for instance, Robert Hatch's review of *The Steel Helmet,* "Hollywood in Korea," *New Republic,* February 12, 1951, 22–23.
12. Robert Hatch, untitled review of *The Big Red One, The Nation,* July 19, 1980, 92–93.
13. John Simon, untitled review of *The Big Red One, National Review,* August 8, 1980, 976.

14. Ezra Goodman, "Low Budget Movies with POW!" *New York Times Magazine,* February 28, 1965, 43.
15. For the best accounts of Fuller's youth, see Goodman, "Low Budget Movies," 42–50; Lipsitz, "New York Intellectuals," 181–94; David Wilson, "Sam Fuller," in *Close-Up: The Contemporary Director,* ed. Jon Tuska et al. (Metuchen, N.J.: Scarecrow Press, 1981), 49–98; and David Selznick, "An Old Pro on the Go Again," *New York Times Magazine,* May 4, 1980, 48–49, 58–80.
16. Samuel Fuller, *The Dark Page,* (Duell, Sloan and Pearce, 1944). The novel was made into the 1952 movie *Scandal Sheet,* directed by Phil Karlson.
17. "Books into Films," *Publishers Weekly,* October 21, 1944, 1662.
18. See, for instance, David Anson, "An Unblinking View of War," *Newsweek,* July 28, 1980, 68.
19. Goodman, "Low Budget Movies," 43.
20. Sarris, *American Cinema,* 93.
21. Fuller, *Dark Page,* 12.
22. Wilson, "Sam Fuller," 77–78.
23. Quoted in *Voices of Film Experience: 1894 to the Present,* ed. Jay Leyda (New York: MacMillan, 1977), 157.
24. Eric Sherman and Martin Rubin, *The Director's Event: Interviews with Five American Film-makers* (New York: Atheneum, 1970), 133.
25. Sherman and Rubin, 177.
26. See especially the fight scene in *Park Row* and the long tracking shot in *Forty Guns.* Phil Hardy, *Samuel Fuller* (New York: Praeger, 1970), 45–47.
27. Raymond Durgnat, *Films and Feelings* (Cambridge, Mass.: M.I.T. Press, 1967), 19.
28. J. Hoberman, "Three American Abstract Sensationalists," in *Vulgar Modernism: Essays on Movies and Other Media* (Philadelphia: Temple University Press, 1991), 23.
29. As David Wilson has commented, "His pictures are constructed like comic books with insane characters and paranoid dream sequences." Wilson, "Sam Fuller," 60.
30. Hoberman, "Three American Abstract Sensationalists," 30.
31. Cf. "The Slaughter on Suicide Hill," reprinted in *Comic Books and America, 1945–1954,* by William W. Savage Jr. (Norman: University of Oklahoma Press, 1990), 60–65. See also Harvey Kurtzman, "The Big If," reprinted in *From Aargh to Zap! Harvey Kurtzman's Visual History of the Comics* (New York: Prentice Hall Press, 1991), 38–39.
32. Michael Gould, *Surrealism and the Cinema (Open-Eyed Screening)* (South Brunswick, N.J., and New York: A. S. Barnes, 1976), 43.
33. Nicholas Garnham, *Samuel Fuller* (New York: Viking Press, 1971), 37–38.
34. Goodman, "Low Budget Movies," 35.

35. Garnham, *Samuel Fuller,* 25–26.

36. Hardy, *Samuel Fuller,* 29; Garnham, *Samuel Fuller,* 118; Lipsitz, "New York Intellectuals," 184.

37. Paul Schrader, "Notes on *Film Noir,*" *Film Comment* 8, no. 1 (spring 1972): 12; and Jon Tuska, *Dark Cinema: American Film Noir in Cultural Perspective* (Westport, Conn.: Greenwood Press, 1984), 168.

38. Frank McConnell, "*Pickup on South Street* and the Metamorphosis of the Thriller," *Film Heritage,* spring 1973, 14.

39. Moullet, "Sam Fuller," 147.

40. Manny Farber, "Underground Films," in *Negative Space: Manny Farber on the Movies* (New York: Praeger, 1971), 16.

41. Dwight Macdonald, "Masscult and Midcult," in *Against the American Grain: Essays on the Effects of Mass Culture* (New York: Da Capo, 1983 [1962]).

42. Macdonald, 28.

43. Sherman and Rubin, *Director's Event,* 151.

44. Sherman and Rubin, 174.

45. Wilson, "Sam Fuller," 97. Ellipses in original.

46. Moullet, "Sam Fuller," 149.

47. Paul Fussell, *Wartime* (New York: Oxford University Press, 1989), 177–80. Jones is quoted on 180.

48. Wilson, "Sam Fuller," 52.

49. Wilson, 57.

50. Joseph Heller, *Catch-22* (New York: Dell, 1961); Kurt Vonnegut, *Slaughterhouse Five* (New York: Dell, 1969).

51. Morris Dickstein, *Gates of Eden: American Culture in the Sixties* (New York: Penguin, 1989), 99.

52. The deterioration was real to a great extent. During the filming of the movie in May 1961, Jeff Chandler suffered a slipped disc and required three operations before he died of blood poisoning on June 17, 1961. *FilmFacts* 5 (1962): 123.

53. Sherman and Rubin, *Director's Event,* 165.

54. Sherman and Rubin, 130–31.

55. Wilson, "Sam Fuller," 97.

56. Quoted in Hardy, *Samuel Fuller,* 21.

57. Sherman and Rubin, *Director's Event,* 163.

58. Ken Kesey, *One Flew over the Cuckoo's Nest* (New York: New American Library, 1962).

59. Manny Farber, "Samuel Fuller," in *Negative Space,* 129.

60. Garnham, *Samuel Fuller,* 21.

61. Robert G. Porfirio, "No Way Out: Existential Motifs in the *Film Noir,*" *Sight and Sound* 45, no. 4 (autumn 1976): 212–17.

62. See, especially, McConnell's critique of Sarris, "Pickup," 9–11. See also the introduction to Sherman and Rubin's interview with Fuller, *Director's Event*, 125. Interestingly, Fuller took the characterization as a compliment. "It doesn't bother me at all. Yes. In a way . . . it intrigues me. It gives me the picture of a hairy ape and a grabber of women's hair." Russell Merritt and Peter Lehman, "'Being Wrong Is the Right Way of Living': An Interview with Samuel Fuller," *Wide Angle* 4, no. 1 (1980).

63. Marshall Berman, *The Politics of Authenticity: Radical Individualism and the Emergence of Modern Society* (New York: Atheneum, 1970), x.

64. Garnham, *Samuel Fuller,* 95.

65. Hardy, *Samuel Fuller,* 9.

Chapter 8: Roger Corman's Low-Budget Modernism

1. Ed Naha, *The Films of Roger Corman: Brilliance on a Budget* (New York: Arco, 1982), 169.

2. Naha, 169.

3. For the story of the making of *The Terror,* see Naha, 52–57, 169–70; Roger Corman and Jim Jerome, *How I Made a Hundred Movies in Hollywood and Never Lost a Dime* (New York: Random House, 1990), 88–94; Fred Olen Ray, *The New Poverty Row: Independent Filmmakers as Distributors* (Jefferson, N.C.: MacFarland, 1991), 49–51.

4. Siegfried Kracauer, *From Caligari to Hitler: A Psychological History of the German Film* (Princeton, N.J.: Princeton University Press, 1947), 5.

5. For a discussion of the definition of exploitation films, see Thomas Doherty, *Teenagers and Teenpics: The Juvenilization of American Movies in the 1950s* (Boston: Unwin Hyman, 1988), 3–9.

6. Quoted in J. Philip di Franco, *The Movie World of Roger Corman* (New York: Chelsea House, 1979), 88.

7. Jay Leyda, ed., *Voices of Film Experience: 1894 to the Present* (New York: Macmillan, 1977), 84.

8. Kracauer, *From Caligari to Hitler,* 5.

9. Ethan Mordden, *Medium Cool: The Movies of the 1960s* (New York: Alfred A. Knopf, 1990), 324.

10. Quoted in di Franco, *Movie World,* 197.

11. See especially di Franco, *Movie World;* Naha, *Films;* and Mark McGee, *Roger Corman: The Best of the Cheap Acts* (Jefferson, N.C: MacFarland, 1988).

12. See especially David Will and Paul Willeman, eds., *Roger Corman: The Millenic Vision* (Edinburgh: Edinburgh Film Festival in association with *Cinema* magazine, 1970).

13. Gary Morris, *Roger Corman* (Boston: Twayne, 1985).

14. On Corman's early years, see Corman and Jerome, *How I Made a Hundred Movies,* 3–21.

15. Corman and Jerome, *How I Made a Hundred Movies,* 18.

16. Naha, *Films,* 94. The movie was distributed by Lippert Productions, one of the few independent film companies in the pre-AIP early fifties. Lippert also produced several of Samuel Fuller's early films.

17. Corman and Jerome, 25.

18. On the history of American International Pictures, see Mark McGee, *Fast and Furious: The Story of American International Pictures* (Jefferson, N.C.: MacFarland, 1984).

19. See Doherty, *Teenagers,* 18–28.

20. Doherty, 29–35. On the growth of drive-ins in the postwar era, see Kerry Segrave, *Drive-In Theaters: A History from Their Inception in 1933* (Jefferson, N.C.: MacFarland, 1992).

21. Naha, *Films,* 102.

22. Samuel Arkoff was interviewed by Tom Weaver in Weaver, *Interviews with B Science Fiction and Horror Movie Makers* (Jefferson, N.C.: MacFarland, 1988), 18–19.

23. Corman's own movies distributed by Filmgroup include *The Wasp Woman, Ski Troop Attack* (1960), *Little Shop of Horrors, The Last Woman on Earth* (1960), and *Creature from the Haunted Sea.*

24. For a brief history of Filmgroup, see Ray, *New Poverty Row,* 23–62.

25. Morris, *Roger Corman,* 4.

26. McGee, *Roger Corman,* 151; Corman and Jerome, *How I Made a Hundred Movies,* 47.

27. Corman and Jerome, *How I Made a Hundred Movies,* 34–35.

28. Morris, *Roger Corman,* 6–10, quote on 8.

29. Peter Biskind, *Seeing Is Believing: How Hollywood Taught Us to Stop Worrying and Love the Fifties* (New York: Pantheon, 1983), 103–5, 124–29.

30. J. Hoberman, *Vulgar Modernism: Writings on Movies and Other Media* (Philadelphia: Temple University Press, 1991), 32–40, quote on 33.

31. Hoberman, 38.

32. Corman and Jerome, *How I Made a Hundred Movies,* 63–69.

33. Danny Peary, *Cult Movies* (London: Vermilion, 1981), 203–5.

34. Quoted in Corman and Jerome, *How I Made a Hundred Movies,* 67.

35. Corman and Jerome, 73.

36. Morris Dickstein, *Gates of Eden: American Culture in the Sixties* (New York: Penguin, 1989), 96–98.

37. Charles Beaumont, "Foreword," in *The Intruder* (New York: Dell, 1962 [1959]).

38. Corman and Jerome, *How I Made a Hundred Movies,* 97–104.

39. Corman's Poe films include *House of Usher* (1960), *The Pit and the Pendulum*

(1961), *Premature Burial* (1961), *Tales of Terror* (1961), *The Raven* (1962), *The Masque of the Red Death* (1964), and *The Tomb of Ligeia* (1964). *The Haunted Palace* (1963) is usually included in lists of the Poe films because its title was taken from a poem by Poe, but it was based on a story by H. P. Lovecraft.

40. Morris, *Roger Corman,* 11.

41. Corman and Jerome, *How I Made a Hundred Movies,* 190. According to Corman, "When I finally met Bergman years later, he mentioned that he thought it was great that we put his film in the drive-ins. 'Nobody ever thought of that before,' he said. 'I've always wanted my pictures to get the widest possible audience. That's an audience that never saw my pictures before New World.'"

42. Susan Sontag, "One Culture and the New Sensibility," *Against Interpretation and Other Essays* (New York: Anchor, 1966), 293–304, quote on 304.

43. Quoted in Corman and Jerome, *How I Made a Hundred Movies,* 184–85.

Chapter 9: Richard Condon and the Paranoid Surreal

1. John Marks, *The Search for the Manchurian Candidate: The CIA and Mind Control* (New York: Dell, 1979), 9–10.

2. Dwight Macdonald, "A Critique of the Warren Report," in *Discriminations: Essays and Afterthoughts* (New York: Da Capo, 1985), 99–139; I. F. Stone, "The Left and the Warren Commission Report," *I. F. Stone's Weekly,* October 5, 1964, 1–3; Stone's "paranoid nonsense" comment is quoted in "Izzy," *Newsweek,* January 22, 1968, 52.

3. Richard Condon, "'Manchurian Candidate' in Dallas," *The Nation,* December 28, 1963, 449.

4. Condon, 449.

5. The extent to which Condon accepted these conspiracy theories and the extent to which he saw them as social metaphors is not certain. In his 1973 autobiography, he repeated the argument made in his *Nation* article ten years earlier, seemingly accepting Oswald's guilt. Richard Condon, *And Then We Moved to Rosenarra* (New York: Dial, 1973), 266–69.

6. Richard Condon, *Winter Kills* (New York: Dial, 1974).

7. Richard Condon, *Death of a Politician* (New York: Ballantine, 1978); Carl Ogelsby, *The JFK Assassination: The Facts and the Theories* (New York: Signet, 1992), 29.

8. Richard Hofstadter, *The Paranoid Style in American Politics* (New York: Vintage, 1964), vii–40.

9. Christopher Lasch, "The Life of Kennedy's Death," *Harper's,* October 1983, 38–39.

10. Michael Rogin, *Ronald Reagan: The Movie, and Other Episodes in Political Demonology* (Berkeley: University of California Press, 1987), xiv.

11. Thomas Pynchon, *The Crying of Lot 49* (New York: Bantam, 1966); Kurt Vonnegut, *The Sirens of Titan* (New York: Dell, 1959).

12. Julian Smith, "The Infernal Comedy of Richard Condon," *Twentieth Century Literature,* January 1969, 221.

13. Whitney Balliett, "Made in the U.S.A.," *New Yorker,* May 30, 1959, 105–7.

14. "Paintless in Armageddon," *Time,* July 6, 1959, 78–79.

15. "The Sustaining Stream," *Time,* February 1, 1963, 82–84.

16. "An Impolite Interview with Joseph Heller," in Paul Krassner, ed., *Best of the Realist* (Philadelphia: Running Press, 1984), 77.

17. Kurt Vonnegut, "The Fall of a Climber," *New York Times Book Review,* September 25, 1966, 5, 42.

18. Herbert Mitgang, "Hollywood-on-the-Rhine," *New York Times Book Review,* September 30, 1967, 21.

19. Roger Sale, untitled review of Richard Condon's *The Whisper of the Axe, New York Times Book Review,* May 23, 1976, 4; Herbert Gold, "Pop Goes the Novel," *New York Times Book Review,* March 12, 1978, 10, 39.

20. Smith, "Infernal Comedy," 221.

21. Richard Condon, "That's Entertainment," *Harper's,* September 1977, 80.

22. Condon, 84.

23. Arthur Cooper, "The Entertainer," *Newsweek,* June 9, 1975, 82.

24. This chapter focuses primarily on the six novels Condon wrote between 1958 and 1966, though his later works are occasionally examined to trace themes that carry throughout Condon's oeuvre.

25. Richard Condon, "Going Hollywood," *Gourmet,* November 1992, 116.

26. Richard Condon, *The Oldest Confession* (New York: Dell, 1958), 11.

27. Condon, 19.

28. Condon, 106.

29. Condon, 106.

30. Condon, 33.

31. Condon, 14.

32. Condon, 58.

33. Condon, 104.

34. Condon, 120.

35. Condon, 131.

36. Richard Condon, *Arigato* (New York: Dial, 1972).

37. Mordechai Richler, "A Captivating but Distorted Image," *Book Week (Sunday Herald Tribune),* September 13, 1964, 19.

38. Richard Condon, *An Infinity of Mirrors* (New York: Random House, 1964), 243–45.

39. Condon, 332.

40. Leo Braudy, "*Winter Kills* by Richard Condon," *Native Informant: Essays on Film, Fiction, and Popular Culture* (New York: Oxford University Press, 1991), 269–70.

41. Richard Condon, *Some Angry Angel* (New York: McGraw-Hill, 1960), 86.

42. Condon, 250.

43. Richard Rovere, *Senator Joe McCarthy* (New York: Harper, 1959).

44. Richard Condon, *The Manchurian Candidate* (New York: Signet, 1959), 87, 102, 146.

45. Condon, 146–48.

46. Condon, 174.

47. Condon, 288.

48. Condon, 290.

49. Arthur Schlesinger Jr., *The Vital Center: The Politics of Freedom* (Boston: Houghton Mifflin, 1949), x.

50. Mickey Spillane, *One Lonely Night* (New York: E. P. Dutton and Sons, 1951).

51. Braudy, "Winter Kills," 268.

52. Richard Condon, *The Vertical Smile* (New York: Dial, 1971).

53. Hofstadter, *Paranoid Style,* 29.

54. Richard Condon, *Prizzi's Honor* (New York: Berkley, 1982); Condon, *A Trembling upon Rome* (New York: Pinnacle, 1983).

55. Richler, "Captivating but Distorted Image," 4; David Dempsey, "Too Real to Live," *New York Times Book Review,* September 13, 1964, 52.

56. Clement Greenberg, "Surrealist Painting," in *One Hundred Years of the Nation,* ed. Henry Christman (NewYork: Macmillan, 1965), 244.

57. Condon, "'Manchurian Candidate' in Dallas," 451.

58. Joe Sanders wrote of one of Condon's later novels, "In *Winter Kills* the hero must resolve mutually exclusive combinations of fact and interpretation to find out who killed his brother, the Kennedy-analogue president, and he also must find out who is killing all the people who could help him answer that question. He is more hindered than helped by the information-gathering services owned by his Pa, which provide so much data that the hero is overwhelmed." Joe Sanders, "The Fantastic Non-Fantastic: Richard Condon's Waking Nightmares," *Extrapolation* 25, no. 2 (summer 1984): 129.

59. I. F. Stone, "A Reply to the White Paper" (1965), in *In a Time of Torment* (Boston: Little, Brown, 1967), 212–18.

60. Sanders, "Fantastic Non-Fantastic," 125.

61. Sanders, 137.

62. Richard Condon, *A Talent for Loving or, the Great Cowboy Race* (New York: McGraw-Hill, 1961), 226.

63. Richard Condon, *Mile High* (New York: Dell, 1969), 40.

64. Condon, *Manchurian Candidate,* 138.

65. Condon, *Death of a Politician,* 80–83.

66. Sanders, "Fantastic Non-Fantastic," 132.

67. Sanders, 131.

68. Condon, *Talent for Loving,* 50–56.

69. Philip Wylie, *Generation of Vipers* (New York: Farrar and Rinehart, 1942), 184–204; Michael Rogin, "Kiss Me Deadly: Communism, Motherhood, and Cold War Movies," in *Ronald Reagan,* 242–43.

70. Stephen Whitfield, *The Culture of the Cold War* (Baltimore: Johns Hopkins University Press, 1991), 43–45.

71. Condon, *Manchurian Candidate,* 84, 325–26.

72. Condon, 81.

73. Condon, 325–26.

74. Condon, 348–51.

75. Condon, *Some Angry Angel,* 56–60.

76. Condon, 85.

77. Condon, 181–82.

78. Condon, 4–5, 274–75.

79. Condon, 78.

80. Condon, 183.

81. Condon, 195–96.

82. Richard Condon, *Any God Will Do* (New York: Random House, 1966), 127.

83. Condon, 124, 128.

84. Hofstadter, *Paranoid Style,* 32.

85. Condon, *Any God Will Do,* 232.

86. Condon, 311.

87. Russell Jacoby, *The Last Intellectuals: American Culture in the Age of Academe* (New York: Farrar, Strauss and Giroux, 1987), 85.

88. Morris Dickstein, *Gates of Eden: American Culture in the Sixties* (New York: Penguin, 1989), 97.

89. Kurt Vonnegut, *Player Piano* (New York: Delta, 1952); Harlan Ellison, "'Repent Harlequin!' Said the Ticktockman" (1965), in *The Essential Ellison* (Beverly Hills, Calif.: Morpheus International, 1991), 877–86.

90. Condon, *Manchurian Candidate,* 190.

Chapter 10: Rod Serling and The Twilight Zone

1. Rod Serling, "Author's Comment," in *Television Plays for Writers: Eight Television Plays with Comment and Analysis by the Authors,* ed. A. S. Burack (Boston: The Writer, 1957), 354–55.

2. This quote comes from a 1959 interview on CBS's "The Mike Wallace Interview."

The interview is available on the Fox videotape, "Video Treasures of the *Twilight Zone:* A Collection of Special Episodes and Rare Footage."

3. "Noon on Doomsday" eventually aired April 25, 1956. For a complete filmography of Serling's work, see Gordon Sander, *Serling: The Rise and Twilight of Television's Last Angry Man* (New York: Dutton, 1992), 225–51.

4. Joel Engel, *Rod Serling: The Dreams and Nightmares of Life in the Twilight Zone* (Chicago: Contemporary Books, 1989), 167–68. "A Town Has Turned to Dust" aired June 19, 1958.

5. Engel, 147.

6. Frank Sturcken, *Live Television: The Golden Age of 1946–1958 in New York* (Jefferson, N.C.: MacFarland, 1990), 90–92.

7. Rod Serling, "About Writing for Television," in *Patterns: Four Television Plays with the Author's Personal Commentaries* (New York: Simon and Schuster, 1957), 25. "The Arena" was televised on CBS's *Studio One* on April 9, 1956.

8. Erik Barnouw, *Tube of Plenty: The Evolution of American Television* (New York: Oxford University Press, 1975), 99–148 passim. See also Victor Navasky, *Naming Names* (New York: Viking Press, 1980).

9. Erik Barnouw related a chilling story involving Daniel Petrie, a director on *Studio One* and *U.S. Steel Hour* (where he directed "Noon on Doomsday"). At two o'clock one morning, Petrie was awakened by a phone call. The caller asked if he were speaking with Daniel Petrie, the director. When Petrie said yes and asked who was calling, the caller responded, "Never mind who I am. Do you have a wife who's tall and blonde?" When Petrie said yes, the caller continued, "I just want to give you a little piece of advice, Mr. Petrie. You better tell your wife to be careful how she talks about the blacklist at cocktail parties," and then hung up. Barnouw, *Tube of Plenty,* 167.

10. Tad Mosel, *Other People's Houses* (New York: Simon and Schuster, 1958), 75.

11. Serling, "About Writing for Television," 19. The show aired on CBS's *Appointment with Adventure,* April 17, 1955. Serling changed the words to "United States" and "fortunate."

12. Michael Kerbel, "The Golden Age of TV Drama," *Film Comment* 15, no. 4 (July–August, 1979): 19.

13. There were, of course, other factors in the exodus of the early television writers. Live television was on the decline, being replaced by westerns and other taped series. And the industry as a whole was moving from New York, where most of these writers lived, to southern California.

14. Quoted in Sander, *Serling,* 162.

15. Engel, *Rod Serling,* 45. This outline of Serling's early years is drawn from Engel, 5–63; and Sander, *Serling,* 9–50.

16. Serling, "About Writing for Television," 3.

17. Sander, *Serling,* 65–79; Engel, *Rod Serling,* 75–88; Serling, "About Writing for Television," 1–6.
18. Engel, *Rod Serling,* 84.
19. Sander, *Serling,* 80.
20. Sturcken, *Live Television,* 28.
21. Barnouw, *Tube of Plenty,* 163.
22. "I Lift My Lamp" appeared on NBC's *Hallmark Hall of Fame,* August 17, 1952.
23. Rod Serling, "The Rack," in *Patterns,* 131.
24. Aired January 20, 1961. For a complete listing of the credits and telecast dates of all *Twilight Zone* episodes, see Marc Scott Zicree, *The Twilight Zone Companion* (New York: Bantam, 1989, second edition).
25. Aired October 20, 1961.
26. *Cincinnati Enquirer,* March 31, 1956.
27. Aired March 4, 1960.
28. Aired April 6, 1962.
29. "The Strike" was telecast June 7, 1954, on CBS's *Studio One.* The script is reprinted in Gore Vidal, ed., *Best Television Plays* (New York: Ballantine, 1956), 163–90.
30. Vidal, 180.
31. Serling, "The Rack," 111.
32. Serling, 124.
33. Serling, 135.
34. "Patterns" was telecast on ABC's *Kraft-Television Theater,* January 12, 1955.
35. Rod Serling, "Patterns," in *Patterns,* 85.
36. Rod Serling, "Author's Commentary on 'Patterns,'" in *Patterns,* 85.
37. "The Rank and File" appeared on CBS's *Playhouse 90* on May 28, 1959.
38. "Requiem for a Heavyweight" aired on CBS's *Playhouse 90* on October 11, 1956.
39. "The Comedian" was telecast on CBS's *Playhouse 90* on February 14, 1957. Serling's screenplay was adapted from a short story by Ernest Lehman.
40. "The Velvet Alley" was telecast January 22, 1959, on CBS's *Playhouse 90.*
41. Both quoted in William Boddy, "Entering 'The Twilight Zone,'" *Screen* 25, nos. 4–5 (July–October 1984): 102.
42. Quoted in Boddy, 106.
43. "The Weary Young Man," *Newsweek,* September 28, 1959, 81.
44. Quoted in Lawrence Venuti, "Rod Serling, Television Censorship, *The Twilight Zone,*" *Western Humanities Review* 35, no. 4 (winter 1981): 357.
45. Venuti, 362.
46. Quoted in Engel, *Rod Serling,* 104.
47. Serling, "About Writing for Television," 25.
48. Serling, "Strike," 178.

49. Rod Serling, "Color Scheme," in *The Season to Be Wary* (Boston: Little, Brown, 1967), 97–192.

50. *Los Angeles Times,* April 8, 1968.

51. For the best discussion of Serling's politics, see Engel, *Rod Serling;* and Sander, *Serling.*

52. Marvin Gottfried, *A Theater Divided: The Postwar American Stage* (Boston: Little, Brown, 1967), 3–26.

53. Gottfried, 48–49. For a broader discussion of the right-wing theater, see 27–54.

54. Gottfried, 57. For a more detailed discussion of the left-wing theater, see 55–89.

55. Kenneth Hey, "'Marty': Aesthetics vs. Medium in Early Television Drama," in *American History/American Television: Interpreting the Video Past,* ed. John E. O'Connor (New York: Frederick Ungar, 1983), 101.

56. Aired April 4, 1961.

57. Aired March 2, 1962. Serling's screenplay was adapted from a short story by Damon Knight.

58. Aired March 7, 1963. Written by Rod Serling.

59. Zicree, *Twilight Zone Companion,* xii.

60. Aired January 1, 1960. Written by Rod Serling.

61. Aired November 27, 1959.

62. Aired October 7, 1959.

63. Aired November 20, 1959. Adapted by Rod Serling from a story by Lynn Veneble.

64. Aired May 15, 1964. Written by Rod Serling.

65. Aired February 21, 1963. Written by Charles Beaumont.

66. Aired October 30, 1959.

67. Rod Serling, "Walking Distance," in *Stories from the Twilight Zone* (New York: Bantam, 1960), 58.

68. Aired May 6, 1960.

69. Aired December 22, 1961.

70. Aired May 5, 1961.

71. For a similar theme, see Rod Serling, "Judgment Night." Aired December 4, 1959.

72. Sander, *Serling,* 109–10.

73. Aired March 4, 1960. Written by Rod Serling.

74. In the episode's conclusion, it is revealed that aliens are watching the residents of Maple Street, but they have only cut off the power as part of an experiment to see how rapidly humans will turn on each other when something inexplicable occurs.

75. Aired January 3, 1964. Written by Earl Hamner.

76. Aired November 1, 1963. Written by Jerry Sohl (though credited to Charles Beaumont) from an idea by Sohl and Beaumont.

77. For similar themes, see Serling's "A Thing About Machines," which aired October

28, 1960; and "From Agnes, with Love," written by Bernard C. Shoenfeld, which aired February 14, 1964.

78. See, for instance, Zicree's criticism of the show as science fiction, *Twilight Zone Companion,* 73, 98, 106.

79. Engel, *Rod Serling,* 215–16.

80. Aired February 26, 1960.

81. For a similar theme, see Serling's "The Parallel." Aired March 14, 1963.

82. Lawrence Sutin, *Divine Invasions: A Life of Philip K. Dick* (Secaucus, N.J.: Carol Publishing Group, 1989), 91.

83. Aired November 3, 1961. Adapted by Rod Serling from a short story by Jerome Bixby.

84. On Serling's post–*Twilight Zone* career, see Engel, *Rod Serling,* 253–344; Sander, *Serling,* 198–223; Zicree, *Twilight Zone Companion,* 430–41.

Conclusion: The Emancipation of Dissonance

1. William L. O'Neill, *American High: The Years of Confidence, 1945–1960* (New York: Free Press, 1986); William Graebner, *The Age of Doubt: American Thought and Culture in the 1940s* (Urbana: University of Illinois Press, 1994).

2. Quoted in Andreas Huyssen, "Mapping the Postmodern," in *After the Great Divide: Modernism, Mass Culture, Postmodernism* (Bloomington: University of Indiana Press, 1986), 189.

3. For a good introduction to modernism, see Daniel Joseph Singal, "Toward a Definition of Modernism," *American Quarterly* 39, no. 1 (spring 1987): 7–26.

4. Huyssen, "Mapping," 190.

5. Singal, "Toward a Definition of Modernism," 16.

6. Charles Beaumont, *Remember? Remember?* (New York: Random House, 1963).

7. The literature on postmodernism is vast, but for a useful introduction, see Huyssen, "Mapping," 178–221; Todd Gitlin, "Postmodernism: Roots and Politics," in *Cultural Politics in Contemporary America,* ed. Ian Angus and Sut Jhully (New York: Routledge, 1988), 347–60; and Fredric Jameson, *Postmodernism, or the Cultural Logic of Late Capitalism* (Durham, N.C.: Duke University Press, 1991).

8. J. Hoberman, "Love and Death in the American Supermarketplace," *Vulgar Modernism: Writings On Movies and Other Media* (Philadelphia: Temple University Press, 1991), 50.

9. Jameson, *Postmodernism,* 4–6.

10. John P. Diggins, *The American Left in the Twentieth Century* (New York: Harcourt Brace Jovanovich, 1973), 156.

11. I. F. Stone, for one, viewed Rubin's appearance before HUAC as a signal event

in the history of the left. Whereas Stone believed his generation acquiesced to established power by playing the role of fearful witnesses, Rubin's satiric performance had disrupted the carefully choreographed ritual to point out the irony and absurdity of the committee's activities. See Andrew Kopkind, "The Importance of Being Izzy," *Ramparts,* May 1974. 43. On the integration movement at the University of Texas, see James Miller, *"Democracy Is in the Streets": From Port Huron to the Siege of Chicago* (New York: Simon and Schuster, 1987), 224.

12. Dwight Macdonald, "Afterword," in *Discriminations: Essays and Afterthoughts* (New York: Da Capo, 1974), 394.

13. Chester Himes, "Prediction," in *The Collected Stories of Chester Himes* (New York: Thunder's Mouth Press, 1991), 420–25.

14. J. Hoberman makes this point in *Vulgar Modernism,* 7.

Bibliography

"Allegory of Any Place." *Time,* October 30, 1964, 85–86.

Amis, Kingsley. *New Maps of Hell: A Survey of Science Fiction.* New York: Harcourt Brace, 1960.

Angus, Ian, and Sut Jhully, eds. *Cultural Politics in Contemporary America.* New York: Routledge, 1988.

Anson, David. "An Unblinking View of War." *Newsweek,* July 28, 1980, 68.

Asimov, Isaac. "Ray: An Appreciation." In *The Bradbury Chronicles: Stories in Honor of Ray Bradbury,* edited by William F. Nolan and Martin H. Greenberg. New York: Penguin, 1991.

Bailey, Frankie. *Out of the Woodpile: Black Characters in Crime and Detective Fiction.* New York: Greenwood Press, 1991.

Ball, John. *In the Heat of the Night.* New York: Bantam, 1965.

Balliet, Whitney. "Made in the U.S.A." *New Yorker,* May 30, 1959, 105–7.

Barnouw, Erik. *The Image Empire.* New York: Oxford University Press, 1970.

———. *Tube of Plenty: The Evolution of American Television.* New York: Oxford University Press, 1975.

Beaumont, Charles. "The Howling Man," "The Jungle," "The Devil You Say," and "The Beautiful People." In *The Twilight Zone: The Original Stories,* edited by Martin H. Greenberg et al. New York: Avon, 1985.

————. *The Howling Man.* Edited by Roger Anker. New York: Tor, 1988.

————. *The Intruder.* New York: Dell, 1962 (1959).

————. *The Magic Man and Other Science-Fantasy Stories.* Greenwich, Conn.: Fawcett, 1965.

————. *Night Ride and Other Journeys.* New York: Bantam, 1960.

————. *Remember? Remember?* New York: Macmillan, 1963.

————. "Something in the Earth." In *The Bradbury Chronicles: Stories in Honor of Ray Bradbury,* edited by William F. Nolan and Martin H. Greenberg. New York: Penguin, 1991.

————. *Yonder: Stories of Fantasy and Science Fiction.* New York: Bantam, 1958.

Bell, Daniel. *The End of Ideology.* New York: Free Press, 1962.

Berman, Marshall. *All That Is Solid Melts into Air: The Experience of Modernity.* New York: Penguin, 1988.

————. *The Politics of Authenticity: Radical Individualism and the Emergence of Modern Society.* New York: Atheneum, 1970.

Biskind, Peter. *Seeing Is Believing: How Hollywood Taught Us to Stop Worrying and Love the Fifties.* New York: Pantheon, 1983.

Block, Lawrence. "A Tale of Pulp and Passion: The Jim Thompson Revival." *New York Times Book Review,* October 14, 1990, 37–38.

Boddy, William. "Entering 'The Twilight Zone.'" *Screen,* July–October 1984, 98–108.

Bogdanovich, Peter. "Hollywood." *Esquire,* September 1972, 12–22.

Bogle, Donald. *Toms, Coons, Mulattoes, Mammies, and Bucks: An Interpretive History of Blacks in American Films.* New York: Continuum, 1989.

Bradbury, Ray. "Afterword: Fifty Years, Fifty Friends." In *The Bradbury Chronicles: Stories in Honor of Ray Bradbury,* edited by William F. Nolan and Martin H. Greenberg. New York: Penguin, 1991.

————. *The Anthem Sprinters and Other Antics.* New York: Dial, 1963.

————. *Dandelion Wine.* New York: Bantam, 1957.

————. *Fahrenheit 451.* New York: Ballantine, 1953.

————. *The Golden Apples of the Sun.* New York: Bantam, 1953.

————. "How to Keep and Feed a Muse." *Writer* 74, no. 7 (July 1961): 7–12.

————. *I Sing the Body Electric.* New York: Bantam, 1969.

————. *The Illustrated Man.* New York: Bantam, 1951.

————. "The Joy of Writing." *Writer* 69, no. 10 (October 1956): 293–95.

————. *Long after Midnight.* New York: Alfred A. Knopf, 1976.

————. *The Machineries of Joy.* New York: Bantam, 1964.

————. *The Martian Chronicles.* New York: Bantam, 1950.

————. *A Medicine for Melancholy.* New York: Bantam, 1959.

————. *A Memory of Murder.* New York: Dell, 1984.

————. *The October Country.* New York: Ballantine, 1955.

———. *R Is for Rocket.* New York: Bantam, 1962.

———. *S Is for Space.* New York: Bantam, 1966.

Braudy, Leo. "*Winter Kills* by Richard Condon." In *Native Informant: Essays on Film, Fiction, and Popular Culture.* New York: Oxford University Press, 1991.

Brody, Meredith. "Killer Instinct: Jim Thompson." *Film Comment* 20, no. 5 (September–October 1984): 46–47.

Brophy, Brigid. "Highsmith." *Don't Never Forget: Collected Views and Reviews.* New York: Holt, Rinehart and Winston, 1966.

Burack, A. S., ed. *Television Plays for Writers: Eight Television Plays with Comment and Analysis by the Authors.* Boston: The Writer, 1957.

Camus, Albert. *The Myth of Sisyphus and Other Essays.* New York: Vintage, 1955.

Carson, Clayborne. *In Struggle: SNCC and the Black Awakening of the 1960s.* Cambridge, Mass.: Harvard University Press, 1981.

Charles, Will [Charles Willeford]. *The Hombre from Sonora.* Lenox Hill Press, 1971.

Christian, Henry, ed. *One Hundred Years of the Nation.* New York: MacMillan, 1965.

Clareson, Thomas. *Understanding Contemporary American Science Fiction: The Formative Period, 1926–1970.* Columbia: University of South Carolina Press, 1990.

Condon, Richard. *And Then We Moved to Rosenarra.* New York: Dial, 1973.

———. *Any God Will Do.* New York: Random House, 1966.

———. *Arigato.* New York: Dial, 1972.

———. *Death of a Politician.* New York: Ballantine, 1978.

———. "Going Hollywood." *Gourmet,* November 1992, 114–20.

———. *An Infinity of Mirrors.* New York: Random House, 1964.

———. *The Manchurian Candidate.* New York: Signet, 1959.

———. "'Manchurian Candidate' in Dallas." *The Nation,* December 26, 1963, 449–51.

———. *Mile High.* New York: Dell, 1969.

———. *The Oldest Confession.* New York: Dell, 1958.

———. *Some Angry Angel.* New York: McGraw-Hill, 1960.

———. *A Talent for Loving or, The Great Cowboy Race.* New York: McGraw-Hill, 1961.

———. "That's Entertainment." *Harper's,* September 1977, 80–85.

———. *The Vertical Smile.* New York: Dial, 1971.

———. *Winter Kills.* New York: Dell, 1974.

Cooper, Arthur. "The Entertainer." *Newsweek,* June 9, 1975, 81–82.

Corman, Roger, and Jim Jerome. *How I Made a Hundred Movies in Hollywood and Never Lost a Dime.* New York: Random House, 1990.

Crouch, Stanley. "Bird Land." *New Republic,* February 27, 1989, 25–31.

del Rey, Lester. *The World of Science Fiction.* New York: Ballantine, 1979.

D'Emilio, John. *Making Trouble: Essays on Gay History, Politics, and the University.* New York: Routledge, 1992.

Dickstein, Morris. *Gates of Eden: American Culture in the Sixties.* New York: Penguin, 1977.

Diggins, John P. *The American Left in the Twentieth Century.* New York: Harcourt Brace Jovanovich, 1973.

Doherty, Thomas. *Teenagers and Teenpics: The Juvenilization of American Movies in the 1950s.* Boston: Unwin Hyman, 1988.

Dostoevsky, Fyodor. *Notes from the Underground.* New York: Dover, 1992.

DuPont, Joan. "Criminal Pursuits." *New York Times Magazine,* June 12, 1988, 60–66.

Durgnat, Raymond. *Films and Feelings.* Cambridge, Mass.: M.I.T. Press, 1967.

Durham, Philip. "The 'Black Mask' School." In *Tough Guy Writers of the Thirties,* edited by David Madden. Carbondale, Illinois: Southern Illinois University Press, 1968.

Ellison, Harlan. "Introduction to Ray Bradbury's 'Christ, Old Student in a New School.'" In *Again, Danger Visions,* edited by Harlan Ellison. New York: Signet, 1972.

———. "'Repent Harlequin!' Said the Ticktockman" (1965). In *The Essential Ellison.* Beverly Hills, Calif.: Morpheus International, 1991.

Ellison, Ralph. *Invisible Man.* New York: Vintage, 1952.

Ely, Melvin Patrick. *The Adventures of Amos 'n' Andy: A Social History of an American Phenomenon.* New York: Free Press, 1991.

Engel, Joel. *Rod Serling: The Dreams and Nightmares of Life in the Twilight Zone.* Chicago: Contemporary Books, 1989.

Fanon, Frantz. *The Wretched of the Earth.* New York: Grove Press, 1963.

Farber, Manny. *Negative Space: Manny Farber on the Movies.* New York: Praeger, 1971.

Franco, J. Philip di. *The Movie World of Roger Corman.* New York: Chelsea House, 1979.

Fromm, Erich. *Escape from Freedom.* New York: Avon, 1941.

Fuller, Samuel. *The Dark Page.* Duell, Sloan and Pearce, 1944.

Fussell, Paul. *Wartime: Understanding and Behavior during the Second World War.* New York: Oxford University Press, 1989.

Garnham, Nicholas. *Samuel Fuller.* New York: Viking Press, 1971.

Gifford, Barry. "The Godless World of Jim Thompson" (1984). In *Nothing More than Murder,* by Jim Thompson. Berkeley: Black Lizard Press, 1948.

Gilbert, James. *A Cycle of Outrage: America's Reaction to the Juvenile Delinquent in the 1950s.* New York: Oxford University Press, 1986.

Gitlin, Todd. "Postmodernism: Roots and Politics." In *Cultural Politics in Contemporary America,* edited by Ian Angus and Sut Jhully. New York: Routledge, 1988.

Gleick, James. *Chaos: Making a New Science.* New York: Viking, 1987.

Gold, Herbert. "Pop Goes the Novel." *New York Times Book Review,* March 12, 1978, 10, 39.

Goodman, Ezra. "Low Budget Movies with POW!" *New York Times Magazine,* February 28, 1965, 42–50.

Gottfried, Marvin. *A Theater Divided: The Postwar American Stage.* Boston: Little, Brown, 1967.

Goulart, Ron. *Cheap Thrills: An Informal History of the Pulp Magazines.* New Rochelle, N.Y.: Arlington House, 1972.

Gould, Michael. *Surrealism and the Cinema (Open-Eyed Screening).* South Brunswick, N.J., and New York: A. S. Barnes, 1976.

Graebner, William. *The Age of Doubt: American Thought and Culture in the 1940s.* Boston: Twayne, 1991.

Greenberg, Clement. "Avant-Garde and Kitsch." In *Mass Culture: The Popular Arts in America,* edited by Bernard Rosenberg and David Manning White. New York: Free Press, 1957.

———. "The Plight of Our Culture." *Commentary,* June 1953, 558–66.

———. "Surrealist Painting." In *One Hundred Years of the Nation,* edited by Henry Christian. New York: Macmillan, 1965.

———. "Work and Leisure under Industrialism." *Commentary,* July 1953, 54–62.

Greenberg, Martin, et al., eds. *The Twilight Zone: The Original Stories.* New York: Avon, 1985.

Guilbaut, Serge. *How New York Stole the Idea of Modern Art: Abstract Expressionism, Freedom, and the Cold War.* Chicago: University of Chicago Press, 1983.

Halttenun, Karen. *Confidence Men and Painted Women: A Study of Middle Class Culture in America.* New Haven, Conn.: Yale University Press, 1982.

Hardy, Phil. *Samuel Fuller.* New York: Praeger, 1970.

Harrison, Russell. *Patricia Highsmith.* New York: Twayne, 1997.

Heller, Joseph. *Catch-22.* New York: Simon and Schuster, 1961.

Hentoff, Nat. "A Brief Note on the Romance of 'The White Negro.'" In *The Jazz Life.* New York: Da Capo, 1961.

———. *Free Speech for Me, but Not for Thee: How the Left and Right Relentlessly Censor Each Other.* New York: Harper Collins, 1992.

Hey, Kenneth. "'Marty': Aesthetics vs. Medium in Early Television Drama." In *American History/American Television: Interpreting the Video Past,* edited by John E. O'Connor. New York: Frederick Ungar, 1983.

Highsmith, Patricia. *The Blunderer.* New York: Penzler, 1956.

———. *The Cry of the Owl.* New York: Atlantic Monthly, 1962.

———. *Deep Water.* New York: Harper and Brothers, 1957.

———. *A Game for the Living.* New York: Atlantic Monthly Press, 1958.

———. *The Glass Cell.* Garden City, N.Y.: Doubleday, 1964.

———. *Plotting and Writing Suspense Fiction.* Boston: The Writer, 1972 (1966).

———. *The Snail-Watcher and Other Stories.* Garden City, N.Y.: Doubleday, 1970.

————. *Strangers on a Train.* New York: Penguin, 1950.

————. *A Suspension of Mercy* (original American title, *The Story-Teller*). New York: Penguin, 1965.

————. *The Talented Mr. Ripley.* New York: Penguin, 1956.

————. *This Sweet Sickness.* New York: Harper and Brothers, 1960.

————. *Those Who Walk Away.* New York: Atlantic Monthly Press, 1967.

————. *The Tremor of Forgery.* Garden City, N.Y.: Doubleday, 1969.

————. *The Two Faces of January.* Garden City, N.Y.: Doubleday, 1964.

Hilfer, Anthony Channell. "'Not Really Such a Monster': Highsmith's Ripley as Thriller Protagonist and Protean Man." *Midwest Quarterly* 25, no. 4 (summer 1984).

Hillier, Jim, ed. *Cahiers du Cinema: The 1950s: Neo-Realism, Hollywood, New Wave.* Cambridge, Mass.: Harvard University Press, 1985.

Himes, Chester. *All Shot Up.* Chatham, N.J.: Chatham Bookseller, 1960.

————. *The Big Gold Dream.* Chatham, N.J.: Chatham Bookseller, 1960.

————. *Blind Man with a Pistol.* New York: Vintage, 1969.

————. *A Case of Rape.* Washington, D.C.: Howard University Press, 1984.

————. *The Collected Stories of Chester Himes.* New York: Thunder's Mouth Press, 1990.

————. *Cotton Comes to Harlem.* London: Allison and Busby, 1965.

————. *The Crazy Kill.* New York: Vintage, 1959.

————. "The Dilemma of the Negro Writer in the United States." In *Beyond the Angry Black,* edited by John A. Williams. New York: Cooper Square, 1966.

————. *The Heat's On.* New York: Vintage, 1966.

————. *If He Hollers Let Him Go.* New York: Thunder's Mouth Press, 1945.

————. *Lonely Crusade.* New York: Thunder's Mouth Press, 1947.

————. *My Life of Absurdity.* New York: Paragon House, 1976.

————. *The Quality of Hurt.* New York: Paragon House, 1972.

————. *A Rage in Harlem.* New York: Vintage, 1957.

————. *The Real Cool Killers.* London: Alison and Busby, 1965.

————. *Run Man Run.* New York: G. P. Putnam's Sons, 1966.

————. *The Third Generation.* New York: Thunder's Mouth Press, 1954.

Hoberman, J. *Vulgar Modernism: Writings on Movies and Other Media.* Philadelphia: Temple University Press, 1991.

Hodgson, Godfrey. *America in Our Time.* New York: Vintage, 1976.

Hoffer, Eric. *The True Believer.* New York: Harper and Row, 1951.

Hofstadter, Richard. *The Paranoid Style in American Politics.* New York: Vintage, 1964.

Howe, Irving. "Mass Society and Post-Modern Fiction." In *A World More Attractive: A View of Modern Literature and Politics.* Freeport, N.Y.: Books for Libraries Press, 1970 (1963).

————. "Notes on Mass Culture." In *Mass Culture: The Popular Arts in America,* edited by Bernard Rosenberg and David Manning White. New York: Free Press, 1957.

Hughes, Dorothy. *The Expendable Man.* New York: Random House, 1963.

Huyssen, Andreas. "Mapping the Postmodern." *After the Great Divide: Modernism, Mass Culture, Postmodernism.* Bloomington: University of Indiana Press, 1986.

Jacobs, Frank. *The Mad World of William Gaines.* Secaucus, N.J.: Lyle Stuart, 1972.

Jacoby, Russell. *The Last Intellectuals: American Culture in the Age of Academe.* New York: Farrar, Strauss and Giroux, 1987.

Jameson, Fredric. *Postmodernism, or the Cultural Logic of Late Capitalism.* Durham, N.C.: Duke University Press, 1991.

Jones, Malcolm, Jr. "Furtive Pleasures from a Pulp Master." *Time,* February 4, 1991, 71.

Kerbel, Michael. "The Golden Age of TV Drama." *Film Comment,* July–August 1979, 12–19.

Kirk, Russell. "Count Dracula and Mr. Ray Bradbury." *National Review,* April 4, 1967.

Knight, Damon. *In Search of Wonder: Essays on Modern Science Fiction.* Chicago: Advent Publishers, 1967.

Kracauer, Siegfried. *From Caligari to Hitler: A Psychological History of the German Film.* Princeton, N.J.: Princeton University Press, 1947.

Krassner, Paul, ed. *Best of the Realist.* Philadelphia: Running Press, 1984.

Lasch, Christopher. *The Culture of Narcissism: American Life in an Age of Diminishing Expectations.* New York: Warner, 1979.

————. "The Life of Kennedy's Death." *Harper's,* October 1983, 32–40.

————. *The True and Only Heaven: Progress and Its Critics.* New York: W. W. Norton, 1991.

Lears, Jackson. "Uneasy Courtship: Modern Art and Modern Advertising." *American Quarterly* 39, no. 1 (spring 1987): 133–54.

Levine, Lawrence. *Black Culture and Black Consciousness: Afro-American Folk Thought from Slavery to Freedom.* New York: Oxford University Press, 1977.

Leyda, Jay, ed. *Voices of Film Experience: 1894 to the Present.* New York: Macmillan, 1977.

Lipsitz, George. *Time Passages: Collective Memory and American Popular Culture.* Minneapolis: University of Minnesota Press, 1990.

————. *Rainbow at Midnight: Labor and Culture in the 1940s.* Urbana: University of Illinois Press, 1994.

Lowenthal, Leo. "Historical Perspectives of Popular Culture." In *Mass Culture: The Popular Arts in America,* edited by Bernard Rosenberg and David Manning White. New York: Free Press, 1957.

Macdonald, Dwight. *Discriminations: Essays and Afterthoughts.* New York: Da Capo, 1974.

———. "Masscult and Midcult." *Against the American Grain: Essays on the Effects of Mass Culture.* New York: Da Capo, 1983 (1962).

———. *Memoirs of a Revolutionist: Essays in Political Criticism.* New York: Farrar, Strauss and Cudahy, 1957.

Madden, David, ed. *Tough Guy Writers of the Thirties.* Carbondale: Southern Illinois University Press, 1968.

Mailer, Norman. "The White Negro." In *Advertisements for Myself.* New York: G. P. Putnam's Sons, 1959.

Marcuse, Herbert. *One-Dimensional Man.* Boston: Beacon, 1964.

Margolies, Edward. "The Thrillers of Chester Himes." *Studies in Black Literature* 1 (June 1970): 1–11.

Margolies, Edward, and Michel Fabre. *The Several Lives of Chester Himes.* Jackson: University of Mississippi Press, 1997.

Marks, John. *The Search for the Manchurian Candidate: The CIA and Mind Control.* New York: Dell, 1979.

May, Elaine Tyler. "Explosive Issues: Sex, Women, and the Bomb." In *Recasting America: Culture and Politics in the Age of Cold War,* edited by Lary May. Chicago: University of Chicago Press, 1989.

———. *Homeward Bound: American Families in the Cold War Era.* New York: Basic, 1988.

May, Lary, ed. *Recasting America: Culture and Politics in the Age of Cold War.* Chicago: University of Chicago Press, 1989.

McCauley, Michael. *Jim Thompson: Sleep with the Devil.* New York: Mysterious Press, 1991.

McCarthy, Todd, and Charles Flynn, eds. *Kings of the Bs: Working within the Hollywood System.* New York: E. P. Dutton and Company, 1975.

McConnell, Frank. "*Pickup on South Street* and the Metamorphosis of the Thriller." *Film Heritage* 8, no. 3 (spring 1973): 9–18.

McGee, Mark. *Fast and Furious: The Story of American International Pictures.* Jefferson, N.C.: McFarland, 1984.

———. *Roger Corman: The Best of the Cheap Acts.* Jefferson, N.C.: McFarland, 1988.

Milliken, Stephen F. *Chester Himes: A Critical Appraisal.* Columbia: University of Missouri Press, 1976.

Miller, James. *"Democracy Is in the Streets": From Port Huron to the Siege of Chicago.* New York: Simon and Schuster, 1987.

Mills, C. Wright. "Nothing to Laugh At." *New York Times Book Review,* April 25, 1954, 20.

Mitgang, Herbert. "Hollywood-on-the-Rhine." *New York Times Book Review,* September 30, 1967, 21.

Modleski, Tania. "Film Theory's Detour." *Screen,* November–December 1982, 72–79.

Mok, Michael. "Chester Himes." *Publishers Weekly,* April 3, 1972, 20–21.

Mordden, Ethan. *Medium Cool: The Movies of the 1960s.* New York: Alfred A. Knopf, 1990.

Morgan, Claire (Patricia Highsmith). *The Price of Salt.* New York: Arno Press, 1952.

Morris, Gary. *Roger Corman.* Boston, Twayne, 1985.

Mosel, Tad. *Other People's Houses.* New York: Simon and Schuster, 1958.

Naha, Ed. *The Films of Roger Corman: Brilliance on a Budget.* New York: Arco, 1982.

Navasky, Victor. *Naming Names.* New York: Viking, 1980.

Nolan, William F. *The Work of Charles Beaumont: An Annotated Bibliography and Guide.* San Bernardino, Calif.: Borgo Press, 1986.

Nolan, William F., and Martin H. Greenberg, eds. *The Bradbury Chronicles: Stories in Honor of Ray Bradbury.* New York: Penguin, 1991.

Novick, Peter. *That Noble Dream: The "Objectivity Question" and the American Historical Profession.* Cambridge: Cambridge University Press, 1988.

O'Brien, Geoffrey. "Afterword." In *After Dark, My Sweet,* by Jim Thompson. Berkeley: Black Lizard Press, 1985 (1955).

———. *Hardboiled America: Lurid Paperbacks and the Masters of Noir.* New York: Da Capo Press, 1997.

O'Connor, John E., ed. *American History/American Television: Interpreting the Video Past.* New York: Frederick Ungar, 1983.

Ogelsby, Carl. *The JFK Assassination: The Facts and the Theories.* New York: Signet, 1992.

O'Neill, William L. *American High: The Years of Confidence, 1945–1960.* New York: Free Press, 1986.

Orwell, George. "Politics and the English Language." In *In Front of Your Nose: The Collected Essays, Journalism and Letters of George Orwell,* vol. 4. New York: Harcourt Brace Jovanovich, 1968.

———. "Wells, Hitler and the World State." In *My Country Right or Left, 1940–1943: The Collected Essays, Journalism and Letters of George Orwell,* vol. 2. New York: Harcourt Brace Jovanovich, 1968.

"Our Country and Our Culture." *Partisan Review* 19, nos. 3–5 (May–June, July–August, and September–October 1952): 282–326, 420–50, 562–97.

Paterson, Thomas, ed. *Cold War Critics: Alternatives to American Foreign Policy in the Truman Years.* Chicago: Quadrangle, 1971.

———. *Meeting the Communist Threat.* New York: Oxford University Press, 1988.

Pearlman, Jill. "Mistress of Fright." *Harper's Bazaar,* February 1989, 52, 180.

Peary, Danny. *Cult Movies.* London: Vermilion, 1981.

Pells, Richard. *Radical Visions and American Dreams: Culture and Social Thought in the Depression Years.* Middletown, Conn.: Wesleyan University Press, 1973.

Pfeil, Fred. "Policiers Noirs." *The Nation,* November 15, 1986, 523–25.

Pohl, Frances K. *Ben Shahn: New Deal Artist in a Cold War Climate, 1947–1954.* Austin: University of Texas Press, 1989.

Polito, Robert. *Savage Art: A Biography of Jim Thompson.* New York: Vintage, 1995.

Prescott, Peter. "The Cirrhosis of the Soul." *Newsweek,* November 17, 1986, 90.

Prosser, Lee. *Running from the Hunter: The Life and Work of Charles Beaumont.* San Bernardino, Calif.: Borgo Press, 1996.

Pynchon, Thomas. *The Crying of Lot 49.* New York: Bantam, 1966.

Ray, Fred Olen. *The New Poverty Row: Independent Filmmakers as Distributors.* Jefferson, N.C.: McFarland.

Reed, Ishmael. "Chester Himes: Black Writer," *Black World* 21 (March 1972): 23–38, 83–86.

Reilly, John M. "Chester Himes' Harlem Tough Guys." *Journal of Popular Culture,* spring 1976, 935–47.

Richler, Mordechai. "A Captivating but Distorted Image." *Book Week (Sunday Herald Tribune),* September 13, 1964, 4, 19.

Rogin, Michael. *Ronald Reagan: The Movie, and Other Episodes in Political Demonology.* Berkeley: University of California, 1987.

Rosenberg, Bernard, and David Manning White, eds. *Mass Culture: The Popular Arts in America.* New York: Free Press, 1957.

Rosenberg, Harold. "Pop Culture and Kitsch Criticism." *Dissent* 5, no. 4 (winter 1958): 14–19.

Ross, Andrew. *No Respect: Intellectuals and Popular Culture.* New York: Routledge, 1989.

Rovere, Richard. *Senator Joe McCarthy.* New York: Harper, 1959.

Sander, Gordon. *Serling: The Rise and Twilight of Television's Last Angry Man.* New York: Dutton, 1992.

Sanders, Joe. "The Fantastic Non-Fantastic: Richard Condon's Waking Nightmares." *Extrapolation* 25, no. 2 (summer 1984).

Sarris, Andrew. *The American Cinema: Directors and Directions, 1929–1968.* New York: E. P. Dutton, 1968.

———. *The Primal Screen: Essays on Film and Related Subjects.* New York: Simon and Schuster, 1973.

Savage, William W., Jr.. *Comic Books and America, 1945–1954.* Norman: University of Oklahoma Press, 1990.

Schaub, Thomas Hill. *American Fiction in the Cold War.* Madison: University of Wisconsin Press, 1991.

Schlesinger, Arthur, Jr. *The Vital Center: The Politics of Freedom.* Boston: Houghton Mifflin, 1949.

Segrave, Kerry. *Drive-In Theaters: A History from Their Inception in 1933.* Jefferson, N.C.: McFarland, 1992.

Selznick, David. "An Old Pro on the Go Again." *New York Times Magazine,* May 4, 1980, 48–49, 58–80.

Serling, Rod. *Patterns: Four Television Plays with the Author's Personal Commentaries.* New York: Simon and Schuster, 1957.

———. *The Season to Be Wary.* Boston: Little, Brown, 1967.

———. *Stories from the Twilight Zone.* New York: Bantam, 1960.

———. "The Strike." In *Best Television Plays,* edited by Gore Vidal. New York: Ballantine, 1956.

Sherman, Eric, and Martin Rubin. *The Director's Event: Interviews with Five American Film-makers.* New York: Atheneum, 1970.

Silver, Alain, and Elizabeth Ward, eds. *Film Noir: An Encyclopedia Reference to the American Style.* Woodstock, N.Y.: Overlook Press, 1992.

Singal, Daniel Joseph. "Toward a Definition of Modernism." *American Quarterly* 39, no. 1 (spring 1987): 7–26.

Smith, Julian. "The Infernal Comedy of Richard Condon." *Twentieth Century Literature* 14, no. 4 (January 1969): 221–29.

Sontag, Susan. "One Culture and the New Sensibility." In *Against Interpretation and Other Essays.* New York: Anchor, 1966.

Spillane, Mickey. *One Lonely Night.* New York: E. P. Dutton and Sons, 1951.

Stampp, Kenneth. *The Peculiar Institution: Slavery in the Ante-Bellum South.* New York: Vintage, 1956.

Stathis, Lou. "Charles Willeford: New Hope for the Living." Introduction to *High Priest of California* and *Wild Wives,* by Charles Willeford. San Francisco: Re/Search, 1987.

Steinbeck, John. *East of Eden.* New York: Penguin, 1952.

Steinberg, Sybil. "PW Interview: Charles Willeford." *Publishers Weekly,* February 6, 1987, 78–79.

Stone, I. F. *The Hidden History of the Korean War.* New York: Monthly Review Press, 1952.

———. "A Reply to the White Paper" (1965). In *In a Time of Torment.* Boston: Little, Brown, 1967.

Sturcken, Frank. *Live Television: The Golden Age of 1946–1958 in New York.* Jefferson, N.C.: McFarland, 1990.

Susman, Warren. "'Personality' and the Making of Twentieth Century Culture." In *Culture as History: The Transformation of American Society in the Twentieth Century.* New York: Pantheon, 1984.

Sutin, Lawrence. *Divine Invasions: A Life of Philip K. Dick.* Secaucus, N.J.: Carol Publishing Group, 1989.

Thomson, David. "The Whole Hell Catalogue." *New Republic,* April 15, 1985.

Thompson, Jim. *After Dark, My Sweet.* Berkeley: Black Lizard Press, 1955.

———. *The Alcoholics.* New York: Vintage, 1953.

———. *Bad Boy.* New York: Mysterious Press, 1953.

———. *The Criminal.* New York: Vintage, 1953.

———. *Cropper's Cabin.* New York: Vintage, 1952.

———. *Fireworks: The Lost Writings.* New York: Mysterious Press, 1988.

———. *The Getaway.* New York: Bantam, 1958.

———. *The Golden Gizmo.* New York: Vintage, 1954.

———. *The Grifters.* New York: Vintage, 1963.

———. *Heed the Thunder.* New York: Vintage, 1946.

———. *A Hell of a Woman.* New York: Vintage, 1954.

———. *The Killer inside Me.* New York: Vintage, 1952.

———. *The Kill-Off.* New York: Mysterious Press, 1957.

———. *The Nothing Man.* New York: Mysterious Press, 1953.

———. *Nothing More than Murder.* Berkeley: Black Lizard Press, 1948.

———. *Now and on Earth.* New York: Vintage, 1942.

———. *Pop. 1280.* New York: Vintage, 1964.

———. *Recoil.* New York: Vintage, 1953.

———. *Savage Night.* New York: Vintage, 1953.

———. *South of Heaven.* New York: Vintage, 1967.

———. *A Swell-Looking Babe.* New York: Vintage, 1954.

———. *Texas by the Tail.* New York: Vintage, 1965.

———. *Wild Town.* New York: Vintage, 1957.

Trilling, Lionel. *The Liberal Imagination: Essays on Literature and Society.* Garden City, N.Y.: Anchor, 1950.

Tuska, Jon. *Dark Cinema: American Film Noir in Cultural Perspective.* Westport, Conn.: Greenwood Press, 1984.

Tuska, Jon, et al., eds. *Close-Up: The Contemporary Director.* Metchuen, N.J.: Scarecrow Press, 1981.

Tygiel, Jules. *Baseball's Great Experiment: Jackie Robinson and His Legacy.* New York: Vintage, 1983.

Venuti, Lawrence. "Rod Serling, Television Censorship, *The Twilight Zone.*" *Western Humanities Review* 35, no. 4 (winter 1981).

Vidal, Gore, ed. *Best Television Plays.* New York: Ballantine, 1956.

Vonnegut, Kurt. "The Fall of a Climber." *New York Times Book Review,* September 25, 1966, 5, 42.

———. "Harrison Bergeron." In *Welcome to the Monkey House.* New York: Dell, 1970.

———. *Player Piano.* New York: Delta, 1952.

————. *The Sirens of Titan.* New York: Dell, 1959.

Watkins, Mel. *On the Real Side: Laughing, Lying, and Signifying: The Underground Tradition of African-American Humor that Transformed American Culture from Slavery to Richard Pryor.* New York: Simon & Schuster, 1994.

"The Weary Young Man." *Newsweek,* September 28, 1959, 81.

Weaver, Tom. *Interviews with B Science Fiction and Horror Movie Makers.* Jefferson, N.C.: McFarland, 1988.

Wertham, Frederick. *Seduction of the Innocent.* New York: Rinehart and Company, 1954.

Whitfield, Stephen. *The Culture of the Cold War.* Baltimore: Johns Hopkins University Press, 1990.

Will, David, and Willeman, Paul, eds. *Roger Corman: The Millenic Vision.* Edinburgh: Edinburgh Film Festival in association with *Cinema* magazine, 1970.

Willeford, Charles. *The Black Mask of Brother Springer.* Berkeley: Black Lizard Press, 1958.

————. "Chester Himes and His Novels of Absurdity." *American Visions,* August 1988, 43–44.

————. *High Priest of California* and *Wild Wives.* San Francisco: Re/Search, 1987 (1953/1956).

————. *I Was Looking for a Street.* Woodstock, Vt.: Countryman Press, 1988.

————. *Pickup.* New York: Vintage, 1954.

————. *Proletarian Laughter.* Yonkers, N.Y.: Alicat Bookshop Press, 1948.

————. *Something about a Soldier.* New York: Random House, 1986.

————. *The Woman Chaser.* New York: Carroll & Graff, 1960.

Williams, John A., ed. *Beyond the Angry Black.* New York: Cooper Square Publishers, 1966.

————. "My Man Himes: An Interview with Chester Himes." In *Amistad,* edited by John A. Williams and Charles F. Harris. New York: Vintage, 1970.

Williams, Raymond. *Marxism and Literature.* New York: Oxford University Press, 1977.

Wilson, David. "Sam Fuller." In *Close-Up: The Contemporary Director,* edited by Jon Tuska et al. Metchuen, N.J.: Scarecrow Press, 1981.

Wright, Richard. *Native Son.* New York: Harper, 1940.

Wylie, Philip. *Generation of Vipers.* New York: Farrar and Rinehart, 1942.

Zicree, Marc Scott. *The Twilight Zone Companion.* New York: Bantam, 1989.

Index